BRITISH PENSIONS POLICY MAKING IN THE 1980s
The rise and fall of a policy community

CASH AND CARE

Editors: Sally Baldwin, Jonathan Bradshaw and Robert Walker

Cash benefits and care services together make a fundamental contribution to human welfare. After income derived from work, they are arguably the most important determinants of living standards. Indeed, many households are almost entirely dependent on benefits and services which are socially provided. Moreover, welfare benefits and services consume the lion's share of public expenditure. The operation, impact and interaction of benefits and services is thus an important focus of research on social policy.

Policy related work in this field tends to be disseminated to small specialist audiences in the form of mimeographed research reports or working papers and perhaps later published, more briefly, in journal articles. In consequence public debate about vital social issues is sadly ill-informed. This series is designed to fill this gap by making the details of important empirically-based research more widely available.

Steven Nesbitt is a Lecturer in Social Policy at the Manchester Metropolitan University.

British Pensions Policy Making in the1980s

The rise and fall of a policy community

STEVEN NESBITT
Manchester Metropolitan University

Avebury

Aldershot · Brookfield USA · Hong Kong · Singapore · Sydney

Published by
Avebury
Ashgate Publishing Ltd
Gower House
Croft Road
Aldershot
Hants. GU11 3HR
England

Ashgate Publishing Company
Old Post Road
Brookfield
Vermont 05036
USA

British Library Cataloguing in Publication Data

Nesbitt, Steven M.
  British Pensions Policy Making in the
  1980s: Rise and Fall of a Policy
  Community. - (Studies in Cash & Care)
  I. Title II. Series
  368.4300941

ISBN 1 85628 498 0

Library of Congress Catalog Card Number: 94-72809

Formatted by
David Geen Database Publishing
Millgate House
Delph
Saddleworth OL3 5JG
England

Printed in Great Britain by Ipswich Book Co. Ltd., Ipswich, Suffolk.

Contents

List of Tables

Table

Schedule of Interviews

The cooperation of the following people who were interviewed in the course of this research is gratefully, acknowledged: –

Name of Interviewee
and Date of Interview   *Position Held During the Inquiry*

Lord Vinson of Roddam   co-author of: *Personal and Portable Pensions*
Dene LVO July 26th 1989   *for All* (Vinson and Chappell, 1983)

Sir Barney Hayhoe MP   Junior Treasury Minister and member of the
August 8th 1989   Inquiry into Provision for Retirement

Marshall H. Field CBE   Chairman, Joint Working Group on
October 26th 1989   Occupational Pensions and a member of the
                               Inquiry into Provision for Retirement

Nick Montagu   Assistant Secretary, DSS and Secretary to the
November 13th 1989   Inquiry into Provision for Retirement

Sir Mark Weinberg   Chairman, Hambro Life and member of
November 23rd 1989   Personal Pension Sub Group of the Inquiry into
                               Provision for Retirement

Graham Mather   Head of IoD Policy Research Unit and a
December 6th 1989   member of the CPS

Ray Whitney MP   Under Secretary of State for Social Security
December 7th 1989

Sir Norman Fowler   Secretary of State for Social Services,
January 26th 1993   Chairman of the Inquiry into Provision for
                               Retirement

The material collected in these interviews is used extensively throughout this thesis and is referenced using the interviewee's surname and the year of interview.

List of Abbreviations

ACA	Association for Consulting Actuaries
ASI	Adam Smith Institute
ASLO	Association of Scottish Life Offices
AVC	Additional Voluntary Contribution
BPF	British Pension Funds
CBI	Confederation of British Industry
Cmnd	Command Number
COMPS	Contracted Out Money Purchase Scheme
CPRS	Central Policy Review Staff
CPS	Centre for Policy Studies
CPU	Central Policy Unit
CSO	Central Statistical Office
DHSS	Department of Health and Social Security (later known as DSS)
DSS	Department of Social Security (formerly known as DHSS)
EOC	Equal Opportunities Commission
FIMBRA	Financial Intermediaries, Managers and Brokers Regulatory Association
FSAVC	Free-Standing Additional Voluntary Contribution
GAD	Government Actuary's Department
GMP	Guaranteed Minimum Pension
HC	House of Commons
IoD	Institute of Directors
IEA	Institute of Economic Affairs
IFS	Institute of Fiscal Studies
IMRO	Investment Management Regulatory Organisation
LAUTRO	Life Assurance and Unit Trust Regulatory Organisation
LOA	Life Offices Associaion
MIBOC	Marketing of Investment Board Organising Committee

NAO	National Audit Office
NAPF	National Association of Pension Funds
NEC	National Executive Committee
NI	National Insurance
NIESR	National Institute of Economic and Social Research
OFT	Office of Fair Trading
OPB	Occupational Pensions Board
PSI	Policy Studies Institute
RPI	Retail Price Index
S.	Section
SERPS	State Earnings-Related Pension Scheme
SFA	Securities and Futures Association
SIB	Securities and Investments Board
	SPC Society of Pensions Consultants
SSAC	Social Security Advisory Committee
SSC	Social Services Committee
TUC	Trades Union Congress

Acknowledgments

This book is based on the writer's doctoral research at the University of Sheffield's Department of Sociological Studies. Among those I must thank are my supervisor, Professor Alan Walker, for his encouragement and guidance, and David Phillips and Mike Reddin for their helpful suggestions. I am also very grateful to those participants in the pensions policy-making process who granted me interviews: Marshall Field CBE, Sir Norman Fowler MP, Sir Barney Heyhoe MP, Graham Mather, Nick Montagu, Lord Vinson of Roddam Dene LVO, Sir Mark Weinberg and Ray Whitney MP.

Preface

Pensions policy is entering an interesting phase, largely because of Robert Maxwell but in part due to the failures of the system of self-regulation introduced by the Financial Services Act 1986. The problems affecting occupational pensions have been detailed in Professor Roy Goode's 1993 report *Pensions Law Reform* and the Securities and Investments Board has investigated allegations concerning consumers being sold inappropriate personal pensions products.

To understand politicians' responses to these pensions problems it is essential to understand how British pensions policy is made. This book describes and analyses pensions policy-making by looking at the process that produced the Social Security Act 1986.

1 Introduction

In post-war Britain pensions policy has never really been off the political agenda. In the early 1990s, thanks to controversies over pension fund surpluses and the efforts of Robert Maxwell and some less than scrupulous financial advisers, politicians find themselves under pressure to produce a new pensions policy. To understand how political responses are formulated we need to know something of the policy-making process.

The days when policy decisions were pragmatic responses to social and economic problems have long gone. We live in an age when political beliefs and pressure group activities have important roles in shaping policy responses. This book is a study of pensions policy-making in Britain. It looks at how pressure for change initially came from such groups as the Institute of Directors, the Centre for Policy Studies and the Adam Smith Institute, while other organisations including the National Association of Pension Funds defended the status quo. In the end the Secretary of State for Social Services, Norman Fowler, set up a unique Inquiry into Provision for Retirement which formed part of a comprehensive review of the social security system.

The Inquiry into Provision for Retirement is the focal point of this book. Using interviews with political and lay participants in the Inquiry, including Sir Norman Fowler and representatives of the pensions industry and right wing pressure groups, a picture is built up of how pensions policy is made in Britain.

There are very few new social, economic or political problems. Most exist for many years before politicians decide to take action. This is particularly true for pensions. Hence it is impossible to understand politicians' responses to pensions policy problems without looking at the way issues were shaped over time. With this in mind, Chapter 2 gives a brief post-war history of pensions policy which takes the reader up to the General Election of 1979. Chapters 4, 5 and 6 identify the economic and ideological changes that provided the background to what has been the most radical review of pensions policy since Beveridge. Then in Chapters 7 and 8 the Inquiry into Provision for Retirement is examined in detail to reveal the workings of the policy-making process. The new pensions policy is then analysed in Chapter 9 in terms of the ideological values that provide its underpinnings and the groups that promoted this ideology. Chapter 10 looks at the implementation problems, stemming mainly from the

1

Financial Services Act 1986, that affected the launch of contracted out personal pensions. Finally, in Chapter 11, there is a brief review of the two main problems currently affecting pensions policy.

For the benefit of readers whose knowledge of the methods of pensions provision is limited, Chapter 3 contains what I hope is an accessible technical account of the different types of occupational and state pensions provision. Chapter 8 describes how these arrangements were changed by the introduction of contracted out personal pensions and the phasing out of the state additional pension.

2 Post-Beveridge pensions policy 1942–1978

Introduction

This book is primarily concerned with the new arrangements for pensions emerging from Norman Fowler's Inquiry into Provision for Retirement and the subsequent Social Security Act 1986. However, in Social Policy there are rarely any 'new' social problems. Most of the issues dealt with by politicians, such as housing and poverty, have developed over a number of decades. The result is that when politicians seek to respond to a current policy 'problem' they have to consider not only the problem itself but also its history and the existing arrangements for dealing with this policy area. Pensions is no exception to this rule; in order to study the policy-making process that gave rise to the Social Security Act 1986 and the measures this incorporated it is essential to understand the pensions framework which the Conservative Government of 1979 inherited. This chapter will therefore review the development of British pensions policy that occurred during the period 1946 to 1978 with the aim of identifying consistencies and changes that characterise the thirty two year period preceding the legislation that forms the subject of this book. It will be seen that despite the very real changes that occurred, there are a number of values which have remained consistent. There is, for example, an almost unchanging theme that workers should pay for their own pensions and thereby alleviate the state of more than minimal responsibility for this area of public expenditure. This fuelled the debate on whether the proposed scheme should be funded or unfunded, the arguments for which are outlined in Chapter 3.

Post-Beveridge Pensions Arrangements

It is tempting to assume that in times of war all social policy-making grinds to a halt but, as the Beveridge Report illustrates, this is far from the case. In July 1941 a highly regarded civil servant, William H. Beveridge, was given the task of heading a committee of inquiry into social insurance. In December 1942 Beveridge's report *Social Insurance and Allied Services* (Cmnd 6404) was

3

published. The Committee had identified five 'giants' which needed to be tackled: Squalor, Want, Ignorance, Disease and Idleness, and it made a series of proposals to tackle these.

Beveridge's proposals included the setting up of the National Health Service; a system of universal flat-rate contributory benefits including Unemployment Benefit, Sickness Benefit and Retirement Pension; non-contributory Family Allowance and, for those who did not qualify for any of the contributory benefits, means-tested National Assistance. It is reasonable to assume that those who appointed Beveridge had no idea that his report would be so radical. Indeed, if Beveridge's report had been published in the late 1980s, he would probably have been branded a Socialist!

This raises the question of why Beveridge's proposals were accepted at all. As mentioned above, the insurance principle, although spurious, made it attractive to people on the political right; there was a favourable disposition towards the idea of government producing central policy initiatives instead of relying on the free market.

This favourable disposition particularly applied to government measures to avoid the unemployment and recession that followed the 1914-18 war. It was now possible for a government to openly pursue a policy of full employment.

A second factor was that Beveridge had shown that the scheme he proposed could actually be afforded, especially if a policy of attaining full employment were pursued by the government. In addition, the proposals caught the public imagination. In part, this was because the war-time Coalition Government allowed the public to believe that the proposals would be implemented. From 1940, following the invasion of Luxembourg and the capture of Radio 208 by German forces, Lord Haw Haw had been broadcasting a propaganda message to the effect that a National Socialist state would be a wonderful country to live in with a comprehensive welfare system that included a state pension. The British government allowed the Beveridge Report to be used to counter this and did nothing to contradict the public's ever strengthening expectation that the proposals would indeed be implemented. It should be added that Sir William Beveridge was himself a very able publicist, appearing in Pathe newsreel films in cinemas across the land to promote his proposals.

According to Shragge (1984), in 1945, as the war drew to a close, the Prime Minister, Winston Churchill, set up a secret committee of Conservative MPs whose task it was to consider ways of 'getting out of' the Beveridge Report's proposals. By now politicians were becoming aware of the enormity of the project they faced. Not least they were concerned that an apparently generous welfare scheme might jeopardise the aid Britain expected to receive from the USA through the Marshall Plan. They feared that the USA might take grave exception to funding a welfare system that was even better than that which USA citizens enjoyed. In the event their only suggestion was that benefit rates be set lower than planned, and this was adopted with benefit rates being set at below subsistence level.

4

It is important to note that what was being created was an instrument of economic management as well as a means of preventing extreme cases of destitution. By using the ideas developed by John Maynard Keynes (1936) the government, when the economy was sluggish, would transfer spending power from the better off (who would probably save a large part of any extra income) to those on benefit who could be relied on to spend any extra money straight away thereby increasing demand in the economy. The transfer could take place through the tax system and the social security system, with the former collecting revenue which the latter then distributed in social security payments to those in need. By raising social security benefits, including pensions, the economy would be kicked into action because the poorer members of society could be relied on to go straight out and buy such commodities as shoes made in Northamptonshire or shirts made from cotton produced in the Lancashire cotton mills. The employers in Northamptonshire and Lancashire, on becoming aware of this increase in demand, would employ extra staff and they, in turn, would be able to spend more money on goods and services so as to increase economic activity. This is known as the 'multiplier effect'. Conversely, when the economy was overheating, rates of benefit could be held down so has to produce a rapid fall in aggregate demand.

For the benefit of older members of the community Beveridge had recommended the creation of a three tier social security system consisting of: –

i)   Contributory National Insurance Pension Scheme

Beveridge recommended the establishment of a universal flat-rate pension scheme run by the state and funded by flat-rate contributions from employers, employees and, to begin with, the Exchequer. This state flat-rate pension was brought into being by the National Insurance Act 1946 with a contributory retirement pension being established for people retiring after July 5th 1948. As will be seen in Chapter 3, this state pension scheme is actually unfunded. Beveridge saw this pension scheme as a means by which the state could provide the basic provision for retirement to which individuals would add their personal provision. Concern over the cost to the state of retirement pensions is not a new phenomenon.

Initially the Exchequer would contribute towards the funding of the Contributory National Insurance Pension Scheme, but it was intended that in the longer term the financing would come entirely from contributions by employer and employee, and it would yield a flat-rate pension whose value was to be set at subsistence level. This was an era when self-reliance was still very much the order of the day. Hence, to assure political acceptance of Beveridge's report, it was essential that individuals should be seen to be paying for their own social security rather than relying on the state. Accordingly, eligibility to receive this pension was to be based on the attainment of a prescribed age and the individual's record of flat-rate contributions during their working life time or, in the case of a married woman, the contribution record of her spouse.

ii) *Private Occupational Pensions and Individually Purchased Pensions*

Beveridge made it plain in his report that individuals should not be discouraged from making personal provision for old age and, from his proposals, it is clear that the state contributory pension was intended to cover only basic needs. In this way the state avoided competing with existing private sector pension arrangements. Nevertheless, according to Shragge (1984), the universal and more or less compulsory nature of the state pension produced a reduction in demand for occupational pensions. Prior to the Social Security Act 1986 individually purchased pensions were largely confined to those who were self-employed.

iii) *National Assistance Benefits*

This was the only means-tested component to Beveridge's scheme and provided a safety net for those whose National Insurance contribution records did not qualify them for the state retirement pension. In 1948 63% of the National Assistance Board's claimants were pensioners (Burden and Campbell, 1985 p.111). In 1966 National Assistance was revised and renamed Supplementary Benefit and, twenty years later, it was revised and renamed yet again to become known as Income Support.

The effect of the newly created Contributory National Insurance Pension Scheme was not as radical as might be supposed. According to Midwinter (1985, p.23) in 1939, before the outbreak of the Second World War, two thirds of those aged over 65 years were already receiving some type of allowance from the state. These were predominantly the poorest in society and were benefiting from the provisions of such legislation as the Widows, Orphans and Old Age Contributory Pensions Act 1925 which, for example, granted pensions to those who were unable to work by virtue of age-related infirmity. This reliance on the state could be viewed as *prima facie* evidence that the market was failing to meet the needs of a large segment of society, but from the reliance Beveridge's proposals placed on the role of Private Occupational Pensions, Individually Purchased Pensions and on encouraging people to make personal provision for retirement, it would appear that he did not see it in this way. Rather, he assumed that everyone had access to some private form of retirement provision.

What Beveridge achieved in terms of pensions, then, was not the *creation* of a pension system but rather the expansion and development of the existing arrangements into a universal scheme based on work testing and age attainment as opposed to means-testing. In this way acceptance of the relatively recent institution of 'retirement age' was enhanced (although at that time Beveridge had hoped that, in view of foreseeable skill shortages, older workers would be encouraged to defer retirement), state pensions were extended to better off workers and their spouses, and the less well-off gained access to a non means-tested retirement pension.

Although Beveridge tends to be remembered as the founder of the welfare state in Britain it must be noted that his proposals on pensions, recommending that both benefits and contributions should be flat-rate rather than progressive, appeared to offer nothing in the way of income redistribution and, if anything favoured the longer-lived middle class. This aspect of the National Insurance Act 1946 might owe something to the intention of keeping the cost of state pensions to a minimum. However, as will be seen, for reasons beyond Beveridge's control the final shape of the Contributory National Insurance Pension Scheme was such that there was scope for income redistribution. It is known that Beveridge would have preferred to have seen a 'funded' state pension scheme which was, by definition, self-financing. In the event what emerged was a 'pay as you go' scheme in which the contributions of the current workforce provided the basic pensions of the current retired population. As will be explained in Chapter 3, herein lay the scope for income redistribution: not between those retirees who were poor and those who were better off, but between the existing workforce and the existing retired population.

This could have been attained by increasing either the flat-rate National Insurance contribution or the revenue produced by direct taxation so as to produce the necessary receipts to the Exchequer that would fund the desired rate of pension. In fact, as the table below shows, retirees did share in the rise in prosperity that prevailed in the 1950s although, because the rates had originally been set very low, poverty was still common among the elderly.

Table 2.1   National Insurance Retirement Pension as a % of U.K. male manual earnings

	SINGLE	MARRIED
July 1948	19.1	30.9
Sept 1951	18.2	30.4
Sept 1952	18.3	30.4
April 1955	18.4	29.9
Jan 1958	19.8	31.6
1976	19.9	31.7

Source: Social Security Statistics, 1981

Concern was growing in the early 1950s that there would soon be a rapid increase in the size of the retired population and an associated rise in demand for retirement pensions (Walker, 1990). The Phillips Committee was established in July 1953 to examine this in terms of the economic and financial issues. That this concern should have arisen so soon after the introduction of the Basic Retirement Pension Scheme implies any or all of the following: –

1) a realisation of the possible long-term consequences to the economy of the absence of any actuarial basis to the relationship between contributions and benefits must have occurred;

2) it had not been politically possible in 1946 to hold the Exchequer's contribution to the scheme to the desired minimum when the rates were originally set, and the opportunity was now being taken to remedy this by raising employers' and employees' National Insurance contributions;

3) the government was concerned about the responsibility that attached to the management of a national pension scheme.

In any event the Phillips Committee produced in 1954 the *'Report of the Committee on the Economic and Financial Problem of the Provision for Old Age.'* According to the report the central problem was the expected rise in demand for pensions. It also looked at the large and increasing numbers of retired people in receipt of National Assistance, this presumably being the result of the relative 'immaturity' of the state pension scheme. It noted the rapid growth of retired workers in relation to non-retired workers, predicting that the retired population would increase by 40% and those receiving state pensions by 80% in the period to 1979. It also noted the rapid growth of occupational pension schemes.

According to Brown and Small the recommendations of the Phillips report were strongly in favour of encouraging employers to set up occupational pension schemes. This would enable employers: –

(a) to meet obligations towards ageing employees, particularly those who had given long service;

(b) to give the employer greater freedom in retiring those employees who were no longer regarded as efficient as a result of age or ill-health;

(c) in conditions of full employment such schemes would help attract and retain labour. (Brown and Small, 1985, p.139)

That this should be contained in a report primarily concerned with the cost of retirement raises the possibility that behind it lay the idea of shifting at least part of the responsibility for pensions away from the state and towards the private sector. A second concern might have been to draw attention to a flaw in the National Insurance Act 1946: Beveridge's three tier system of benefits assumed that the entire workforce had access to private sector pensions with which to top up the subsistence level state pension, yet this was patently not the case. The Phillips Committee, rather than press for legislation to remedy this flaw and thereby risk fuelling further public alarm, placed its faith in the goodwill of employers. This trust was not to be rewarded.

Despite the declared urgency of the problem of funding, it was another five years before the government took any steps to resolve the matter. This reflected the government's hope that employers would respond to the Phillips Committee's recommendations, thereby causing the problem to disappear without the need for any legislation, but this would still leave the problem of financing the state pension scheme. That the government took so long to respond to this aspect of the report gives an indication of how politically sensitive and alarmist the issue was. Nevertheless, in the years following the Phillips Report both main political parties published clear proposals on the sorts of refinement to the state pension scheme they saw as necessary.

1957-1967: A Period of Debate

After an initial post-war consensus a public debate developed over the nature of the role of the state in providing a basic retirement pension. In this debate the two main views held were those of the Labour Party which wanted to extend the state scheme into one which provided an earnings-related pension, while the Conservative Party wanted to encourage private sector solutions to the problem of retirement provision.

By the mid-1950s the opposition Labour Party had become concerned that two thirds of the workforce did not enjoy membership of an occupational pension scheme, even though a large proportion of them worked for employers who ran schemes for at least some categories of employee. The remedy which they proposed was the establishment of a compulsory National Superannuation Scheme to be managed on an actuarial basis (Brown and Small, 1985 p.144). In exchange for earnings-related contributions, members would receive a pension of 50% of their wage. Those who already belonged to occupational pension schemes whose benefits matched those being proposed would be able to choose between retaining their membership of their employer's scheme or contracting into the state earnings-related scheme. In this way the Labour Party hoped that the gap between those with occupational pensions and those who only bene-fited from the flat-rate state pension would be narrowed.

It is notable that the Labour Party, which might have been expected to regard the welfare state as a mechanism for increasing social equality by means of the redistribution of income, should have come up with a proposal whose key feature was an earnings-related pension that could only partially reduce the extent to which the inequalities of working life were carried over into retire-ment. If it had been enacted, the National Superannuation Scheme would have brought earnings-related pensions to within every worker's reach. The Labour Party could not have adopted a policy which undermined or eliminated occu-pational pensions because by now a significant minority of the working class population enjoyed membership of such schemes. Hence the proposals gave private sector pensions a definite role, albeit relatively minor, in the provision of retirement pensions. However, the contracting out arrangements would have undermined the principle of universalism while ensuring that the state scheme became the least advantageous earnings-related scheme to belong to, thereby attracting only those segments of the workforce which the pensions market had either little ability or no desire to cater for. Furthermore, because of their location within a capitalist economy, pension funds are prevented by legal and ideological constraints from adopting such policies as income redistribution.

9

The Labour Party's proposals would therefore have reinforced inequalities of income in retirement.

Like the Labour Party, the Conservative government had realised by the mid-1950s that, in contrast with Beveridge's presumption, a large proportion of the workforce did not belong to occupational pension schemes (Burden and Campbell, 1985 p.111). However, whereas the Labour Party saw the answer as being a state-run earnings-related scheme that would run in direct competition with the private sector, the Conservative approach was to foster the private sector's growth. Evidence of this intention is to be found in a White Paper published in 1958 by the Conservative government, entitled: *Provision for Old Age* (Ministry of Pensions, 1958). This contained a section entitled: 'Occupational Pension Schemes: A National Asset' in which attention was drawn to the value of pension funds as a vehicle for savings and the danger that the private sector would be adversely affected by the expansion of the state pension system. The resulting legislation was the National Insurance Act 1959, creating the Graduated Pension Scheme which was implemented in 1961. This was carefully designed so as to minimise the extent of state funding and offer no threat to the market for private and occupational pensions. Nor did it alter the adverse position of married women that had been created by the National Insurance Act 1946.

Contributions to the Graduated Pension Scheme were on a progressive scale and based on earnings between £9 and £15 per week (Shragge, 1984 p.95). However, benefits were not in strict accordance with contributions. Had it been funded, the scheme would have had the apparent quality of achieving a modest measure of income redistribution within each generation of workers. However, its 'pay as you go' nature meant that at best the scheme might, in time, achieve a redistribution of income from the existing workforce to the existing retired population and, in so doing, afford the retired population both a share of the current prosperity and a measure of inflation-proofing. In fact none of these goals was adopted. The rate of benefits even to less well-paid contributors was set so low that this scheme constituted a progressive tax on income and a strong, though not wholly successful, incentive to employers to set up contracted out schemes, with attendant tax advantages, for their workers. (The Labour Party, it should be noted, was against tax concessions for occupational pensions, on the grounds that it amounted to a state subsidy to the private sector.)

The inadequacy of Graduated Pensions levels points to the use of an *apparently* earnings-related state pension scheme to raise additional funds through a politically acceptable means to cover the cost of the flat-rate retirement pension (Hannah, 1986 p.57), and a fear on the part of government, perhaps still unused to the responsibilities created by the 1946 Act, of being both burdened with the cost of retirement and responsible for directing fresh capital away from industry. Hence what must have been a conscious effort on the part of politicians to make occupational pensions an attractive proposition and thereby weaken Beveridge's principle of universalism.

During the period from 1956 to 1963 occupational pension schemes experienced growth, even though the returns on contributions were not particularly attractive (Brown and Small, 1985 pp.143 144). Many occupational pension schemes had been set up by medium and large employers as an incentive to potential employees to join their staff and as a disincentive to current employees who might otherwise have considered changing jobs. Although the proportion of the workforce belonging to such schemes has grown over the years, peaking at around 1967-70, it has long been realised that such schemes did not extend maximum potential benefit of an earnings-related pension (usually based on final salary) to more than a very small percentage of all members. In fact members often only benefited from their contributions to their last employer's pension scheme because earlier job changes resulted in refunds of contributions. In other instances, retirees who drew occupational pensions from a succession of employers received considerably less than would have accrued had their entire working lives been spent with one employer.

By 1967 the growth of occupational pension schemes had reached a plateau. According to the 1967 *Report of the Government Actuary's Department* (GAD, 1967) nearly 94% of workers (22 millions out of 23.6 millions) were employed by firms with occupational pension schemes but only 12.2m benefited from membership (Brown and Small, 1985, p.144). Any ability that the National Insurance Act 1959 might have had to persuade employers to create occupational pension schemes for their workers had now been exhausted, in part because the skill shortages of the 1950s had long since ended. Among those excluded from membership of occupational pension schemes were those who had not yet completed a minimum period of service, usually two years. Then there were workers who failed to satisfy conditions of maximum and minimum age. Of greatest concern, however, were those workers who were excluded by virtue of gender and occupational characteristics. For example according to Brown and Small (1985, p.148), for those organisations with schemes in 1967, membership extended to 67% of the male workforce and 33% of the female workforce, and while over 67% of non-manual workers were in schemes, only 46% of all manual workers and 15% of female manual workers benefited from membership. Throughout industry blue collar workers had been benefiting from their trade union strength at the expense of their mostly non-union white collar counterparts. The resulting erosion of pay differentials between white and blue collar workers meant that membership of an occupational pension scheme was often the last vestige of the higher status clerical staff had once enjoyed. Thus far this privilege had not been threatened since trade unions had tended to ignore pension rights in favour of the short term gains of higher wages. What was called for now was a means of persuading both those employers with schemes to widen their scope to overcome the gender and occupational differences that existed, and trade union negotiators and members to see the value of occupational pensions as a form of deferred income.

11

1968-1975: A Period of Economic Crises and Compromises

In 1969, while Richard Crossman was Secretary of State for Social Services, the White Paper *National Superannuation and Social Insurance: Proposals for Earnings-Related Social Security* was published (DHSS, 1969). As a consequence of the recent pressure on sterling and the very large balance of payments deficits this document was more favourably disposed towards occupational pensions than were the 1958 proposals, recognising their value as investment vehicles which could at once lead to increased productive capacity while constraining domestic consumption. That a government should, at a time of economic crisis, propose a generous state earnings-related pension scheme (which would pay up to 60% of half average earnings plus 25% of the remainder [Brown and Small, 1985 p.149]) indicates the political value of any device which can painlessly reduce personal spending, in this case by deferring wage earners' consumption until retirement. Although this came before Parliament as a bill, the Conservative victory in the 1970 General Election prevented it becoming law.

According to the Government Actuary's Department (GAD, 1972) membership of occupational pension schemes, having peaked around 1967-1970, declined in 1971. This occurred at a time of rising unemployment. In 1970 the Conservative government, in the course of a major overhaul of the taxation system, introduced taxation changes in the Income & Corporation Taxes Act 1970 to foster the development of occupational pensions but, despite this, during the period from 1971 to 1975 occupational pension levels did not keep pace with state pensions (Shragge 1984, p.122).

The 1971 White Paper reaffirmed the Conservative government's support for pension funds as a source of capital and expressed the desire for the state and private sector to work in partnership on pensions. This scheme, introduced by Sir Keith Joseph, was more modest than the subsequent Castle Plan.

The proposals of the Castle Plan, contained in the White Paper *Better Pensions: Fully Protected Against Inflation* (DHSS, 1974) and enacted in the Social Security (Pensions) Act 1975, were essentially a compromise between those of Richard Crossman and Sir Keith Joseph. It set out proposals for the integration of the state and private sector pension schemes.

A crucial factor in the Castle Plan's acceptability to the pensions industry was the economic climate that had recently prevailed. For a long while all had gone well with the post-war welfare state. There had been an economic boom and this had helped sustain a cross-party consensus that the British post-war welfare state was a 'good thing' towards which as much revenue as possible should be directed. In the mid 1970s, however, the situation began to change: –

1.   the balance of payments deficit grew;
2.   inflation kept rising (27% in 1974);
3.   taxation rose to fund government spending. In particular, spending on such high technology areas as health and defence rose by more than the rate of

either wage or price inflation;

4. there was increasing industrial unrest, accompanied by large wage demands;

5. crude oil prices were subject to a threefold price increase in a matter of months in 1975;

6. according to a Sunday Times survey, the average rate of return for occupational pension funds in between 1970 and 1976 was 6% while inflation for that period had averaged 14% per annum, reaching a peak of 27% between January 1975 and June 1975 when the Castle plan was being developed (Bell, 1977);

7. such low returns on investment led serious investors to put money in property rather than productive capacity;

8. unemployment began to rise as inflation rose, which defied economic theory.

This had been a time of acute industrial and financial crisis extending to the property market in which many funds had become heavily invested. What saved the pension funds from immediate financial embarrassment was their relative immaturity and, probably, the surpluses accruing from an increase in the numbers of redundant workers. The occupational pension schemes' 'immaturity' meant that they had lots of contributors supplying a regular inflow of cash but very few retired members drawing only limited pensions, thereby creating a net inflow of funds. Fund managers were able to meet immediate liabilities using incoming cash and were therefore not forced to sell investments at unfavourable prices in order to pay pensions. This situation would not pertain today. It seemed that the government had lost control of the economy. Conventional Keynesian methods of controlling the economy just did not work; in fact if anything they made matters worse. With the benefit of hindsight, it would seem that what had happened was that the economy had become 'globalised'. In contrast to 1936, when Keynes produced his General Theory of Employment, Prices and Money, the British economy was now a relatively open system which more than ever depended on international trade. The result was that when Keynesian measures were taken to kick the economy into action by increasing government spending on personal social services and social security, the effect was to worsen the balance of payments deficit and weaken the value of sterling. This happened because people would use the extra income to buy such essentials as shoes from Poland and clothes from South Korea, rather than from domestic producers in Northamptonshire and Lancashire.

All the government could do was focus its attention on controlling wages in the hope that this would curb growth in future demand and thereby enable the economy to cool down.

The Castle Plan

In spite of the emerging doubts about the efficacy of Keynesianism, a cornerstone of which was the role of government intervention in economic management,

13

the measures embodied in the White Paper *Better Pensions* (DHSS, 1974) were enacted in the Social Security (Pensions) Act 1975. Its objective was to ensure that the entire full-time workforce would have not only the state flat-rate retirement pension but also an earnings-related pension. To achieve this the state would provide a State Earnings-Related Pension Scheme (SERPS) to which all full-time workers would contribute unless they were members of occupational pension schemes which were qualified to 'contract out' by virtue of the ability to provide a 'Guaranteed Minimum Pension' (GMP).

In addition, the state would underwrite the investments of occupational pension schemes so that if a fund was unable to produce for its members a pension equal to that which would have resulted from the same contributions being paid into SERPS, the deficit would be met by the Exchequer. This represented a major extension of the state's role in welfare and the end of a long debate about the second tier of pension provision.

That the 1975 legislation should have been accepted despite the reservations concerning interventionist activity on the part of the state was due to several factors. First, the government of the day was Labour and was less antagonistic to state activity than a Conservative government would have been; secondly, as mentioned above, a period of economic crisis is no time for a government to begin an experiment with entails putting the country at the mercy of market forces; and, thirdly, this was the third attempt at legislating in this area of policy in six years, and it was felt by both main political parties that the pensions industry needed a break from what had been a long period of uncertainty. As stated by the Conservative Party:

> "We have made it clear that we can accept the compromise reached last year. After years of chop and change it is important to have a period of stability. Nevertheless we reserve the right to improve the contracting out arrangements so that the terms enable the pensions industry to operate efficiently." (*Conservative Party Campaign Guide*, 1977, p.426, cited in: Shragge, 1984, p.149).

The passage of the Social Security (Pensions) Act 1975 did not halt the demise of either Keynesianism or, by implication, that of Keynesian Beveridgism which had underpinned the country's entire welfare system during the post-war era. In the sphere of policy-making the ideas of such right wing thinkers as Hayek and Friedman were gaining a new relevance (Ferris, 1985) and by the 1980s, as the Green Paper *Reform of Social Security* (DHSS, 1985) clearly shows, the role of the state in pensions provision was being reformulated.

Causes for Concern

A number of factors combined to cause grave concern among the post-1979 governments with regard to what has been referred to as the 'burden of dependency'. In addition to the failings of occupational pensions mentioned above, the most widely publicised focus of attention has been the set of demographic changes predicted to occur over the next fifty years. The two main aspects of this are the increase in longevity and the change in the dependency ratio (in particular, the number of retired people as a proportion of those who are in paid employment).

The increase in longevity is something Beveridge did not foresee when he made his recommendations for a flat-rate universal state retirement pension. At that time a significant proportion of the predominantly male workforce could be relied on to die within a few years of retiring, if not while they were still in the workforce. As table 2.2 below shows, post-retirement life expectancy has increased significantly during this century: –

Table 2.2   **Life Expectancy at 60 Years**

	1901	1989	2001
Men	13.3	17.4	22.7
Women	14.6	21.7	22.7

CSO, Source Social Trends No.21, 1991

Hence even without any improvement in benefits, the population's improved life expectancy has meant that the financing of the flat-rate Basic Retirement Pension has become a more expensive proposition than had originally been envisaged.

The predicted change in the dependency ratio, which will be the product of both the increase in longevity described above and the declining birthrate in the period following the late 1960s, is predicted to result in a contracting workforce at a time when the retired population, particularly the elderly retired, is expected to continue growing. It is important to qualify this by pointing out that such a prediction does not take into account the possibility of a sharp increase in the numbers of women who in future comprise part of the workforce.

The interaction of SERPS and occupational pensions has three adverse aspects: –

1. SERPS, despite its modesty, is inflation-proofed. Since a very large number of its contributors will be among the lowest paid who can ill afford to absorb the impact of inflation, this gives the scheme a certain strength. However, the cost of inflation-proofing, which would have to be borne by the state and therefore the tax payer, could be higher than the post-1979 Conservative government considered justified in bearing.

2. Occupational pension schemes must, in order to contract out of SERPS, provide a 'Guaranteed Minimum Pension' (GMP) on retirement. This means that an occupational pension fund must produce for each of its members a pension roughly equal to that which would have been produced had the

same contributions been paid into SERPS and, should it fail to do so, it is the employer's responsibility to 'top up' the fund's assets. Where the occupational pension fails, after retirement, to keep pace with price inflation, the state would supplement the pensions of retired members. In this way a Labour government accepted the need to protect occupational pension schemes and their members against intolerable levels of inflation.

However, there are those who believe that the state should not take on such a responsibility, not least because of the large financial responsibility that would result from a protracted period of inflation. The risk should instead be borne by individuals and the private sector.

3. Furthermore, what was perhaps not fully appreciated in 1975 was the extent to which SERPS would become a source of income for the majority of workers. Job changes described above together with the unprecedented levels of redundancies that featured in the early 1980s combined to give SERPS a far greater membership than was originally foreseen.

It has been said that it would take a very pessimistic view of the economic future to produce the conclusion that the country cannot afford SERPS. What is more probable is that there is a strong ideological objection to pensions being shielded from the worst effects of the markets.

3 Pensions: a technical account

Introduction

An important aspect of this book is the argument that despite policy makers' rhetoric, pensions policy in the 1980s was based on ideological considerations rather than practical ones. To facilitate a proper assessment of this case and, at the same time, provide those readers who perhaps are unsure of how pensions operate with a basic level of understanding, this Chapter provides a technical description of the different methods of pensions provision. Attention will be drawn to the advantages and disadvantages of the different types of pension.

When the Secretary of State for Social Services, Norman Fowler, came to office in 1981, he inherited a complex set of pension arrangements that had accrued over the years since Beveridge's proposals had been enacted. The arrangements for retirement pensions were composed of those managed by the state, including the flat-rate state pension and the state earnings-related pension scheme (SERPS), and those provided by the private sector, in the form of occupational pensions and, for self-employed people, there were personal pensions. The technicalities of these methods of pension provision are explored below.

Contributory National Insurance Pension Scheme

In providing this Basic Retirement Pension since 1948 (and the non-contributory pension that preceded it) the state has performed a valuable service to capital by facilitating the removal from the labour market of older workers who were deemed to be inefficient. While workers were expected to make personal provision for additional retirement benefits, the cost of providing a basic pension was effectively 'socialised' perhaps in part because it served the interests of capital, and what was in the interests of capital was in the interests of the state.

Proposed by Beveridge in his 1942 report, this pension was to be paid at a flat-rate to retired men aged 65 years or over and to retired women aged 60 years or over. To qualify for this pension a retiree, together with his/her employer, has to have made sufficient flat-rate National Insurance contributions during the employee's working lifetime. Those who were self-employed were eligible to join this scheme.

17

It was originally intended that this scheme would be self-funding. However, in practice it is managed on a 'pay as you go basis'. This means that the Basic Retirement Pension is unfunded; unlike occupational pension schemes, there is no investment fund into which contributions are paid and invested to produce a yield to pay for the contributor's future pension. Instead, the National Insurance contributions of today's workforce are used to pay the Basic Retirement Pensions of today's retirees, thereby forming part of what is sometimes called the 'intergenerational contract'. This method of funding has the advantage that it can enable the current retired population to share in current economic prosperity and thereby reduce relative poverty often experienced by members of this group. This arises because pension contributions are calculated and levied as a percentage of earnings, which means that a large rise in wages automatically produces an increase in the monetary value of contributions, thereby facilitating a similar increase in pensions if politicians deem it appropriate. A pension scheme that ties retirees' incomes to the National Insurance contributions that were levied many years ago prevents them from sharing in current prosperity. However, a scheme which is funded by the contributions of today's workforce can be used to enable current retirees to share in current prosperity. As earnings rise so will National Insurance Contributions, making it possible to fund higher pensions. For a while this happened, with the Basic Retirement Pension keeping pace with earnings. Indeed in 1978 the Labour government, having regard for the then high levels of wage inflation, installed, along with a prices and incomes policy, a method of uprating the Basic Retirement Pension based on the higher of price or wage inflation (Lynes, 1985, p.11), thereby making this link between the Basic Retirement Pension and earnings a formal one. After the 1979 General Election the first suggestion of a change in the government's attitude towards retirees came in the 1980 Budget presented to the House of Commons by Sir Geoffrey Howe. With effect from 1981 the basis of uprating the Basic Retirement Pension would be prices rather than earnings.

A disadvantage of the 'pay as you go' basis to Beveridge's Basic Retirement Pension is a demographic one. The scheme is viable if the numbers of workers leaving the workforce through retirement is approximately equal to the numbers of new recruits, thereby ensuring that the ratio of retirees to contributors is stable. If, however, there are changes in fertility and longevity resulting in a growing number of retirees whose pensions must be paid by a diminishing number of workers then, in theory, there is the potential for funding difficulties in years to come. As will be seen, these 'funding problems' have little basis in reality although they served as valuable ammunition for those seeking to influence pensions policy in the 1980s. A more serious threat to the funding of the Basic Retirement Pension has been the abandonment by post-1979 Conservative governments of the policy of full employment whose pursuit was fundamental to the Beveridge plan.

In accordance with Beveridge's 1942 proposals different pension ages were adopted for men and women, that for men being 65 years and that for women

18

being 60 years. This is because at the time Beveridge was formulating his proposals this was the typical age difference between men and women who were marrying. By building this into pensions policy Beveridge hoped that it would enable husbands and wives to retire at about the same time. This assumption has long since become redundant and indeed Britain's membership of the European Community obliges the government to equalise pension ages in accordance Article 119 of the Treaty of Rome. This has been implemented where occupational pensions are concerned and, in the November 1993 Budget, the Chancellor of the Exchequer announced proposals to equalise pension ages at 65 years for the Basic Retirement Pension or the State Earnings-Related Pension.

Despite political efforts, such as the recommendations of the Phillips Committee (1954), to persuade employers to accept a part of the cost of retirement through occupational pension schemes, unsatisfactory coverage of the workforce led the state, in 1975, to accept part of this additional cost through the creation of the State Earning-Related Pension Scheme.

State Earnings-Related Pensions Scheme

The State Earnings-Related Pension Scheme (SERPS) was created by the Social Security (Pensions) Act 1975 which was implemented in 1978. The aim was to ease some of the problems, described below, which characterised occupational pensions. This scheme provided a modest earnings-related retirement pension based on a worker's best 20 years' earnings, in addition to the Basic Retirement Pension, to all workers whose employers did not provide an occupational pension scheme. The legislation provided that from 1978 all full-time employees had to contribute to either an employer's occupational pension scheme which had been authorised to contract out of SERPS, or to SERPS itself. Henceforth there were two possible outcomes for any worker who changed employers. One possibility was that the employee's contributions to the occupational pension fund to date would be frozen until retirement and, in the meantime, the employee would commence contributing to his or her new employer's occupational scheme (if one existed). Alternatively, the worker may be allowed to withdraw from the first employer's occupational pension scheme, usually where the period of membership has been less than five years (though precise regulations vary between schemes). Where this occurred the employee received a refund of contributions (often valued at somewhat less than their actuarial worth) from which a sum had been deducted in order to 'buy into' SERPS for the period no longer covered by the (former) employer's occupational pension scheme. A third, but unlikely, outcome was for the worker's contributions to be transferred to the occupational pension scheme of the new employer.

The Castle Plan's aims were to provide a generous index linked/earnings-related pension based on the individual's best 20 year's 'relevant' earnings in addition to the existing flat-rate Basic Retirement Pension, while allowing ample scope for the development of the market for private pensions through

19

contracting out arrangements for approved occupational schemes. Whereas Sir Keith Joseph's 1973 proposals for a state earnings-related pension scheme had essentially been aimed at providing a reserve scheme, SERPS as introduced by Barbara Castle was intended to run in 'competition' with occupational schemes so as to encourage a higher standard of benefits than had hitherto existed.

To exercise the contracting out option occupational schemes had to be able to produce a Guaranteed Minimum Pension (GMP) that would at least match that produced by SERPS. Where the occupational pension fails, after retirement, to keep pace with price inflation, the state would supplement the pensions of retired members. In this way a Labour government accepted the need to protect occupational pension funds and their members against intolerable levels of inflation. However, there were those who believed that the state should not take on such a responsibility, not least because of the large financial responsibility that would result from a protracted period of inflation. The risk should instead be borne by individuals using the market.

Behind the decisions in 1975 to create SERPS and in 1985 to phase it out, lay important political, ideological and economic considerations. The creation of SERPS owes as much to the prevailing economic climate of the 1970s as to the need to ensure that all workers were adequately provided for in retirement. At a time of high inflation and correspondingly high wage claims, SERPS provided a painless means of reducing workers' spending power by promising future benefits.

Since April 1978 SERPS has produced a net inflow of funds for the Exchequer. Most of this consists of workers' contributions minus the pro rata additional pensions paid to retirees who contributed to the scheme for at most five years prior to the Inquiry's announcement. SERPS does have several advantages although, as will be seen in Chapter 8, these have been modified by the Social Security Act 1986: –

(1) the main advantage of SERPS is that as with the Basic Retirement Pension it enjoys total portability. This is especially valuable for those workers who for one reason or another experienced frequent job changes;

(2) for a significant proportion of women and blue collar workers the principle that a SERPS pension would be based on the best twenty years' relevant earnings gave the scheme its best qualities. In contrast with white collar workers, manual workers on piecework tend to reach their peak earnings at the age of about thirty years, so that schemes based on final earnings disadvantage them by not reflecting the most productive phase of their working lives. By giving greatest weight to these most productive years SERPS went some way to redressing this. This principle was also advantageous to women who, having interrupted their working lives to have children, could not enjoy continuous membership of an occupational scheme, or who found that they could only return to work at a lower income level and in consequence end their working lives on a lower final salary than would otherwise have been the case;

(3) SERPS is valuable for those employed by small firms or employed on a part-time basis and who therefore would not, prior to the 1986 legislation, have had access to any form of contracted out additional pension provision;

(4) in its original design, a SERPS pension could be inherited in full by a surviving spouse already in receipt of such a pension. Hence the surviving spouse can be well-provided for. As will be explained in Chapter 8, this will end after April 2000;

(5) up to the point of retirement SERPS entitlements are inflation-proof through an index-linking with wages, although thereafter entitlement is linked to the Retail Price Index (RPI);

(6) a final, though only partial, advantage to blue collar workers is that whereas contributions to occupational pension schemes are often based on basic pay, contributions to SERPS are based on gross earnings. With contributions to occupational pension schemes commonly calculated on basic pay, those blue collar workers for whom overtime has been a large component of their wage are at least discouraged from making adequate provision for retirement and experience an even greater fall in income on retirement than would otherwise be the case. Such workers could contract to make Additional Voluntary Contributions (AVCs) but the uncertainty of future overtime earnings and the reluctance of younger workers to give priority to the financial implications of retirement do not make this an attractive proposition. In any case, it is only since the Social Security Act 1986 that employers with occupational pension schemes have been compelled to provide AVC facilities.

SERPS does have several weaknesses: –

(1) as described above, contributions to SERPS are only based on 'relevant earnings'. Hence even SERPS does not allow blue collar workers to make full provision for retirement;

(2) what was perhaps not fully appreciated in 1975 was the extent to which it would become a source of income for a large proportion of the workforce. Job changes described above together with the unprecedented levels of redundancies that featured in the early 1980s have combined to give SERPS a far greater membership than was originally foreseen;

(3) at a general level, and with the benefit of hindsight, it is arguable that the Labour government of 1975 should have foreseen the impact on future governments of the rapidly escalating cost of SERPS arising from maturity. In its early years the state scheme had a substantial net inflow of funds but, as both the number of benefiting retirees and the size of their earnings-related pensions increased, the cost of SERPS increased geometrically. The only check on this growth is that while post-retirement earnings-related pensions are annually revalued according to the RPI, contributions grow by a percentage that exceeds wage rises. This occurs because SERPS

contributions are based on 'relevant earnings' which are calculated by taking the gross wage and subtracting the exempt component which is increased annually in line with the basic state pension and, therefore, the RPI. As wages rise faster that prices, this means that 'relevant earnings' comprise an ever increasing proportion of wages;

(4) the most glaring weakness of SERPS is that it endorses income inequalities. Where previously inequality existed between those workers who were members of occupational pensions schemes and those were not, a new dichotomy was created of state and private sector earnings-related pensions. The Castle Plan's contracting out conditions were to be a means of setting a standard which occupational schemes would have to match. To put it another way, the schemes which contracted out would be those which could match or improve on the benefits of the state scheme. The inevitable consequence of this must be that the state scheme would be the worst (or joint worst) performer among all providers of earnings-related pensions. Hence the state scheme could never provide a generous pension for those workers who did not have access to occupational schemes. Nor is it likely that the extra income provided for SERPS retirees would have greatly improved their living standards. Because the membership of SERPS consists predominantly of lower-paid workers, retirees with entitlements to relatively small additional pensions have found that either they are disqualified from earnings-related benefits or their level of benefit has been reduced by the amount of their additional pension. The savings on earnings-related benefits such as supplementary pension and housing benefit have, of course, been an extra source of gain to the state. The inequality between SERPS and occupational pension contributors has been heightened by the strong downward pressure on wages that characterised the early 1980s;

(5) there is a weakness in SERPS which arises from the following features. First, the level of a SERPS pension is the determinant of the GMP, i.e. the point below which the state will intervene to top up occupational pensions. Secondly, despite the illusion of a scheme with an actuarial basis, SERPS is unfunded. As with the Basic Retirement Pension, the rate of return on contributions is ultimately dependent on the policy of the government of the day. From the first of these features emerges a strong disincentive to any government to raise the return on contributions delivered by SERPS. While pension funds might be obliged to raise their contribution levels for existing contributors in order to match the new GMP created by the higher SERPS rate, it would be the state which funded the resulting deficit where retired members of pension funds were receiving occupational pensions below the new GMP level. Hence while many but not all occupational pension schemes improve their conditions of membership the return on the state's earnings-related pension scheme at best remains unchanged;

22

(6) related to this, and equally important, is the second feature whereby the level of SERPS benefit is determined by government policy. For example, as a consequence of the Social Security Act 1986 the value of SERPS contributions will, from the year 2000, be reduced in phases from 1/80 of a contributor's relevant earnings to 1/100. In the meantime SERPS will continue to provide the state with a net inflow of cash until the late 1990's;

(7) according to Fogarty (1982, pp.32/3) the number of women aged between 60 and 74 years and men aged between 65 and 74 years will decline modestly until the next century and then, according to Reddin (1986, p.11) begin to rise, with a significant increase between 2000 and 2030. The main immediate population increase is among those aged 75 years and over who will need increased assistance. In the longer term there is a population trend which will cause the proportion of workers/SERPS contributors to decline in relation to the proportion of retirees/beneficiaries. This change in the dependency ratio will be the product of both the increase in longevity described above and the declining birthrate in the period following the late 1960s. Such a prediction does not take into account the possibility of a sharp increase in the numbers of women participating in the labour force.

By the early 1980s, and prompted by this demographic trend, researchers such as John Kay of the IFS were suggesting that the future cost of SERPS would place an intolerable burden on the working population (Helowicz, 1987, p.7). Coming at a time when a Conservative government had already declared its intention to reduce state spending, such research must have provided right wing politicians and 'think tanks' with credible support for their ideas on personal freedom, people's capitalism and personal pensions. That a plan of such long-term importance for the integration of private and state earnings-related pension schemes should possess as many flaws as the 1975 Social Security Bill and yet succeed in being enacted is a reflection more of the sense of urgency felt by politicians to get something into law than of any real consensus. Its most immediate attraction was the need to give pensions providers a period of stability. In addition, at a time of high wage inflation, both SERPS and occupational pension schemes offered ways of instantly and painlessly reducing the workforce's spending power. SERPS is especially potent in this respect because the combined employer/employee contributions of approximately 10% are based not on gross pay but on 'relevant earnings' which in 1993/4 consisted of earnings in excess of £56 per week. Hence in 1993/4 a 10% increase on a weekly gross wage of £120 would cause the worker's 'relevant earnings' to rise from £64 (£120 less £56) to £76 per week (£132 less £56) producing a rise in contributions. In this way a 10% pay rise would produce a 12% increase in state revenue from SERPS.

Initial reactions on the part of employers to the measures in the Social Security (Pensions) Act 1975 were mixed. Some employers widened the scope of their existing occupational pension schemes' membership; some formed new or additional pension schemes; others closed their pension schemes and contracted back into the state earnings-related scheme. According to Brown and Small (1985), some employers purposely contracted back into and then out of the state scheme so as to benefit from the financial assistance made available to new funds under the terms of the Castle Plan.

Final Salary Occupational Pension Schemes

Final salary occupational pensions are paid for either partly by employer and partly by employee, with the employer usually paying the larger share or, where the scheme is non-contributory, by the employer alone. These contributions are calculated as a percentage of the payroll. This type of pension scheme is sometimes known as a 'defined benefit' scheme; the benefit is defined in advance in terms of employees' final salaries. It is useful at this stage to acknowledge the extent to which occupational pension schemes are not homogeneous in their methods of financing and management.

The two main types of pension scheme are: Unfunded and Funded.

i) Unfunded Occupational Pension Schemes

As the term suggests, unfunded (sometimes known as 'pay as you go') pension schemes do not have at their foundation a pool of accumulated contributions in the form of an investment portfolio. Rather, the contributions of the employer and the current workforce are paid out immediately in the form of pensions to the retired members of the pension scheme. As was explained earlier when discussing the Basic Retirement Pension, unfunded pension schemes have the merit of enabling the current retired population to share in any increase in the living standards of the working population. In practice, however, such a system can only work where there is an absolute guarantee of the employer's continued existence and scale of operations. A significant level of redundancies could produce a funding crisis with a reduced workforce being required to pay for the pensions of a proportionately large number of current retirees. Even a very large private sector company can go into liquidation, and with an unfunded occupational pension scheme this would leave the current workforce, who perhaps for years had contributed towards the pensions of their employer's retired workers, with no provision for their own retirement and no subsequent workforce on which to rely for a retirement income. The result is that only the state is capable of operating a pension scheme on such a basis, and it does so for both the State Retirement Pension and Civil Service pensions. Indeed, civil servants are unique in having their occupational pensions indexed to current earnings, and it was Margaret Thatcher who as Prime Minister appointed Sir Bernard Scott to report on ways of ending this unusually generous arrangement. (Scott, 1981)/. This is described in Chapter 4.

ii) Funded Occupational Pension Schemes

By contrast, with a funded pension scheme the contributions of the employer and employees are not used to provide immediate pensions for current retirees. Instead these contributions are invested in order to provide pensions at some future date when the current employees reach pensionable age. Many occupational pension schemes were set up by medium and large employers as an incentive to potential employees to join their staff and as a disincentive to current employees who might otherwise have considered changing jobs.

The majority of occupational pension schemes are funded, which is to say that contributions in respect of an employer's current workforce are made to a fund held by a trust created for that purpose. Large employers have their own pension fund and fund managers whose expertise may be augmented with the services of outside advisers. Employers whose pension schemes are perhaps not so large may still have their own pension fund but employ a firm of fund managers look after the day to day investment decisions. Life offices offer fund management facilities, but they also market an alternative pension product in the form of insured pensions. With a managed fund the life office invests the contributions from the client company to produce the necessary sum to meet future pensions liabilities. The contributions include a life insurance component to cover the eventuality of employees dying in service. Any surplus or deficit in the fund accrues to the client. However, with an insured pension the client company pays a premium to the life office in exchange for which the life office guarantees to pay pensions as employees, including early leavers, reach normal retirement age. The contributions go into the life office's general investments and any surplus or deficit that would otherwise have accrued to the client company is absorbed into the life office's earnings.

Since 1978 and the implementation of the Social Security (Pensions) Act 1975, full-time workers have been obliged to contribute to the State Earnings-Related Pension Scheme (SERPS) unless they contributed to an occupational pension scheme which had been able to qualify for contracted out status. As mentioned earlier, such status was attained if the occupational scheme undertook to produce a Guaranteed Minimum Pension (GMP). This is a pension at least equivalent to that which the same contributions would have been produced had they been paid into the state scheme. To achieve this, where an employer has an occupational pension scheme with its own pension fund, the flow of revenue provided by the contributions to the pension fund is invested by the fund managers: –

(1) in accordance with statutory restrictions on the range of permissible investments;

(2) in accordance with the broad guidelines of the fund's trustees; and in such a way as to be likely to yield sufficient assets as to meet future liabilities. Such liabilities will be in the form of: (a) occupational pensions that will

25

become payable to retirees (and/or their surviving spouses); (b) the transfer values of the contributions in respect of early leavers who choose to transfer accrued contributions to their new employer's fund, and (c) the transfer values of the contributions in respect of any past or present employee who, since April 1988, has elected to set up a personal pension fund.

Most occupational pension schemes are geared to produce pensions equal to a proportion of final salary. The definition of 'final salary' can vary from one scheme to another. Most commonly it means the last full year's earnings, but it can mean an average of the last three years' earnings or the best year of the last three years' earnings. The proportion of final salary is usually one sixtieth or one eightieth for each year of employment. Hence an employee who retires after twenty years of working for a firm which runs pension scheme based on sixtieths will receive an occupational pension equal to one third (20/60) of their final salary.

The explanations for the ease with which fund managers have achieved apparently high returns on investments lie in aspects of the design of occupational pension schemes and their effects on the distribution of pension fund assets.

The design of occupational pension schemes is such that the pension received by each member is not merely the product of their accrued contributions and the return on their investment as would be the case with personal pensions. Occupational pensions entail transfers of resources both from one member to another and from employer to member. These transfers occur at different stages in the process of making provision for an occupational pension and take a number of forms which can be loosely categorised as: (1) insurance and (2) cross-subsidy (Kaye, 1987, pp.59-62).

Both features entail the transfer of resources from some scheme members to others, but there is a major difference:

(1) an insurance element involves the sharing by scheme members of a future risk, such as unexpected longevity. The precise effect of differences in members' lifespans on the distribution of pension fund assets is, for a homogeneous workforce, unforeseeable by the contributing members and is not the result of the design of the pension scheme.

(2) a cross-subsidy, by contrast, involves a straightforward, foreseeable and largely inevitable transfer of resources from one group within a pension scheme's membership to another. In some cases it might be purposely designed into the scheme while in others it is an inadvertent consequence of the pension scheme's regulations. By systematically examining the components and processes that together make up a pension scheme, elements of insurance and cross-subsidy will be identified.

External sources of cross-subsidy lie in tax treatment. There are two inequalities deriving from the difference in tax treatment for contributions to SERPS and occupational pension schemes whose effect is to create a cross-subsidy.

First, SERPS contributions are not subject to the exemption from income tax that attaches to contributions to occupational pensions, so that it can be argued that tax payers who contribute to SERPS are subsidising those who belong to occupational pension schemes. Secondly, there is an inequality between workers who pay income tax at the standard rate and those whose income is taxed partly at higher rates. Because occupational pension contributions are, together with allowances, deducted from gross pay to produce a figure for taxable pay, relief is given at the contributor's highest tax rate. Hence within a given occupational pension scheme the highest earners will tend to pay less, pound for pound, for their pensions than those who are on average or low earnings. In this way, income which has been redistributed through progressive taxation is promptly returned to its source.

There are also several internal sources of cross-subsidy in occupational pension schemes. The first concerns the earnings profiles of different types of employee. For a given occupational pension scheme, contribution levels are calculated actuarily to produce a final salary pension which takes account of the pay increases awarded during the employees' working lives. This assumes that over the years all employees receive similar wage increases but, in reality, managers' incomes normally rise faster than those of manual workers and tend to continue rising right up to the point of retirement. Managers also stand to receive significantly higher pay increases than manual workers. The earnings of manual workers usually peak at around middle age, and thereafter prospects of wage increases resulting from either internal or external promotion diminish. Where, as is usually the case, an occupational pension is calculated on a final salary basis this will inevitably disadvantage the manual worker. By the time of retirement the manual worker's peak contributions will have been invested for considerably longer and yielded a higher return than those of most managers whose highest contributions will usually be those which immediately precede retirement.

Large pay increases of the order recently enjoyed by British managers can have the effect of creating a deficit within a pension fund since the future liabilities of the fund are promptly increased and the existing assets may become inadequate to the point of threatening the solvency of the fund. The increase in the pension fund's liabilities must be met from any of:

(1) the employer's resources;
(2) an adjustment of contribution levels, or
(3) the capitalising of any surplus currently held by the pension fund which might otherwise have been applied to give a discretionary increase in pension levels or used to fund either a cash refund or a 'contribution holiday' for the benefit of the employer.

Any of these options could be disadvantageous to workers on average or low earnings who belonged to the same scheme. As before, within a given occupational pension scheme one occupational group can find itself subsidising another.

As mentioned earlier, another component in the calculation of occupational pension contribution rates is the average post-retirement life expectation. The effect of this mechanism is to build into the occupational pension scheme an element of insurance for each individual against the possibility of unexpected longevity. Resources are thus transferred from those whose lifespans are shorter than average to those whose lives are, at least in theory, unexpectedly long. However, this insurance element is only present in a pure form where all members of a scheme have similar biographical and occupational characteristics.

Where members' biographical and occupational characteristics are not homogeneous this same insurance feature can produce a cross-subsidy. For example where senior managers and manual workers belong to the same occupational pension scheme it is probable that the latter subsidise the former. In contrast with most workers, managers will probably have better life chances in the shape of better working conditions and housing, better health education, good diet and private health care, leading to greater longevity and therefore a greater claim on the assets of the fund. Herein lies another form of cross-subsidy in which managers will tend to pay less for their pensions than manual workers. The result is that within a given occupational pension scheme one occupational group (e.g. manual workers) can find itself subsidising another (e.g. senior managers).

Longevity can also create a cross-subsidy in an occupational pension scheme where and men and women pay the same contribution rates. This arises because women will tend to draw their pensions for a longer post-retirement period than men. The impact of this has been lessened since all occupational pension schemes were required to provide a surviving spouse benefit, usually in the order of half of the full pension, making women's life expectancy the key factor in any pension calculations. However, this means that women occupational pension contributors are being required to pay for a surviving spouse benefit which their spouses are unlikely ever to receive.

Yet another form of cross-subsidy is from younger workers to older workers and is particularly important in terms of producing ageist employment practices. It is more expensive to provide an occupational pension for older workers because their contributions will be invested for a shorter period and therefore have less time in which to yield a appropriate return. Employees' contributions to a pension fund are calculated as a percentage of gross earnings (though normally excluding overtime). However the percentage can vary according to the age of the employee on joining the scheme, with older recruits paying a fractionally higher percentage of their earnings in pension contributions than younger ones. In part the extra cost of pension provision is met by older recruits to a workforce who may find that their pension contribution amounts to a fractionally larger percentage of their income than that of their younger counterparts. To this extent older and younger workers are self-sufficient in their provision for retirement. However, the employee's contribution is not alone in being affected by age. Employers pay a higher contribution towards the occupational pensions of older workers than towards for younger ones which sometimes discourages employers from taking on older workers. Where older workers are recruited it is arguable that a subsidy is taking place. What is harder to discern is whether there is a cross-subsidy: do older workers, by raising labour costs, consume resources that would otherwise be available to provide higher wages or pensions for younger workers or perhaps higher pensions for current retirees?

A final type of cross-subsidy that occurs within occupational pension schemes is that which exists between early leavers and stayers. In its original form, when an employee changed jobs they could leave their accrued pension contributions with that employer's pension scheme and, on retirement, draw a pension from their last employer and from all previous employers in whose occupational pension schemes they had left their accrued contributions. Prior to the 1985 it was common for occupational pension schemes to pay pensions based on the earnings when they were last employed with that firm plus any discretionary revaluation of those contributions that might have occurred in the intervening period. This meant that little regard was given to wage inflation that occurred in the intervening period. An early leaver's pension was therefore often a fraction of what would have been provided if only the employee had been allowed to transfer their accrued contributions to the pension fund of their new employer or even take a refund and use the proceeds to purchase an annuity. As will be seen in Chapter 10 the 1985 Act went some way to reducing this inequity though it could not compensate for the early leaver's loss of access to the final salary basis.

The interaction of SERPS and final salary occupational pensions has three adverse aspects: first, SERPS, despite its modesty, is inflation-proofed. Since a very large number of its contributors will be among the lowest paid who can ill afford to absorb the impact of inflation, this gives the scheme a certain strength insofar as it might ease poverty. However, the cost of inflation-proofing, which would have to borne by the state, could be higher than the present government considers justified in transferring to the tax paying population; secondly, occupational pensions must, in order to contract out of the state earnings-related scheme, provide a GMP on retirement. This means that an occupational pension scheme must produce for each of its members a pension approximately equal to that which would have been produced had the same contributions been paid into SERPS and, should it fail to do so, it is the employer's responsibility to 'top up' the fund's assets to match liabilities in respect of active members. Where the occupational pension fails, after retirement, to keep pace with price inflation, the state would supplement the pensions of retired members. In this way a Labour government accepted the need to protect occupational pension funds and their members against intolerable levels of inflation. However, there are those who believe that the state should not take on such a responsibility, not least because of the awesome financial burden that could result from a protracted period of inflation. The risk should instead be borne by employed individuals using the market, and thirdly, what was perhaps not fully appreciated in 1975 was the extent to which it would become a source of income for a very significant proportion of the workforce. Job changes described above together with the unprecedented levels of redundancies that featured in the early 1980s have combined to give SERPS a far greater membership than was originally foreseen.

Personal Pensions

Personal pensions were created in 1956. The tax allowances that attach to them were created by Section 226 of the Income and Corporation Taxes Act 1970 and thereafter they became known as 'Section 226 contracts' or as 'self-employed pensions'. The latter term is misleading because although they were primarily associated with self-employed, there was also a small proportion of employed people using personal pensions as an addition to either their employer's occupational pension scheme or, where none existed, as an additional provision to that made through SERPS. In fact it was possible, prior to July 1st 1988, to take out a Section 226 contract if a person was: self-employed, in employment that did not offer an occupational pension scheme, or in freelance employment as well as in full-time pensionable employment.

The absence of a Guaranteed Minimum Pension (GMP) that characterised this type of pension meant that under the Social Security Act 1975 such a pension could not be used to contract out of SERPS. Hence Section 226 contracts, which under the Finance Act 1988 are now known as 'Section 620 contracts', tended to be used only as a means by which SERPS pensions could be topped up.

The most significant feature of personal pensions is their inherently speculative nature. In contrast with most occupational pensions where, in theory at least, the main determinant of pension level is final salary, the crucial factors in determining the level of income arising from a personal pension plan are:

1. the quality of investment management and the performance of shares generally;

2. the ability of the retiree to get a good rate of return on the annuity which is purchased at the point of retirement, and

3. the rate of inflation during the post-retirement period. The fixed rate of return on annuities can leave their beneficiaries extremely vulnerable during periods of high inflation.

In view of what was said earlier when discussing occupational pensions, it could be argued that personal pensions, with their 'defined contribution' basis, are more equitable than occupational pensions with their 'defined benefit' basis. They may not redistribute wealth away from the rich towards the poor but

30

nor does the reverse occur, as frequently happens with occupational pension schemes. Other differences will be that:

(1) pension funds surpluses are non-existent in defined contribution pension schemes since all assets are allocated according to the levels and timings of contributions and are not be affected by length of service. Hence the long stayer is not be subsidised by the early leaver nor the manager by the worker, and

(2) employers will not be able to utilise any surplus by taking refunds and contribution holidays. But nor will they be obliged to top up final salary occupational funds whose assets are inadequate to meet future commitments in respect of active members. There will therefore be a fall in the incidence of cross-subsidies.

Historically, money purchase schemes have proved inadequate and this is one reason why final salary bases are preferred. But it could be argued that if contributions to personal pension plans are invested in the same securities as would have been selected by the employer's final salary fund, the gains accruing will be identical. Indeed Kaye (1987, p.53) goes further than this and argues that if as much had been contributed to personal pensions as has been to occupational pensions the benefits for most members would have been considerably greater. The key differences would lie in how these gains were distributed among the different types of employee described earlier and in the employer's immunity from the responsibility that goes with sponsoring a defined benefit scheme of having to top up the pension fund in the event of the scheme being unable to meet all final salary pension liabilities.

4 1979-82: Economic crises and an ideological shift

Introduction

There were two distinct phases to the post-1979 development of pensions policy; the first between 1978 and May 1983 was cautious, penny pinching and based on a short-term view, while the second which began with the Conservative's re-election was bold, aimed at achieving major savings and based on a long-term view. With this in mind, the first part of this account contained in this Chapter examines the main post-1979 circumstances and events which may have played a role in shaping pensions policy until 1982. Chapter 5 provides the second part of the account and covers the events preceding the 1983 General Election. Chapter 6 looks at the post-general election events leading up to the announcement of the Inquiry into Provision for Retirement, at the end of which there is an assessment of the pensions debate thus far and an examination of the positions of the various participants in this unfolding debate. In this way the ground will be prepared for Chapters 7 and 8. Chapter 7 consists of a detailed examination of the pensions policy-making process while Chapters 8 analyses the proposals and legislation contained respectively in the Green Paper *Reform of Social Security* (DHSS, 1985) and the Social Security Act 1986, and Chapters 10 looks at the implementation of these measures.

Causes of the Inquiry Into Provision For Retirement.

It is impossible to state conclusively or exhaustively what triggered the Inquiry. Nevertheless, it is possible to identify a series of events that took place over a period of approximately two years which, taken together, can be seen as producing increasing pressure for change. Subject to this qualification it will be seen that there are three factors which stand out as having influenced the initiation and outcome of the Inquiry: the early leavers problem; concern over the impact of demographic trends on the future cost of SERPS, and the emergence of a rightward ideological shift that favoured private sector solutions to problems currently tackled by the state. These factors are examined in depth below.

Events During the Period: 1978-1983.

i) General

By the late 1970s Britain was facing what was widely perceived, though not empirically demonstrated, to be a serious economic situation. Inflation was high, unemployment was rising and there was reported to be an unprecedented level of industrial unrest. The Conservative government which was elected to office in May 1979 came complete with both a causal explanation of the nation's economic problems and a commitment to remedy them using monetarist methods. In particular they expressed concern about:

1. Inflation: this reached 21% in 1979 (Watsons Statistics, 1988) having been exacerbated by a large rise in oil prices. A substantial part of the responsibility was nevertheless attributed to the inability of the previous Labour government to control either public spending or powerful trade unions.

2. Public spending: the Conservative government saw the extent of public expenditure as excessive. They believed that it resulted from government spending increasing more quickly than economic growth and from the involvement of the state in activities better left to the private sector.

Among the solutions employed by the government to curtail what it perceived to be the excessive power of trade unions were legislative measures which restricted the ability of trade unions to take strike action, and the fostering of an economic slump that severely damaged the country's manufacturing base (Gamble, 1988). However, of greater interest at this stage are those measures which were adopted with a view to cutting back the level of public expenditure and the scale of state activity.

The earliest measures taken to control public expenditure were contained in Chancellor of the Exchequer Sir Geoffrey Howe's June 1979 Budget. It was proposed that public expenditure would be cut by £1.5 billion and that a further £1 billion would be saved through the tightening of cash limits (Gamble, 1988, p.98).

A further and much broader undertaking to reduce government expenditure was given in the Conservative government's first public expenditure White Paper in the following November. This document opens with the sentence: 'Public expenditure is at the heart of Britain's present economic difficulties.' (HM Treasury, 1979, para.1). This marked a watershed for what remained of Keynesian economic management. The post-war orthodoxy had been that through high spending the state had a leading role to play in regulating the economy. Monetarism, by contrast, dictated that the state's primary economic responsibility was the maintenance of a strong currency. Controlling the level of public expenditure was the essence of the Conservative government's 'monetarist' policies. This proved to be an important principle in subsequent social security policy.

It was intended that the adopted measures would reduce or freeze levels of government expenditure on selected programmes. To the government of the day the most obvious targets were those types of expenditure which came under the heading of social security. The social security budget was the largest category of expenditure. As can be seen in the table below, between 1970 and 1980 expenditure had grown sixfold through a combination of inflation and the creation of new types of benefit; it was also consuming 34% more of the gross national product though this can in part be accounted for by the decline in output that occurred in the late 1970s:

Table 4.1   Total Expenditure on Social Security as a % of GNP
1960-83   United Kingdom

Year	Total Expenditure on Social Security £million	Total Expenditure as a % of GNP
1960	1,499	6.6
1970	3,927	8.8
1980	23,508	11.8
1983	33,901	13.1

Source: CSO Annual Abstract of Statistics for 1960-83 cited in: Halsey, 1988, p.501.

From the Treasury's point of view much of this spending would have con-stituted an avoidable drain on the economy at a time when what was needed was less public expenditure and more private investment. As mentioned earlier, social security was the largest expenditure head in the late 1970s accounting for approximately a quarter of all government spending, and within the social security budget retirement pensions comprised the largest component. Hence it must have seemed inevitable that social security in general and retirement pensions in particular would be among the main targets for expenditure cuts. Yet this attention was initially slow in coming.

The 1979 Public Expenditure White Paper makes no specific reference to pensions and, on social security generally, says merely that expenditure is deter-mined by the number of claimants which in turn depend on economic and demographic factors (HM Treasury, 1979, para.39). In so doing it omits to mention that the Treasury's ability to determine both the rates at which benefits are paid and the qualifications for claiming have a significant effect on the level of spending. Only in the case of unemployment benefit did the Conservative government seem able to take a firm line, indicating: '... the Government's intention to intensify efforts against fraud and abuse of the social security system.' (HM Treasury, 1979, para.39), and later, in 1981, abolishing earnings-related unemployment benefit.

According to Gamble (1988, p.114) the explanation for the restraint shown towards social security is that: 'Certain areas of spending, notably the health and social security budgets, were judged too sensitive for major direct cuts.'

Another possible explanation lies in the difference between social security and other types of government expenditure. Most expenditure by the state has the objective of producing particular quantities and qualities of services. The extent to which this is achieved depends not just on the adequacy of the budget but on the efficiency with which the organisation charged with providing a service is managed. It was possible (though not necessarily reasonable) for the government to transfer the responsibility for achieving savings in expenditure without reductions in services to such agencies as the Civil Service and local authorities. Transferring responsibility to these agencies had two advantages: firstly, they are traditionally unpopular; this unpopularity was boosted by senior Conservative politicians who alleged that bureaucracy and red tape within the Civil Service and the profligacy of 'loony left' local authorities were impeding economic progress and, secondly, their running costs are high in relation to the direct cost of the service to be delivered, affording scope for significant expenditure cuts without a proportionate deterioration in the level of the service (if any) provided.

In contrast, only a fraction of the expenditure on social security is absorbed by overheads incurred through the provision of the service. Most of the cash expended is the end product, in the shape of benefits paid. As a result there was very little scope for savings through increased efficiency. An exception to this principle is the increase in the use of means testing and 'targeting' benefits whose political acceptability permitted the abolition of the universal earnings-related unemployment benefit and compelled most unemployed workers to apply instead for both unemployment benefit and supplementary benefit.

Hence during the Thatcher government's first term of office radical steps to reduce public expenditure were usually indirect, carefully chosen so as to minimise electoral hostility, and justified on the economic grounds of a need to improve value for money. That unemployment benefit seems to have been an exception to this is perhaps explicable in terms of a 'moral panic' which fostered the notion that many claimants were 'undeserving'. It may also have been the case that the government foresaw the continuing rise in unemployment (see table 4.3 below) and the abolition of earnings-related unemployment benefit was a way of pre emptively minimising the escalating cost. However, the early steps to control expenditure on pensions were cautious in the extreme.

ii) Change in Government Attitude Towards Retirees

The first suggestion of a change in the government's attitude towards retirees came in the 1980 Budget presented to the House of Commons by Sir Geoffrey Howe. The previous Labour government, having regard for the then high levels of wage inflation, had recently installed, along with a prices and incomes policy, a method of uprating the basic state retirement pension based on the higher of price or wage inflation (Lynes, 1985, p.11). In this way the Labour government had sought to protect the well-being of retirees against the adverse state of the economy. However, at a time when wages were rising faster than prices the

Chancellor of the Exchequer, Sir Geoffrey Howe, replaced this recently introduced basis for uprating with one based entirely on price inflation as measured by the retail price index. This reversed the priorities set by the previous government and risked considerable criticism for the sake of what in the short term could only be minor savings. The impression was given that this was a temporary setback for pensioners which would be reversed when economic circumstances permitted. This impression was reinforced by the Social Security Act 1980 which gave a long-term undertaking that the Basic Retirement Pension would not be revalued by less than price inflation, thereby implying that it would at least occasionally be subject to a higher uprating. As is explained below, this was then further reinforced by the 1981 DHSS White Paper *Growing Older,* which quite explicitly promised that when the economy improved pensioners would share in that improvement.

In other words, political statements of the day suggested that what was influencing pensions policy was, in O'Connor's terms, a 'fiscal crisis', but the measures on the uprating of basic pensions only made sense if viewed as a 'crisis of values' and therefore part of a longer term strategy to restructure the arrangements for retirement pensions (O'Connor, 1973). This observation will be re-examined later.

iii) Publication of the Scott Report

In February 1981 the Inquiry Into The Value Of Pensions, chaired by Sir Bernard Scott, presented to Parliament its report in which it compared the value of private and public sector occupational pensions. The Prime Minister, Margaret Thatcher, had initiated the Inquiry because of what was said to be public concern for the value and cost of inflation-proofing public sector pensions. The 'problem' had arisen as a consequence of the Pension (Increase) Act 1971 which had give civil servants protection against the effects of inflation. This arrangement afforded retired civil servants a protection of benefits which no private sector pension schemes came close to matching during that period of rising inflation (Scott, 1981, para.46). In subsequent years, however, the rate of inflation climbed to levels which the Conservative government of the day could not have foreseen and the prospective cost to the state of the inflation-proofing of civil service retirees' and early leavers' pensions rose to unexpected proportions.

It is not clear why civil service pensions attracted the Prime Minister's attention when they did; these were problems to be faced in the distant future and as such did not form an obvious target for a cost cutting government, except perhaps with a view to privatising some parts of the Civil Service. If the Prime Minister hoped the Inquiry would support the removal of indexation for public sector pensions then she was to be disappointed; instead, Sir Bernard Scott's committee recommended that ways be found of improving the protection of benefits accruing from private sector occupational pension schemes, for example through state provision of index linked bonds with which pension funds could hedge against the effects of inflation (Scott, 1981, para.28).

Although the Scott Report was primarily concerned with public sector pensions, it demonstrates that at a time when the Conservative government seemed preoccupied with finding ways of quickly reducing public expenditure, the Prime Minister at least was already interested in long-term cost reductions. Furthermore, this report is one of the earliest to recognise the 'problem' of inadequate private sector occupational pensions. It is true that David Ennals, as Secretary of State for Social Services, had in 1977 and 1978 asked the OPB to study the 'inadequacy' of occupational pensions, but neither report had been completed yet.

In the short-term the Scott Report's recommendations for inflation-proofing occupational pensions made no impression on the government. The recommendation that occupational pension funds be provided with opportunity to purchase index linked bonds was eventually taken up by a later government, but by that time (1985) the problem of inflation was receding.

iv) DHSS White Paper: Growing Older.

In March 1981 the Secretaries of State for Social Services, Scotland, Wales and Northern Ireland published the White Paper Growing Older which was '... the outcome of the first comprehensive review of all issues which determine the well-being of older people,' (DHSS, 1981, pp.iii iv). This White Paper, which was high on ideology and low on substance, seems to have been concerned not so much with retirees in general as with the very old and such issues as the future level of social services and health care provision. In this context it indicated quite clearly that economic considerations must take precedence and that social need would be met as a consequence of lower inflation and increased growth (DHSS, 1981, p.iii). It did state that retirees should share in the nation's prosperity through increased basic pensions when economic recovery materialised (DHSS, 1981, para.2.4), but otherwise it said little of importance about future pensions policy.

Of the three main causes of pension reform outlined above, two appear to have their existence confirmed by the White Paper Growing Older :

1. The ideological shift: there was a noticeable emphasis on individual rights and responsibilities and on the role of government being to maintain a strong economy rather than to provide health and social care. This implies that the ideological shift which was to influence future pensions policy was underway.

2. The future cost of SERPS: the White Paper drew attention to the demographic trends (DHSS, 1981, para.1.2) and commented that they would lead to an increase in the cost of pension provision to be borne by corporate and individual tax payers (DHSS, 1981, para.1.6). This was one of the earliest indications of government concern for the long-term costs of pensions provision. By contrast there was a notable lack of concern by

37

policy makers for the effects of demographic trends on the cost and stability of occupational pension schemes.

3. The early leaver problem: just as the White Paper ignored the impact of demographic factors on the cost of private sector pensions, so it gave no recognition to the problem of early leavers, although as shown below, it was soon to become an important issue.

v) Occupational Pensions Board Report (1981)

The OPB was commissioned in March 1978 by the then Secretary of State for Social Services, David Ennals, to report on the inadequacy of occupational pension schemes' preservation of early leavers' rights. The terms of reference were:

> To consider what further steps should be taken to protect the occupational pension rights and expectations of employees who change employment, the transfer of rights between pension schemes; to review the financial and other implications and to make recommendations. (OPB, 1981, para.1.1)

As a result, in June 1981 the OPB published its report: *Improved Protection for the Occupational Pension; Rights and Expectations of Early Leavers* (OPB, 1981). The report recognised that for many workers, particularly those subject to frequent job changes and periods of unemployment, contributions to occupational pension schemes did not yield a worthwhile retirement income. The main flaw lay in the failure of most pension funds to preserve and upgrade the value of early leavers' accrued contributions. This was not a new problem; rather, its solution had been put off because, first of all, it would inevitably increase the cost of occupational pensions and thereby raise employers' costs, fuelling inflation; secondly, it was generally believed that the real problem lay in high rates of inflation which eroded the value of early leavers' pensions and, thirdly, trade unions were not interested in improving the pension rights of ex members. The OPB recommended what has been described as an evolutionary rather than radical approach to the early leavers problem on the grounds that: '... changes of such magnitude would take a long time to agree and implement.' (Rogers, 1982, p.11).

The key recommendation was that an annual revaluation of early leavers' contributions should be carried out using 'limited price indexation' (although this entailed the risk of giving early leavers better protection than current retirees), combined with the possibility of transferability of contributions. However, a promise by government that the OPB recommendations would be implemented was not forthcoming.

Perhaps the OPB's ideas had become less compelling by virtue of the rightward ideological shift that was taking place; the change of government in 1979 and their different response to economic and social problems of the day altered the way in which the pensions 'problem' was seen. An alternative explanation is that the OPB addressed the 'right' problem insofar as the future cost of maintaining the retired population was of concern to the Conservative government but, by making recommendations that would raise employers' labour costs, it produced the 'wrong' answers. However, it is crucial to remember that what the OPB recommended was a voluntary rather than mandatory solution and therefore there was no compelling ideological reason for the government not to support their report. There were, however, economic reasons, as described below.

In 1991 Sir Norman Fowler wrote that the plight of early leavers was a cause with which he had some sympathy (Fowler, 1991, p.203), but unfortunately the timing of this OPB report was not very propitious in that the nation's economy was not yet deemed to have recovered from its period of crisis. Although stock market share indices had been rising for some time and inflation was falling:

Table 4.2   Changes in the General Index of Retail Prices

79/80	80/81	81/82	82/83
21%	11%	9%	3.5%

Source: Watsons Statistics 1988

unemployment was still very high in 1981 and was continuing to rise:

Table 4.3   Percentage Rate of Unemployment
(Official Series) – UK

1980	1981	1982	1983
7.4%	11.4%	12.1%	12.9%

Source: Department of Employment cited by: Halsey, 1988, p.174.

As mentioned above, the inadequacy of private sector occupational pensions had previously been excused on the grounds that the real enemy was high inflation. As inflation fell it became apparent that this was patently not the case and that the real problem lay in the structure which determined the distribution of funds assets among the four classes of member: contributors employed by the sponsoring employer; early leavers whose accrued contributions continued to be held by the pension fund; early leavers who accepted a refund of their accrued contributions and rejoined SERPS, and retired members. The early leaver problem had been compounded by the iniquitous practice of 'franking' contribution refunds so that the amount refunded was considerably less than the value of accrued contributions.

Although concern for inadequate pensions was initially promoted by the Labour government's Secretary of State, David Ennals, through the commissioning of the OPB study, it would seem that the OPB adopted the cause as its own, becoming the main promoter of the view that deferred pensions should be subject to at least some minimal revaluation. Hence a change of government in 1979 did not result in this cause being dropped. If this is correct, it could be argued that pensions never actually came off the political agenda. The period from 1969 to 1986 was one of almost continuous review and obfuscation; the only respite had been during that period between the passing of the 1975 legislation and its implementation in 1978.

vi) Social Services Committee Report (1982).

Soon after the publication of the 1981 OPB report (OPB, 1981) came the decision by the Social Services Committee in July 1981 to undertake the inquiry that produced the report *The Age of Retirement* (SSC, 1982a, para.2). The purpose of the inquiry was: '... to consider whether ... any change in pension age and the age for actually ceasing work should be made' (SSC, 1982a, para.6) and although it was not the Inquiry's purpose to look at the cost of pensions it was nevertheless felt that:

> high and rising pension costs, better pension entitlements, and the trend towards earlier retirement are all highly relevant to our inquiry. (SSC, 1982a, para.7).

The dual subjects of pensionable and retirement ages had probably been brought to the fore by the increase in *de facto* early retirement. The large numbers of redundancies in the early 1980s produced a formidable number of unemployed workers at both ends of the age range. There were redundant older workers who had no prospect of re-employment and there were school leavers who on completing a one year Youth Training Scheme faced unemployment. The government's response to the continued high rate of unemployment affecting the latter group had been two fold: it increased the duration of Youth Training Schemes from one to two years, and they introduced an early retirement scheme which enabled older workers, including those who were unemployed, to take early retirement on full state pension. Where unemployed older workers were involved this had the effect of reducing the unemployment statistics while removing the stigma of long-term unemployment from the individuals concerned. Where employed older workers were involved, it was hoped that by allowing early retirement for workers whose employers undertook to fill the resulting vacancy with a new employee, younger workers would find employment and the unemployment statistics would accordingly be reduced. It was generally accepted that early retirement might be feasible for a greater number of workers if they could be allowed to draw their occupational pensions at an earlier date than the Normal Retirement Date which was usually built in to an occupational pension scheme's terms and conditions. The SSC began taking evidence in November 1981 (SSC, 1982a, para.2) and published its report in October 1982. The report will be discussed later in this Chapter.

vii) Activities of the Institute of Directors

Also in November 1981, Walter Goldsmith, the Director General of the IoD, addressed the Autumn Conference of the NAPF. He drew attention to the cost of pensions provision:

> British industry has reached the point at which it is going to be unable to shoulder significant burdens arising from pension funding. (Goldsmith, January 1982, p.21)

This seems to have been a broad hint that whatever measures were adopted in response to the OPB's call for the revaluation of early leavers' accrued contributions, they should not involve any extra cost for employers. Walter Goldsmith expressed concern too at the cost to the tax payer of funding what he regarded as very generous public sector pensions, on which the Scott Committee had recently reported, and called for the privatising of public sector pensions. He did not, however, express concern at the future cost of SERPS.

Of greater interest, however, is Walter Goldsmith's statement that: 'It is neither the case, nor is it desirable, that the economy should be run by the pension funds.' (Goldsmith, January 198 p.21). The IoD's contribution at this stage was confined to expressing concern about the cost of funding both private and public sector occupational pensions. It had no objections to the financial power exerted by life offices. Nor had they developed the idea that personal pensions would solve the early leavers problem. As will be seen, these latter two positions were to change by May 1983.

It appears from the above that by November 1981 the issue of pensions was high on the agenda. It had achieved this position mainly because of the OPB's 1981 report and despite the government's failure to promise the implementation of its recommendations. The SSC entered the forum with its inquiry into the *Age of Retirement*, but this was not a direct contribution to the debate; rather, it served to stract the attention of actual and potential participants in the debate who instead devoted their energies to preparing submissions for the SSC. At the same time, and for the same reason, politicians who might otherwise have been under pressure to respond to the OPB report were given a 'breathing space'. This view is supported by the decline in activity on the pensions front during the period in which the SSC was preparing its report.

viii) NIESR, PSI and IFS Symposium in December 1981

In December 1981 a symposium was held by the NIESR, PSI and IFS. It was entitled: 'Retirement Policy The Next Fifty Years'. Distinguished economists presented seven papers exploring such issues as future dependency ratios and the needs of future retirees (Pilch, 1982). This represents one of the earliest academic analyses in the 1980s to portray the elderly as a 'problem'.

Thus far, and with the exception of the joint NIESR/PSI/IFS Conference mentioned above, the pensions debate had focused on the problem of early leavers with some attention being given to demography. However, in July 1982 attention was focused sharply on the future cost of state pensions. This was the first of the Government Actuary's Quinquennial Reviews: *National Insurance Fund Long Term Financial Estimates* (1982) and while not providing evidence of an imminent crisis the Government Actuary's estimates did show that after 2005 the cost of pensions provision would rise sharply (SSAC, 1983). In part this was due to an unexpected rise in SERPS membership precipitated by redundancies in the early 1980s which had led workers with less than five years' contributions to an occupational scheme to cease membership and contract back into SERPS. The situation was not helped by the failure of occupational pension scheme membership to expand during the previous decade. The interrelationship between the private and public parts of that pension cost were obviously of interest to a government that was seeking always to encourage greater private sector participation in welfare provision. Hence the Government Actuary's projections for the cost of SERPS was an important causal factor in the Inquiry into Provision for Retirement being held.

ix) Rise of Demographic Concerns

Mounting concern about the future cost of SERPS against demographic projections into the next century was probably heightened by the publication on June 30th 1982 of the latest decennial census data (Charlton, 1982). At about this time, two internal groups of civil servants had been looking at the implications of future pensions obligations and it seems that this, together with the realisation that there had been virtually no growth in occupational pension membership for a decade, were contributory factors towards the initiation of the Inquiry into Provision for Retirement. So the field of pensions was becoming fertile ground for policy makers eager to introduce a New Right agenda.

x) Activities of the Central Policy Review Staff and the National Association of Pension Funds

Two developments occurred in September 1982: the more important was the leak of the CPRS proposals for reducing welfare spending, and the less important was an NAPF response to the early leaver problem. The CPRS became involved in the public expenditure debate on two occasions. The first concerned a short paper commissioned by the Treasury in the Summer of 1982 and covered options for reducing the full range of public expenditure. The paper was completed in September 1982 and was immediately leaked. From this emerged evidence of a more radical approach towards reducing welfare spending than had previously seemed politically acceptable. The report argued that for the foreseeable future public expenditure would continue to absorb 45% of GDP only one per cent less than it did in the highest year during the Labour government. It further argued that more radical cuts required more radical policies, recommending that the link between social security benefits and inflation should be broken. It outlined proposals for major reductions in public expenditure on education, health care and defence. According to *The Economist* (September 18th, 1982) the report, which was circulated among Cabinet members:

> ... *came with the seal of approval of the Treasury,* which recommended that it form the basis of a six month study of a public spending strategy for the rest of the decade. *This means that its ideas were not pulled out of the ether and that it has more significance than most think tank papers.* (*The Economist,* September 18th, 1982, p.25 italics added).

It would therefore seem that by 1982 the Conservative government was undertaking a quiet but radical Treasury-led review of expenditure policy covering social security and, therefore, including pensions. Although:

> Cabinet wets were so appalled at the think tank's suggestions that they argued successfully that it would be wrong to give it serious and instant consideration. (*The Economist,* September 18th, 1982, p.25),

the indications remain that the review of public spending strategy was carried out, resulting in the Treasury Green Paper *The Next Ten Years: public expenditure and taxation into the 1990s* (HM Treasury, 1984) which was published the following year.

This leak, coming so soon after the Scott Committee's failure to give the government the justification it needed to reduce spending on public sector pensions, established beyond doubt that reducing the cost of state involvement in pensions provision was on the political agenda. The second CPRS report referred to above dealt with long-term public expenditure and the future cost of retirement pensions. Significantly, this study had been approved by the Prime Minister in the Summer of 1982 and was completed in the Spring of 1983. According to Blackstone and Plowden (1988, p.127) one of the focal points of this study was: 'occupational pensions and the need for them to be more 'portable''. Furthermore, when the report was produced in 1983:

> It, *(the report)* started with four premises: the state pension scheme *(SERPS)* cost too much; it did not focus enough on the genuine poor; there was too little scope in the pensions system as a whole for the individual to look after himself; and that the system of occupational pensions was rigid and inflexible and acted as a disincentive to career change. (Blackstone and Plowden, 1988, p.127).

Given that the issues of portability, flexibility and freedom were approved, if not stipulated, by the Prime Minister it is hardly surprising that they were to become an essential ingredient to any acceptable pensions policy. It is also significant that the idea that SERPS cost too much was taken as given.

xi) Activities of the Adam Smith Institute.

Also during 1982 the ASI produced a document entitled: *Privatizing Pensions*. It was a private memorandum addressed to the Secretary of State and, since the CPRS report on pensions was not completed until the following year, it appears to have been one of the first suggestions that SERPS should be replaced by personal pensions.

xii) National Association of Pension Fund's 'Central Fund'.

Of rather less significance was the NAPF adopting as policy an idea developed by Maurice Oldfield and Dennis Blair that the early leavers problem should be solved by the creation of a central fund into which early leavers' accrued contributions would be paid (Blair, 1982). This was intended not as a perfect solution to the early leavers problem but rather as a means of alleviating the worst effects. In fact the proposal was naive and impractical; if implemented the result would have been the creation of an investment house that would soon have grown to form the largest and most powerful financial institution in the land. In fact the idea of a central fund for early leavers' accrued pension contributions was similar to a measure contained in Sir Keith Joseph's 1973 pensions legislation. However, the ideological climate had changed in the intervening period. A 1980s Conservative government, whose words and deeds had repeatedly demonstrated its commitment to increasing competition and minimising the role of the state in the economy, could not possibly have adopted such a proposal.

xiii) Occupational Pensions Board Report (1982).

Pressure for change in pensions arrangements increased still further in October 1982. This month was probably the busiest so far in terms of exchanges on the subject of pensions policy. The OPB published a report which in some ways reinforced the message of that published in 1981. Entitled: *Greater Security for the Rights and Expectations of Members of Occupational Pension Schemes* this report had actually been commissioned on February 21st 1977, prior to that which was presented in 1981. The delay in completion arose because in the aftermath of the oil crisis and economic and financial disturbances the OPB was: '... reluctant to pronounce on the long term security of funded pension schemes ... ' (OPB, 1982, para.1.4).

The OPB again highlighted the early leaver problem by drawing attention to how rarely the final salary basis of occupational pension provision actually

44

produced an adequate pension (OPB, 1982, paras.1.8 & 3.28). It also called for a statutory requirement for disclosure of information by pension funds (OPB, 1982, paras.7.3 & 11.3). Recommendations on the subject of disclosure requirements had been made by the OPB in 1975 but it had been decided not to make these mandatory (OPB, 1982, para.1.5). In addition the Board had looked at an area previously covered by the Wilson Committee (1971) concerning the adequacy of trust law as a basis for regulating pension funds, calling for a complete review of the law relating to pension schemes arrangements. This issue was to lie dormant until, following the Maxwell pensions scandal, Professor Roy Goode was appointed to examine this subject (see Chapter 11).

Norman Fowler welcomed the OPB proposals, particularly those affecting the disclosure of information to scheme members (*Pensions World*, 1982, p.635). However, while he promised legislation to outlaw the practice of 'franking', Norman Fowler declined to introduce legislation to compel disclosure and said that he hoped there would be improvements in the early leaver situation. In other words, he preferred to leave the problem to sponsoring employers and pensions providers in the hope that they would arrive at a voluntary solution. In view of the pension sponsors' and providers' inertia over 'franking' this was an optimistic view to take.

xiv) Stewart Lyon's Presidential Address

Only six days after the publication of the above OPB report Stewart Lyon, in his capacity as President, addressed the Institute of Actuaries. His presidential address was entitled: *'The Outlook for Pensioning'* (Lyon, 1983, pp.41-44 & 93-97). This was a particularly pessimistic view of future demographic, social and economic trends. His view was also unfavourable on the subject of SERPS whose future cost he thought would be burdensome to the economy, partly because he believed the scheme was too generous, and partly because:

> although more than half of all full-time employees are contracted out, the indications are that by 1995 Guaranteed Minimum Pensions may be outweighed by 3:1 by the earnings-related pensions being paid by the state scheme. Thirty years later the ratio could have deteriorated to 5:1. (Lyon, 1983, p.44).

Stewart Lyon's address was seminal. His case was reinforced in October 1982 when an article by the Government Actuary Edward Johnston appeared in *Pensions World* (Johnston, 1982, pp.569 571). The Government Actuary's recently published quinquennial (review (1982) had indicated that if between 1985/6 and 2025/6 prices rose by 6% per annum and wages rose by 8%, the change in ratio of employed to retired sections of the population would necessitate an increase in Class 1 National Insurance contributions of 42% (Haberman, 1987, p.193). It should be pointed out that the accuracy of this projection will depend on future retirement patterns; as Reddin (Reddin and Pilch, 1985, p.28) observes:

> ... the prime determinant of the number of pensioners is the pension age: we *choose* that age. Raise the age and we get fewer pensioners: decrease it and we get more. ... 'The elderly' are a social category; their current numbers are determined by the fertility of their parents. The number of pensioners, however, is determined by legislation.

A further qualification concerns the comparison of dependency ratios over long timescales. Over such periods major changes in technology tend to occur, with increased productivity making it possible for a greater proportion of the population to depend on the economic output of a reduced workforce (Haberman, 1987, pp.153/4). Nevertheless, commenting on the implications of the quinquennial review for the future for SERPS Edward Johnston (1982, pp.569 71) said: 'This picture appears less favourable than that shown by the projections made when the Scheme was passed through Parliament. Both Stewart Lyon and Edward Johnston were to become members of the Inquiry in to Provision for Retirement.

xv) Social Services Committee's Report: 'Age of Retirement'

Finally in October 1982, just two days after Stewart Lyon's presidential address, the report of the Social Services Committee, *The Age of Retirement* (SSC, 1982a) was published. Though a very muddled document, it contained an argument for flexibility of pensionable ages and gave consideration to the idea of a common retirement age. Ultimately it favoured the idea of a 'decade of retirement' which would give potential retirees the right to choose their retirement age from anywhere within a ten year age range and with an adequate pension. The Committee also spent a considerable amount of time arguing in favour of higher state pension rates.

The Report noted that the maturity of SERPS and the eventual reversal of the existing favourable demography would make the future cost of pensions formidable (SSC, 1982a, para.38). The SSC went on to insist that future pensions policy must be constructed on the basis of demographic trends (SSC, 1982a, para.33) and while very sceptical of their value, they noted with what now seems remarkable prescience that: 'an optional return to money purchase is a possibility that must be borne in mind.' (SSC, 1982a, para.28).

When, in 1983, he set up the Inquiry into Provision for Retirement the Secretary of State, Norman Fowler, said he had decided that the Review would take account of findings of *The Age of Retirement* inquiry. Yet it is difficult to judge whether this document had any impact on subsequent pensions policy. The principal problem is that the report contains many conflicting views and unresolved discussions; whatever measures had ultimately been incorporated into the Social Security Act 1986 it would probably have been possible to find their *apparent* origins in *Age of Retirement*. It should also be said that select committees tend not to contribute directly to policy-making. Nevertheless, this document does display the full range of opinions on that existed on this subject at the time, and it is possible that the preparation and submission of evidence to the Committee by employers' organisations, trade unions and pension fund managers provided a dress rehearsal for the consultations to be held within a very short time scale by the Inquiry into Provision for Retirement.

5   1982-83: General Election

Introduction

By 1983 the economy was coming out of recession and entering a prolonged period of growth. As is usually the case, it was only possible to recognise this trend with the benefit of hindsight, and so policy shaping continued to be influenced by a negative picture of the economic future. This Chapter continues the chronological account of the increasing pressure for a change in pensions policy and shows how right wing groups were becoming increasingly confident and determined in their campaigning.

xvi) Social Security Advisory Committee's 1983 Report.

Almost alone in defending pre-1979 pensions policy in the face of growing hostility was the SSAC whose membership consists of political appointees but not politicians. In January 1983 they produced their Second Report (1982/83). In this they seem to have had in mind the purposes of publicly defending SERPS against recent threats and, to a lesser extent, putting the case for uprating the basic state pension (SSAC, 1983, chap.6.11). Hence they only made passing reference to the 'early leaver' problem (SSAC, 1983, chap.6.5). They rejected the idea of any major reorganisation of SERPS (SSAC, 1983, chap.6.20) and thereby openly indicated their disagreement with the course of government policy. In adopting a traditional welfarist approach this report takes the side of labour rather than that of either capital or the Treasury.

The SSAC is a knowledgeable body of people, undoubtedly capable of making a valuable contribution to the pensions debate; they noted with satisfaction that ten of the fourteen recommendations in their First Report had been implemented (SSAC, 1983, chap.1.4). Yet it is certain that their Second Report had little or no impact on the direction of pensions policy. Their ideas, particularly their belief in a contract between workers and retirees (SSAC, 1983, chap. 6.6) and their espousal of an important role for the state in pension provision, were not in tune with those which were gaining credibility with the Conservative government. The SSAC's members are political appointees and yet until quite recently, when David Willetts, then Director of Studies at the CPS and a Conservative parliamentary candidate (*The Times* , December 10th 1989) was appointed as a member (*Guardian* , November 2nd, 1989), there was no evidence of appointees deliberately being drawn from the right wing of the Conservative Party or from industry or the City. This confirms how little influence the SSAC had on the policy-making process and how irrelevant its perspective was deemed to be by policy makers.

xvii) Financial Times and Joint BPF/NAPF Conferences.

In the following month, on February 9th and 10th 1983, a conference organised by the *Financial Times* entitled: 'Pensions in 1983' was held in London. The Conference might not have been an occasion of great importance except that in addition to Edward Johnston giving a warning on the future cost of SERPS, Madsen Pirie of the Adam Smith Institute (ASI) presented an argument in favour of personal pensions which was not dissimilar to that stated in the 1982 ASI memorandum entitled *Privatizing Pensions* (ASI, 1982). The ASI was still the only organisation to be presenting an argument explicitly in favour of personal pensions. Although several participants in the Inquiry into Provision for Retirement discounted the possibility of the ASI having played any part in the policy-making process, it would be understandable if ASI members felt entitled to some credit for the way in which pensions policy subsequently developed.

Soon after, on February 25th 1983 at a joint BPF/NAPF conference Maurice Oldfield, chairman of the NAPF, gave a speech entitled: 'Property in a Democracy' in which he referred to:

> ... reports in the press of a move by some advisers to the Conservative Party to give employees so called freedom to make their own pension arrangements. (*Pensions World* , April 1983, p.222)

In the same speech, he later made reference to what he called: 'anonymous pressure groups...' (*Pensions World*, April 1983, p.222); apparently the activities of the CPS and its supporters were becoming known, in part because of a recent publication discussed below. It is clear that by now the pensions debate was gathering momentum. Thus far it had mainly been concerned with the future cost of SERPS and the 'early leaver' problem, and these issues tended to be analysed strictly in terms of the perceived burden to the economy and to employers. As was shown earlier, Madsen Pirie of the ASI appears to have been the only person to argue for the introduction of personal pensions. Walter Goldsmith, Director General of the IoD, had argued in November 1981 that employers should not have to bear the costs of improving occupational pension schemes, but he had not yet presented a case for personal pensions; indeed he seemed favourably disposed towards occupational pension funds. Most of the individuals and organisations described here and in Chapter 4 either were or were soon to become part of what is hypothesised to have been a pensions policy community, and yet even at this stage it was not very clear who would eventually support the personal pensions approach. What was becoming clear, however, was that whatever the policy outcome it would almost certainly be favourable to the interests of capital. The interests of labour were not being adequately represented.

xviii) Central Policy Review Staff: Second Report.

In March 1983 CPRS produced its second report which was in two parts and concerned the arrangements for state and occupational pensions. The study had included an examination of the impact of pensions on long-term public expenditure and how this could be reduced, and the introduction of 'portability' to occupational pensions, and, as stated above, it had been undertaken because the Prime Minister had approved it. The first part of the report described SERPS as inadequate and recommended phasing it out while raising the basic pension to reduce public hostility. According to Blackstone and Plowden (1988, pp.127 8).

> The DHSS did not like it because they saw it as breaking the 'pensions consensus'. The Treasury disliked it because it would cost money initially, a good example of the Treasury's inability to concede the desirability of spending money in order to save later.

Although the study had been undertaken with the Prime Minister's approval, its completion came immediately before what was to be a general election. According to Blackstone and Plowden, Margaret Thatcher was furious and demanded the recall of all copies of the CPRS report from ministries. But Peter Shore MP leaked parts of it in the run up to the General Election (Blackstone and Plowden, 1988, p.96). The key proposal was that: '... the scheme (SERPS) should be phased out and the basic pension raised to buy off some of the key hostile reaction' (Blackstone and Plowden, 1988, p.127). The second part of the report:

> ... made recommendations on how to develop personal pension schemes as a credible alternative particularly for more mobile employees unsuited to the form of compulsory final salary company schemes. (Blackstone and Plowden, 1988, p.127).

Had there not been an impending general election it is conceivable that given the Prime Minister's support the CPRS proposals might have been implemented despite their unpopularity with both the DHSS and the Treasury.

There was no evidence that the CPRS had had any impact on the Inquiry into Provision for Retirement. Yet given that these ideas were produced at the instigation of the Prime Minister Margaret Thatcher and that they resemble both the CPS paper (Vinson and Chappell, 1983) and the DHSS Green Paper (DHSS, 1985), it is hard to believe that it was not a significant if indirect contribution to the debate. Indeed Blackstone and Plowden do not consider the CPRS role to have been crucial; they attach far greater importance to the activities of the CPS and the CPU (Blackstone and Plowden, 1988, p.128). Nevertheless, there remains the implication that the pressure for change began in Downing Street and spread outwards.

xix) Centre for Policy Studies' 1983 Paper.

In April 1983 the CPS published the paper entitled *Personal And Portable Pensions For All* (Vinson and Chappell, 1983). This paper marked the formal entry of the CPS into the pensions debate, though in view of comments of the chairman of the NAPF Maurice Oldfield, in his speech 'Property in a Democracy', made two months earlier at the joint BPF/NAPF conference (see above), it is possible that CPS supporters of the personal pension cause had been involved informally for some time.

Within the CPS there was a study group responsible for producing the April 1983 paper. At the time it was known as the Personal Capital Formation Group and its members were: Nigel (Lord) Vinson, Philip Chappell, Philip Darwin and Brian Kingham . It is significant that Nigel Vinson and Philip Chappell were both clearly in sympathy with the ideas soon to be promoted by the IoD which was to make an important contribution to the pensions debate, and that the membership of the Group was 'fluid'. Hence Graham Mather was both head of the IoD Policy Unit and a member of the CPS and took part in the CPS discussions that led to the above paper even though he was not formally a member of the study group. This overlap of membership is characteristic of policy communities and will be explored more fully later.

The CPS paper of 1983 contains a brief but well-developed philosophy concerning the ownership of property which is simplistically applied to the problems of pensions; evidence of this is to be found in the approach taken to the 'early leaver' problem (Vinson and Chappell, 1983, paras.3 & 4), disclosure of information (Vinson and Chappell, 1983, para.5) and mobility of labour (Vinson and Chappell, 1983, para.3). In each of these three examples the CPS paper has taken an issue to which the OPB attached some importance in its 1981 report and then sought to give a crude demonstration of how a free market philosophy can provide solutions. This suggests that the paper was motivated by opportunism; the government needed to take action on the recommendations the 1981

OPB report, and the pensions debate was seen as vehicle on which to launch the CPS ideas on a share-owning democracy. Indeed this was effectively confirmed on September 28th 1983 when a letter from Nigel Vinson and Philip Chappell headed: 'Financing pensions in a weak economy' appeared in the pages of *The Times*. This explained that:

> ... Our proposals did not start from trying to resolve the balance between leavers and stayers but rather because we perceived a lack of personal identification and involvement by the member in the wealth represented by the £120 billion of pension fund assets. It happens to be a beneficial and most timely by-product of our proposals that they would, over a period, also solve the 'early leaver' problem. (Vinson and Chappell, 1983a, p.13).

Both the CPS paper (Vinson and Chappell, 1983) and the above letter fail to argue that personal pensions should replace SERPS. This is an interesting omission since a primary market for personal pensions would have to be SERPS contributors. The welfarist principles underpinning SERPS are in direct contradiction to the market ideology of the CPS, and yet the 1983 paper implicitly supported the continued existence of SERPS. This might indicate that the authors were neither motivated nor even influenced by the growing concern over the future cost of SERPS, but it is more probable that the CPS paper was written in the knowledge of the fate which had befallen the CPRS report. It suggests that for tactical reasons chiefly in order to avoid embarrassing the Prime Minister and to a lesser degree to avoid incurring the immediate hostility of the Treasury and DHSS which the CPRS proposals had provoked in the previous month they refrained from explicitly putting this controversial argument while promoting their cause. Indeed, like the CPRS report, the CPS paper advocated higher basic pensions (Vinson and Chappell, 1983, para.4b iii); that such a proposal should emanate from the CPS is hard to imagine and can only be understood in terms of a crude attempt at producing a politically acceptable launch to a campaign for personal pensions.

In some ways the CPS paper is less radical than the subsequent DHSS Green Paper (DHSS, 1985). For example, whereas the Green Paper favoured allowing employees to opt out of their employers' occupational schemes at will, the CPS paper recommended that in order not to destabilise occupational funds, opting for a personal pension should only be permitted with the employer's consent (Vinson and Chappell, 1983, para.5e). This is a strange restriction in a paper otherwise concerned with individual freedom of choice. Nor, as mentioned, did it advocate the phasing out of SERPS. It must surely be unusual for a 'think tank' to be outdone by the DHSS.

This is probably evidence of the influence possessed by such insider groups as the IoD, many of whose members are involved in pensions-related activities such as insurance and would not want funds managed by their life offices to suffer; alternatively it may have been an attempt by the CPS to avoid causing embarrassment to the Conservative government as it neared a general election.

51

It seems more than coincidental that the CPS should launch its campaign for personal pensions the month after the Prime Minister 'killed' the CPRS report whose proposals appear to have been so similar in essence and two months before the CPRS was wound up.

As mentioned above, it is likely that CPS activity in the field of pensions began before the CPRS report was published and appears to be a response to the 1981 OPB report. However, one possibility is that the April 1983 CPS paper might have been a bowdlerised version of the March 1983 CPRS report, the Prime Minister's intention being to continue the pressure for personal pensions and the abolition of SERPS in a campaign that could at once be tightly controlled from Downing Street and yet kept at arm's length. A campaign run at arm's length would have the advantages of avoiding allegations of Prime Ministerial meddling while making it possible for the government to deny any connection with CPS proposals which happened to be particularly controversial. Later CPS publications, such as Chappell (1988, p.20), are unequivocal about SERPS:

> SERPS is part of the tradition of the consensus of the mid-1970s and should be scrapped along with all other intellectual impedimenta of that decade.

A question worthy of consideration is whether the CPS, as distinct from its supporters, can be said to have had a particular view on pensions policy. Lord Vinson felt the CPS did indeed have a position on pensions policy which he described in interview as deriving from a philosophical view on the control and distribution of wealth rather than a pragmatic attempt to solve a current pensions problem. The study group which had overall responsibility for preparing the paper consisted of:

> People who are interested in spreading and diffusing the ownership of wealth because of the philosophical background to this is that a free society ... depends on well-diffused, well-spread economic power and the multiple patronage that flows from that. (Vinson, 1989).

Accordingly, the 1983 CPS paper argued for the right of individuals to determine their methods and levels of investment and pensions provision, each individual having the right to contribute and manage their 'personal portable pension' portfolio. The authors of the CPS paper also argue that part of the solution to the 'early leaver' problem is for a condition to be included in OPB regulations that: '...preserved pensions of early leavers be increased in line with pensions in payment.' (Vinson and Chappell, 1983, para.4d) which might suggest an attempt to make the cost of occupational pensions more onerous for employers, but in fact it is no more onerous than the OPB's own recommendation and would hardly bring about the disestablishment of pension funds.

As has been shown, the proposals put forward by Vinson and Chappell frequently display a lack of empathy with the government's private thinking.

Their paper is a poorly written and presented document which received hostile and dismissive reactions from pensions providers; it contrasts sharply with the ASI: publication *The Future of Pensions*. (ASI, 1983) which was well-written, seven times as long, contained detailed and carefully developed arguments, and was well-produced with a glossy cover. Yet almost all members of the Inquiry into Provision for Retirement who were interviewed by the writer were convinced that it was the CPS paper which had a crucial effect on the pensions debate.

The CPS case received a boost when in late April 1983 the World Markets Company, which monitors the performances of pensions funds, published a survey of nearly 700 pension funds with a market value of £47 billion and 56% of all UK pension fund assets. The survey showed that the average monetary return on investments had been 28.9% during 1982 and that in real terms pension funds had shown an average return of 4.8% per annum over the previous five years while actuaries had been assuming a return of 3%. According to an article in *The Times*:

> These figure bear out the contention held by CPS in their review of pensions that pension funds are currently over-funded, providing an ideal opportunity when surplus cash is available within the funds, to improve the benefits of deferred pensioners (early leavers). It also accounts for the decline in real terms of pension fund contributions, down 20% on the previous year as employers cut back on the cash going into funds. (*The Times*, April 29th, 1983, p.17)

xx) Institute of Directors' 'Three Point Plan'.

In May 1983 the IoD's position moved beyond that of merely opposing moves that would increase employers' occupational pension costs. An article appeared in *Pensions World* (May 1983, p.306) reporting that Walter Goldsmith, Director General of the IoD, had recently addressed the Institute's Sussex branch where he had proposed a 'Three Point Pension Charter'. In this he proposed:

(1) Introducing greater competition to the pensions market by allowing the entry of banks, insurance companies, building societies, unit trusts etc.;

(2) The mandatory provision by employers' occupational schemes of Additional Voluntary Contributions (AVCs) as a condition of contracting out. This condition, which has since been legislated into being, seems to deliberately make the provision of occupational schemes onerous for employers.

(3) The unitisation of occupational pension funds.

On changing employers the employee would be able to take the full value of their accrued units and use the funds in one of the following ways:

(a) to set up their own fund, to which they could make additional voluntary contributions in the future;

53

(b)   to pass over to their new employer;

(c)   to invest in their own business. *(Pensions World*, May 1983, p.306).

This was the first time that Walter Goldsmith had, on behalf of the IoD, explicitly argued in favour of personal pensions. The case that was made closely resembled that of the CPS paper of the previous month both in its philosophical basis and in that it avoided discussing the obvious issue of the future cost of SERPS. Given the extent to which finance capitalism is represented in both the CPS (e.g. Philip Chappell is a retired merchant banker) and the IoD, it is likely that both organisations appreciated the arguments in favour of retaining SERPS for those for whom personal pensions could not be profitably provided. However, the IoD did eventually oppose SERPS.

xxi) National Association of Pension Funds' Annual Conference 1983.

In May 1983 the NAPF held its Annual Conference at Brighton. The Chairman, Maurice Oldfield, noted that the pensions industry was under 'great pressure' (Oldfield, 1983, p.377). He was particularly scathing towards the CPS paper on personal portable pensions, saying: 'Let us hope that the Centre for Policy Studies document is never taken seriously by any politician who sees half a chance to gain a vote or two.' (Oldfield, 1983, p.378). The Conference was addressed by Stewart Lyon, President of the Institute of Actuaries and a General Manager of the Legal & General Assurance Society, who gave a talk entitled 'Pensions can we afford the existing commitment?' (Lyon, 1983, pp.454 8). In this he reiterated his pessimistic view of the future for SERPS and NI contributions. He argued that high inflation, which had eroded the value of both pensions in payment and preserved pensions, had concealed the true cost of pension provision. This is consistent with the idea that pensions, though never really off the agenda despite the 1975 legislation, once again became a serious political issue as inflation began to fall. However, he was against abolishing SERPS, presumably recognising the need for a residual additional pension system, suggesting instead that the return on SERPS contributions should be reduced. He did not recommend money purchase schemes as a solution and he was particularly critical of the ideas of both the ASI and of Nigel Vinson and Philip Chappell. He referred to the ideas in the 1983 paper by Vinson and Chappell: '... which in my opinion is superficial and seriously lacking in balance.' (Lyon, 1983, p.458). On the matter of 'early leavers' Stewart Lyon said that the problem could not be solved without cost. He also argued that workers' expectations of pensions must be lowered but that pensions should be protected against inflation.

The Deputy Director General of the CBI, Bryan Rigby, addressed the NAPF Conference and expressed the CBI's concern that the cost of improvements to pension schemes, presumably including better terms for early leavers, should not be borne by employers (Rigby, 1983, pp.453 4). At the same time he was against the use of money purchase schemes as a solution, preferring what he described as an 'evolutionary' rather than radical approach to pensions change. By implication, he expected employees to either accept lower pensions or bear the full cost of improved conditions but was in favour of retaining SERPS.

With delegates arguing that workers' retirement expectations should be lowered and that any additional pensions costs should be borne by workers rather than employers, it would seem reasonable to expect the TUC delegates to put up a spirited defence of workers' especially early leavers' interests; instead, according to the *Pensions World* report, they seem to have used this opportunity at the NAPF Conference to advise trustees against investing funds in South Africa (Pensions World, June 1983, p.382).

On May 8th 1983, the final day of the NAPF Annual Conference and the day before the June General Election was called, the Secretary of State for Social Services, Norman Fowler, addressed those gathered in Brighton. In what was undoubtedly a reference to the forthcoming DHSS Early Leavers Conference he assured them that there would be no change in pensions legislation without consultation. He did make it known that he was not keen on the 'Central Fund' solution to the 'early leaver' problem which had been adopted by NAPF as policy, and with regard to what he called 'portable personal pensions', he said: 'I can see the attraction...' (Fowler 1983, p.381) though in this context he seemed to be referring to executives rather than the majority of workers. In the same speech Norman Fowler said:

> But the problems of transferability can be tackled without replacing employers' occupational schemes by personal pensions. The problems are essentially of costs and priorities. ... Personal pensions are a separate matter ... .
> (Fowler, 1983, p.381)

thereby indicating that the two issues of portability/early leavers and personal pensions were not to be linked. However, later in the same address he said:

> There are some fundamental questions about choice to be resolved here. There are also difficult questions of whether a personal money purchase pension will be a more attractive choice than a final salary occupational pension ... and of the effects on occupational schemes if a substantial number of young employees are allowed to opt out. I hope that all concerned will join in the debate and that the early conference which I am proposing to hold on early leavers will provide an opportunity for the strength of various competing ideas to be tested out in public against one another.
> (Fowler, 1983, p.382).

This speech is significant because Norman Fowler, having first indicated the separateness of the early leaver and personal pensions issues, then goes on to confuse the two issues, deliberately or otherwise, by suggesting that both subjects should be discussed at the forthcoming Early Leavers Conference. As will be seen, this 'confusion' was to be a important characteristic of both the DHSS

Early Leavers Conference and the Inquiry into Provision for Retirement. It may have had a decisive role in influencing the shape of the arguments that were submitted and the ideas that emerged from the latter.

In the course of the same speech Norman Fowler announced that legislation would be introduced to remove 'franking' and that he had set up a Joint Working Group to look at the OPB report of 1981 and its recommendations on early leavers.

xxii) General Election, 1983.

Then came the General Election. As mentioned, it was called on May 9th 1983, the day after Norman Fowler's speech to the NAPF, and held one calendar month later on June 9th. The Conservative Party emerged with a majority of 144 seats over all other parties and a majority of 188 seats over the Labour Party.

While the General Election campaign was in progress, on May 24th, Norman Fowler repeated that unless occupational pension funds made satisfactory arrangements to protect the interests of early leaver he would introduce legislation (The Times, May 25th, 1983, p.5). The Conservative manifesto committed the future Conservative government to improving the lot of early leavers but otherwise left improvements in occupational schemes to the pensions industry (Lorna Bourke, 1983).

6   Post-1983 General Election

Introduction

Following the General Election of June 9th 1983 there was a change in the nature of the Conservative approach to policy-making. According to Peter Young of the ASI the re-elected Conservative government acquired a sense of immortality and this had profound effects on both their policies and the justifications put forward to explain them (Rose, 1989). Where hitherto the approach to pensions policy had been penny pinching, with changes to the basis and implementation dates of upratings, the approach adopted after May 1983 was different in at least two respects: –

(1) most obviously, and as a consequence of the overwhelming Conservative majority in the House of Commons, the post-1983 policies on retirement pensions were of a more uncompromising nature than before. There was no need to concede amendments to bills in order to secure their passage through Parliament. Their implemented policies tended to represent the operationalisation of Conservative philosophy in an almost pure form. As will be shown, a notable exception to this concerned attempts to abolish SERPS on which the government backed down, and

(2) the perspective upon which policies were based was decidedly more long-term than had previously been the case. Previously, policy makers had been influenced by three factors:

(a) *The goal of re-election.*

   With five-year terms of office British governments have usually been reluctant to make radical changes to existing policies. Policies take time to formulate and implement and may not be in place in time for the next general election. This appears to have held true for the first Thatcher government since it is apparent from the Cabinet's hostile reaction to the proposals for cutting state spending (described in Chapter 4), that although it was in order for the Treasury to ask the CPRS to produce such radical plans for cutting government expenditure, the proximity of a general election was instrumental in those proposals being disowned,

(b) *The fear that a successive government would simply repeal radical legislation before implementation was complete.*

This happened both in 1971 when the recently elected Conservative government was able to repeal as yet unimplemented sections of the Children and Young Persons Act 1969 which had been enacted by the previous Labour government, and in 1975 when the Labour government's Secretary of State, Barbara Castle, repealed unimplemented sections of the 1973 Conservative pensions legislation.

(c) *The need to deal with whatever economic crisis the country was currently facing.*

Since the mid 1960s there had been a perception of Britain experiencing an almost unbroken series of economic crises, beginning with a balance of payments crisis that precipitated the devaluation of sterling in 1967 and including a series of rises in oil prices implemented by OPEC in 1973 and again in 1979. Whether these crises were real or otherwise, a considerable part of all political debate and decision-making was nevertheless occupied by attempts at devising solutions.

Post-1983 Conservative Policies

With the sense of immortality that affected the Conservative government after May 1983 a longer term view in policy-making was possible, and with the revenues that flowed from North Sea oil on top of the economic recovery that began in 1982, the government was no longer preoccupied with controlling the next economic crisis. As a result the bases and justifications for policy changes became more overtly ideological. In the absence of a preoccupation with either the next general election or some impending crisis it became possible for the Conservative government in general and the Treasury in particular to pursue policies not because of the need for urgent action but simply because they believed them to be right. It became possible too for the Conservative government to look at the long-term implications of current policy-making. Consideration was given, for example, to the burden which SERPS would comprise for future generations of tax and national insurance payers. As Norman Fowler was to comment in 1985:

> Neither I nor the Government generally are interested in securing temporary change. We want change to last. (Norman Fowler, 1983a)

However, the formulation of radical policies was conditioned by a belief, deeply held by the Conservative right wing, that governments should avoid interfering with the running of private sector institutions wherever possible. The result was that Conservative politicians, brimming with ideas for privatising such state run enterprises as British Gas, British Telecom and the Trustee Savings Bank, were very coy about getting involved in occupational pensions.

58

Hence, it was only after a prolonged period of exhortation and cajolery had failed to persuade the pensions industry to do something about the inequitable treatment of early leavers, that Norman Fowler finally organised a major conference to resolve this matter.

This conference is described below, but for now it is important to recognise that this predisposition to inaction opened the door still wider for previously marginal think tanks and pressure groups to make influential contributions to the development of pensions policy.

Equal Opportunities Commission

In June and November 1983 the EOC made efforts to persuade pension providers to make a commitment to equality. The provision that men and women should receive equal annual incomes from annuities in spite of gender differences in longevity might have represented a limited success for women but it was not implemented. In their attempts to influence policy the EOC could not compare with such organisations as the IoD. Despite their apparent insider status the EOC had no overlapping memberships with influential groups and they were ideologically out of sympathy with the New Right agenda that was gaining ground.

Institute of Directors

On September 3rd 1983, shortly before the DHSS Early Leavers' Conference (September 14th 1983), Walter Goldsmith of the IoD was reported as having written in an information sheet produced by Pointon York, a financial services group, on the advantages of personal pensions and the disadvantages of occupational pension scheme. He argued that:

> ... employees fail to take into account in their remuneration package the value of non-pay benefits. If pensions were expressed as capital of each individual it would undoubtedly have a useful impact on employees' attitudes in the annual pay as workers saw their pensions grow. (Walter Goldsmith, cited in: *The Times* , September 3rd, 1983)

Walter Goldsmith also argued for all occupational funds to provide for additional voluntary contributions and transferability of the full value of employees' accrued contributions: into a new employer's pension fund, into a personal pension portfolio, or to be used by the ex employee to capitalise a new business. He continued:

> The political advantages of these proposals are clear. While dealing with the problems of the early leaver, a nation of capitalists would be unleased on a massive scale. A wider interest in the success of industry would be identified. In particular, any Socialist plans to take control of pension funds would receive short shrift from 15 million owners. (Walter Goldsmith, cited in: *The Times*, September 3rd, 1983)

This appears to have been the IoD's most partisan statement to date on the subject of pensions. As with the CPS, the economic and ideological objectives seem to be of greater importance than solving the practical problems of providing for 'early leavers'. It seems unlikely that Walter Goldsmith did not realise how onerous the measures on transferability were; rather, the whole package served three political purposes:

1   they forestalled any attempt by a future left wing government to 'nationalise' the pensions industry. Since the publication of the Wilson Report (1980) there had from time to time been calls from the left wing of the Labour Party to nationalise occupational pension funds and use them to regenerate industry (Bose, 1985) and the Conservatives were generally sensitive to possibility that their policy changes might be reversible;

2   they generated support for the twin concepts of individual capitalism and personal pensions while undermining the credibility of the main opponents to such proposals: the occupational pensions lobby, and

3   the measures on transferability were necessary in order to ensure financial neutrality between occupational and personal pensions.

The IoD proposals met the government's policy objectives on SERPS and the OPB report, they were compatible with the government's ideological predilections and they would be difficult for a future government to reverse. That the IoD and others had canvassed support for these proposals and in doing so provoked only half hearted opposition would have made them all the more attractive to the government.

DHSS Conference on Early Leavers

On September 14th 1983 the DHSS Conference on Early Leavers was held at the then DHSS Headquarters at Alexander Fleming House. The expressed purpose of the Conference was to look at the problem of early leavers and to see if any developments in opinion had occurred since the NAPF annual conference in May. Speaking at the Conference, the Secretary of State for Social Services, Norman Fowler said:

> There is a consensus view that actions should be taken on the problem of early leavers and I think the case for legislation has got very much stronger. There is no question that the representatives at today's conference also accept it. … If we wait for a decision on portable pensions, we would be waiting rather longer. I think we can act separately on early leavers. (cited in: Bourke, 1983a).

This appears to have been an attempt by Norman Fowler to both consult and shape the pensions policy community. Only the previous week (September 8th 1983) he had given one of the most positive acknowledgements of his favour-

60

able predisposition towards using the private sector to solve welfare problems. He announced the private firms could tender for NHS contracts for cleaning, catering and laundry.

According to a key participant the purpose of the Early Leavers Conference was to get ideas on personal pensions and unitising. This is in stark contrast with the Conference's declared aim but it confirms the confusion sown by Norman Fowler's earlier remarks. At the Conference established pensions interests said, personal pensions were not feasible, creating an image of administrative chaos in which pension providers would have to pursue employees and small employers whose contributions were in arrears. However, (later – Sir) Mark Weinberg challenged this view, saying that personal pensions were indeed feasible. He was subsequently appointed to the Inquiry Sub Group, although this was probably due to his previously work on personal pensions. Among those represented at this meeting were the NAPF, the OPB, the CPS, the Society of Pensions Consultants (SPC), the Association for Consulting Actuaries (ACA), the Life Offices Association/Associated Scottish Life Offices (LOA/ASLO), the Government Actuary's Department (GAD), the TUC and the CBI.

In attempting to understand forces at work in this Conference it is helpful to categorise the participating organisations in terms of the groups they represented and their interests: the NAPF represented employers who sponsored occupational pension schemes. Others representing vested interest groups included the IoD and TUC, although these two could be said to have a strong ideological base.

There were representatives of such professional bodies as the Institute of Actuaries and the Society of Pension Consultants who were present because of their technical expertise in this field. Of course, the relationships between these organisations and the individuals representing them was a little more complex than this; there were frequent cases of cross-membership in which an individual belonged to two organisations present, and there were other instances where an individual was present because of their technical expertise and the office they held in a professional institute, but where they also held senior posts with such an organisation as a life office.

The NAPF continued to play a defensive role in the pensions debate. At the Early Leavers Conference Tom Heyes, chairman of NAPF, could only say that his organisation accepted legislation 'reluctantly' (Bourke, 1983a). In a subsequent editorial comment on the Early Leavers Conference Tom Heyes was scathing about both OPB and CPS. He described the OPB proposals for escalating the value of deferred pensions as 'simplistic' and doing nothing for pensions already in payment (Heyes, 1983). He was referring to the fact that early leavers who had already retired would not benefit from the measures proposed by the OPB, which while true was little more than a diversion from the fact that the OPB recommendations would increase pension costs for NAPF members.

However, by publishing his criticisms of personal pensions in an editorial of *Pensions World* he was probably preaching to the converted and failing to reach the the most important audience which consisted of policy makers. By being generally negative and actively trying to avoid a solution to the early leavers problem the NAPF gave the appearance of being primarily concerned with the defence of its members' material interests, these being employers with an interest in holding down labour costs. A different interpretation was provided by a representative of the Society of Pensions Consultants who said that providers of pensions 'froze' because they were uncertain of what the government was about to legislate, and the government was holding fire in the hope that the pensions industry would produce a collective solution (*Pensions World,* October 1983, p.704). In any event, the NAPF's refusal to compromise meant that at this stage at least their ideas, and therefore their members' interests, had no influence on the pensions policy-making process.

The CPS was represented at the Conference by Nigel Vinson. In his presentation to the Conference he argued that in circumstances of 'catalytic change' such as withdrawal from an occupational pension scheme through redundancy, the individual should be allowed to create his or her own pension investment portfolio with the proceeds of their accrued pensions contributions. This represented a narrowing of the proposal contained in their April 1983 paper (Vinson and Chappell, 1983) that every individual should be allowed a self-administered pension scheme.

The very presence at this Conference of Nigel Vinson, who was a leading protagonist of the personal pensions cause, seems peculiar if it was accepted by Norman Fowler that personal pensions and early leavers were separate issues. It appears to confirm that in Norman Fowler's mind the two issues were still confused. However, an alternative interpretation might be that Norman Fowler had little alternative but to give a representative of CPS a hearing at the Conference, such was that organisation's standing within hierarchy of the Conservative Party and its strength within the pensions policy community.

The OPB was represented, presumably defending its recommendation for the revaluation of deferred pensions. The TUC was firmly against the CPS personal pension proposal. They also said that leavers and stayers should be subject to equal treatment with regard to revaluation of deferred pensions up to the wage levels of retirement age, and that this should be achieved without reducing benefit levels. In effect they rejected the idea that those retired workers who had been 'stayers' were subsidised by the early leavers, arguing instead that employers had been able to underfund their schemes; henceforth employers should increase their contributions. A Conservative Secretary of State could not possibly have adopted such a policy, and by taking this position the TUC ensured its continued exclusion from any pensions policy community.

The CBI, represented by Bill Ashley, favoured a voluntary solution by employers and scheme members. He insisted that pension funds had in the past shown themselves to be adaptable to changing circumstances. The CBI had prepared and circulated among its members a set of seven alternative solutions to the early leavers problem, all equally vague and unenforceable.

The announcement of the Inquiry into Provision for Retirement

More than a year after the SSC report was published the Government produced its response entitled *Reply to the Third Report of the Social Services Committee* (DHSS, 1983). The Government appeared to gently criticise the Committee for not strictly adhering to their own terms of reference and focussing instead on pension levels, and in part this a fair point to make; it had argued, for example, that priority should be given to raising the income levels for poorer pensioners rather than providing funding for earlier retirement (SSC, 1982a, para.55). In addition, the Government refused to accept the SSC's estimates of the costs of the altering/equalising male and female pensionable ages and of introducing flexible retirement (DHSS, 1983, para.7). The Government's response ended with the announcement that:

> ... the Government is setting up an Inquiry chaired by the Secretary of State for Social Services to consider pensions issues. Members of the Inquiry's Steering Committee will include experts in the field of pensions, and the aim will be to encourage wide spread public debate on all the issues relating to the future development of pensions. The Inquiry has been given the following terms of reference:

>> 'To study the future development, adequacy and cost of state, occupational and private provision for retirement in the United Kingdom, including the portability of pension rights, and to consider possible changes in those arrangements, taking account of the recommendations of the Select Committee on Social Services in their report on retirement age'. (DHSS, 1983, para.11.)

Despite this statement that the Inquiry would take account of the SSC's report: *The Age of Retirement*, it is difficult to judge whether this document had any impact on subsequent pensions policy. It does display the full range of opinions that existed on this subject at that time and most of the issues raised were ultimately dealt with in the Inquiry into Provision for Retirement. However, as mentioned in Chapter 5, select committee reports are noted for their lack of impact on policy and just as the SSC report did not trigger the Inquiry so it is improbable that it had any effect on the Inquiry's policy outcome.

Not only was the Inquiry into Provision for Retirement announced but so too were the identities of some of the expert members. A letter by Norman Fowler was published in the Sunday Times detailing the expert members' roles:

> The other members of the Inquiry are there to help us in evaluating the evidence because of their experience of occupational pensions or other relevant fields. But it is the Government which in the end has to reach conclusions and the main responsibility for the Inquiry will be mine. (Norman Fowler, 1983).

Until now the main 'public' forums in which an essentially ideological pensions debate had taken place had been the NAPF Annual Conference, conferences on pensions and the letters columns of *The Times*. The pensions policy debate had become dominated by an elite group of actuaries, financiers and right wing ideologues, supported at least in principle by the Prime Minister and the Chancellor of the Exchequer. Those who favoured the personal pension option were turning out to be very able at securing press and political attention. It seemed that the debate was now beyond the control of the Secretary of State for Health and Social Services. By setting up the Inquiry into Provision for Retirement Norman Fowler was regaining the initiative.

With the announcement of the Inquiry into Provision for Retirement, Norman Fowler began to take control of the pensions debate. He was under pressure on at least two fronts to reform pensions. Firstly, he had given the pensions industry every opportunity to produce a solution to the early leavers problem and they had failed to do so. To the extent that reduced pensions entitlement was likely to leave retired early leavers more dependent on means-tested social security than retired stayers, there was a long-term incentive for the Conservative Government to act. Secondly, pressure was now coming from the Prime Minister and the Chancellor of the Exchequer (and perhaps some other Cabinet members) to reduce the long-term cost of SERPS, and this resulted in a show of disunity which is described below.

At exactly the point in time when the Review was being set up there was an unusually public disagreement between Norman Fowler and both Margaret Thatcher and Nigel Lawson. On November 23rd, the day the announcement of the Inquiry into Provision for Retirement was made, a report appeared in *The Times* that:

> Cabinet ministers complained last night *(ie Nov. 22nd)* that they were kept in ignorance of the consequences of their recent decisions to cut public spending. And as the Prime Minister arrived in India ... two cabinet members made speeches heavily critical of her views and attitudes. Mr Norman Fowler challenged the belief of Mrs Thatcher and Mr Lawson that public spending would have to be curbed because of long-term increases in the number of pensioners. *(Bevins, 1983)*

The other cabinet minister referred to above was Peter Walker and the cost cutting in question concerned measures introduced by the Treasury to save money by increasing parental contributions to student grants. Cabinet ministers complained that they had had to agree to them under pressure without being given enough time or information to weigh up the consequences (Haviland, 1983). This report, and the public protest by Norman Fowler and Peter Walker, demonstrate the extent to which spending policy was being dominated by the Prime Minister and the Chancellor of the Exchequer working in close cooperation.

This protest was one of two such expressions of dissent. In the same edition of *The Times* Norman Fowler was reported as having made a speech at Brent that was strongly critical of Margaret Thatcher and Nigel Lawson on the day before the Review was announced:

Mr Norman Fowler last night *(Nov. 22nd)* shot down one of the key arguments used by Mrs Thatcher and the Chancellor of the Exchequer for long-term spending cuts the prospective increase in the pensioner population. He said in a speech at Brent:

'The numbers of people over 65 years who will have risen over the last 20 years will now remain more or less stable until about 2010.'

But Mr Fowler last night took his challenge to Mrs Thatcher and Mr Lawson further ... arguing that social policy needed to be subject to 'rational appraisal' and that this debate should be 'responsible, realistic and open'. He then directly took on Thatcher and Lawson when he said:

'The fundamental case for open debate is, of course, that it provides the opportunity for agreement on the problems and the cost of resolving them. And let us be clear; facts do not all run one way. A view being put around with increasing frequency is that the emerging cost of the elderly is going to place "unbearable strains" on the population at work. Is this a fair summary? The answer is far more complex than might be imagined. It is anything but clear that as is often stated we risk being pushed off course by a further uncontrollable tide of spending.' *(Bevins, 1983a; in Italics: writer's addition.)*

Norman Fowler's justification for this last assertion that there was no certainty of an 'uncontrollable tide of spending' was that inflation had fallen and the numbers of people aged over 65 years would remain roughly stable over the next 20 years. In a subsequent ITN interview Margaret Thatcher said 'By the time people like me are old age pensioners, there are going to be more than there are now' (Bevins, 1983). There is an identifiable point of disagreement between Norman Fowler and Nigel Lawson. This took the form of a comment by Nigel Lawson on London Weekend Television's *Weekend World* the previous Sunday, saying that there was '... a constant pressure from the ageing population' (Bevins, 1983). This view is in total disagreement with Norman Fowler's thinking at that time, as the speech at Brent clearly shows. Norman Fowler was in agreement with Nigel Lawson's aim of cutting taxation, but he felt that:

the reduction of taxation was not our only objective. We had other social policy commitments and we also needed to keep these. (Fowler, 1991, p.202)

Norman Fowler's Brent speech suggests that although he was under political pressure to adopt a cost cutting approach towards pensions, he did not favour the scrapping of SERPS. The timing, coinciding as it did with the announcement of the Inquiry into Provision for Retirement, also suggests that he was distancing himself from the Prime Minister and the Chancellor of the Exchequer in an attempt to assert control over the pensions debate.

In fact, no Secretary of State could have excluded either the Prime Minister or the Chancellor of the Exchequer from pensions policy decisions. Changes concerning this area of policy invariably have enormous long-term implications in terms of taxation, public spending and the electorate's perception of the government of the day. However, Norman Fowler's public rejection of their ideas and setting up of a highly public inquiry can be seen as an attempt to take the policy-making process, in the short-term at least, out of the Cabinet's influence (save to the extent that some Cabinet members were appointed to the Inquiry by Norman Fowler). This would allow Norman Fowler to develop support for his policy ideas while making it difficult for other interested parties to impose their ideas without appearing meddlesome.

If this was not enough, the Inquiry's membership and format, to which a lot of thought was given, was designed to further reduce political interference through the recruitment of technical experts. In effect, Norman Fowler had created his own think tank which would produce technical arguments that could be difficult for political opponents to challenge; their ideological arguments would be rendered invalid. The use of selected Cabinet members on the Inquiry would provide an opportunity to canvas support and secure ministerial commitment prior to the proposals going before the appropriate cabinet committee.

On the same day as he announced the Inquiry into Provision for Retirement, Norman Fowler also announced: first, the future enactment of the OPB recommendations on the preservation of early leavers' pension rights on which a consultative document would be published the following week (in fact it was published on November 29th 1983 and reported in *The Times,* November 30th 1983); secondly, that he was concerned about the need for disclosure of information to pension fund members; thirdly, that he had set up a working party of officials to consider the implications of Professor Gower's study of investor protection, and finally the Inquiry would consider the possibility of personal pensions:

> This proposal deserves careful study.... My aim is to produce conclusions for example on personal pensions by the spring. (*Pensions World,* December 1983, p.788)

It would have been understandable if Norman Fowler had been dissatisfied with the OPB recommendations on early leavers. Even the OPB recognised that what they put forward was not a perfect solution:

> We realise that our conclusions will be disappointing to those who had hoped for a larger scale extension of transfer arrangements in a way which would have resolved most early leavers' problems. (OPB, 1981, chap 9.33).

The Secretary of State's intention to enact the OPB proposals implies that the early leaver problem had been solved to his satisfaction and therefore it ought to have had no place on the Inquiry into provision for Retirement. However, as will be seen in Chapter 8, this issue continued to cloud the pensions debate and indeed receive the Inquiry's attention. It will also be apparent that personal pensions were not seen as a solution to SERPS but would probably have come about anyway.

7 Inquiry into Provision for Retirement

Choice of Inquiry Format

The formal nature of the Inquiry and its invitations to interested parties to submit evidence rendered alternative forums of debate illegitimate. Henceforth the pensions debate took place under the chairmanship of Norman Fowler who also decided who could participate and which submissions would receive how much, if any, consideration.

Norman Fowler had decided against the conventional approach of setting up an internal committee of civil servants to review pensions arrangements:

> The last thing I wanted was to have an internal departmental inquiry on this because frankly, although there are some extremely able people inside the Department of Social Security I think some of the best civil servants I have ever worked with are in there I don't think necessarily that occupational pensions is, for example, the number one issue in the life of the DSS.
> (Sir Norman Fowler, 1993)

The likelihood was that a ministerial element would take policy forward more sharply and more politically than an internal civil service inquiry.

Nick Montagu was an Assistant Secretary in the Civil Service who, having only recently been transferred from another department, came to the Inquiry as secretary when the proposal for it was fully fledged. There were other civil servants with both experience in the field of pensions and established formal contacts with the pensions industry, several of whom could have performed the role of secretary to the Inquiry. However, among these would have been civil servants whose experience in maintaining the existing pensions system gave them a conservatism that made the development and implementation of radical measures anathema. It is possible that this formed one of a series of measures with which Norman Fowler sought to break up the existing policy community in that Nick Montagu had only recently joined the DHSS and therefore had not had time to be socialised into their particular culture. Nor had he had time to establish formal or informal relationships with interested parties. This argument is supported by the fact that the DHSS Research Unit was deliberately not consulted on the proposed contents of the Green Paper.

The implication is that tactical considerations and the need to win political support within the Cabinet were also important factors. The Inquiry format was a political device to ensure that these aims were achieved. Involving people from the pensions industry in the review process was essential, partly because of the need for their support and cooperation for any changes to existing pensions arrangements, and partly to provide Norman Fowler with the opportunity to develop the technical arguments that would support his personal pensions proposals. Whereas some parts of the pensions industry had, in the past, resisted the pressure for change, with the Inquiry into Provision for Retirement:

> It was not possible for anyone to refuse to co operate with this process, so one got it *(the pensions debate)* out in the open and one also made it incumbent on the pensions industry to give evidence to it, to give their best advice but also to be put under question. (Sir Norman Fowler, 1993).

In this way Norman Fowler was able to take control of the debate on pensions. He was very keen that it should be a public inquiry and so the DHSS advertised for evidence and held public sessions. These public sessions gave the Inquiry a fairly high profile and to some degree reduced the influence of pressure groups.

As mentioned, Norman Fowler chose to approach the perceived problems of the social security system by setting up a series of inquiries, each looking at a particular aspect of that system. Most inquiry teams, including that responsible for pensions, were chaired by ministers, which Meacher (1985, p.1) describes as both 'unprecedented' and 'an obstacle to impartial conduct'. However, this is to miss the point that Norman Fowler already knew what policy outcomes he wanted; an alternative format such as a committee of the sort chaired by Sir William Beveridge or a Royal Commission would not have allowed him to have control over the early stages of the policy making process:

> The difference between the way I did it and the way, say, the Beveridge Committee did it is that Beveridge simply made his proposals to the government. They were *his* proposals. He stood by them *but* it was the government that in the end made the decision on whether they accepted them or not. I was a government minister my role was different. I had to make proposals not only

proposals I believed in and supported but proposals which I could get past my colleagues. So I had to do both roles at the same time, and obviously things were changed and obviously there were battles. (Sir Norman Fowler, 1993).

How the Inquiry Functioned

Unlike a Royal Commission the Inquiry was not intended to produce findings in any formal sense. According to Norman Fowler, its purpose was to educate ministers so that they could then go on to produce a viable pensions policy. In other words, the Inquiry served as an advisory group to ministers who could formulate policies in the light of their discussions without being in any way bound by them. However, other participants in the Inquiry described the external members as having a more critical role in terms of actually coming up with ideas for future pensions policy. Indeed it seems unlikely that a Secretary of State would chair a series of 37 meetings purely in order to educate himself and other government ministers. Such a series of meetings could only have been intended to produce practical ideas to be incorporated into new a pensions policy, enabling Norman Fowler to keep the promise made when he announced the Inquiry into Provision for Retirement: 'My aim is to produce firm conclusions, for example on personal pensions, by the Spring.' (*Pensions World*, December 1983, p.788). As will be seen, the Inquiry into Provision for Retirement was really two inquiries held in parallel and whose membership overlapped to very a considerable degree.

Frequency of Meetings

The Main Team had 23 meetings. There were also three public sessions at which a total of eleven external bodies or individuals were met. These meetings ran from December 1983 to January 1985. The Inquiry's activities peaked in July 1984 when there five internal meetings and all three public sessions. All meetings of both the Main Team and the Sub Group were chaired by Norman Fowler. The Sub Group had seven internal meetings between January and May 1984. There were also four open sessions attended by representatives of 14 external bodies, at which a wide range of the views was presented.

The first public sessions were on personal pensions so as to complete the personal pensions task first. The Consultative Document was published by summer 1984 and the Main Pensions Inquiry went on until January 1985.

Constraints on the Review

Soon after the Inquiry into Provision for Retirement was announced the Treasury stepped in and laid down a zero cost constraint. Only later did the scope of the Review broaden to cover other aspects of social security so that the Inquiry into Provision for Retirement became one of a series of five reviews which undertook a study of the entire social security system. The reviews were commissioned ostensibly on the grounds of a need to overhaul the social security system and there was wide agreement that this was necessary. With this broadening in scope of the Social Security Review it was made clear by the Treasury that the zero cost principle applied across the board, allowing cross subsidies between expenditure heads. In the event this did not happen; rather, the Inquiry into Provision for Retirement was cost neutral in a self contained way, save to the extent that when considering modifying SERPS in the way proposed in the White Paper, *Programme for Action* (DHSS, 1985), the effect on income-related social security benefits and claims was taken into account.

Despite this, cost neutrality might have been considered a difficult goal to achieve when so many aspects of the costs, for example taxation, were not taken into account until the Inquiry had finished. However, the Social Security Review as a whole and its pensions component were conducted in public expenditure terms rather than in terms of revenue foregone. Hence taxation was not important; nor apparently was the loss of revenue from SERPS contributors who went over to personal pensions. The Inquiry's concern was with the level of actual public spending; the issue of revenue foregone became salient once the proposals got into the network of cabinet committees.

Critics have argued that the review process as a whole was flawed from the outset in that none of the review teams had a remit to examine the taxation system and, as described elsewhere in this Chapter, attempts to discuss tax issues were blocked by the Treasury representative on the Inquiry. Perhaps this was hardly surprising since it was a DHSS rather than a Treasury initiative; at least this was the formal position. Yet the cost to the Exchequer of personal allowances and relief from taxation is considerable, with relief on mortgage interest and contributions to private sector pension schemes amounting to almost £10bn. in 1984/5 (GLC, undated, p.8). Taxation was not discussed during the Inquiry, although the Treasury put in a note for information just to give the Inquiry some background on existing tax concessions which were discussed later on. One reason for the lack of discussion on taxation was because although the taxation implications would be considerable if there was a mandatory occupational or personal pension scheme of the sort outlined in the Green Paper, this would be revenue foregone rather than a change in costs; the amount of revenue foregone by virtue of tax relief on contributions would have been considerable. As will be seen in Chapter 8 it was this factor, rather than easing the hardship and trauma that would accompany the sudden ending of access to SERPS, which led to the Green Paper's abolitionist proposals being replaced by the White Paper's proposals to phase in personal pensions.

Support

As mentioned earlier, Nick Montagu was Secretary to the Inquiry. He was assisted by two people at principal level: an administrator (Ian Alexander) who acted as the Deputy Secretary; an economist who acted as the civil service special adviser to the Inquiry, and clerical and executive staff.

Membership

The Main Team which conducted the Inquiry into Provision for Retirement had twelve members, half of whom were Conservative parliamentarians: it was chaired by the Secretary of State for Social Services Norman Fowler, other politicians included Minister of State for Social Security Dr Rhodes Boyson (until September 1984) and Tony Newton (from September 1984), Under-secretary for Social Security Ray Whitney; Undersecretary for the DTI Alex Fletcher, Minister for Employment Peter Morrison, and the Treasury was represented by Junior Treasury Minister Sir Barney Hayhoe. There were two senior representatives from the pensions industry though they did not attend on behalf of their life offices; these were Marshall Field, Chairman of the Life Offices Association and the Occupational Pension Schemes Joint Working Group (also General Manager of the Phoenix Assurance Company) and Stewart Lyon, President of the Institute of Actuaries (also a member of the Joint Working Group on Occupational Pensions, and General Manager of Legal and General Assurance). Mark Weinberg, chairman of Hambro Life was a member of the Sub Group on personal pensions, did not appear to represent any partic-ular organisation. Professor Alan Peacock, Vice Chancellor of the University of Buckingham and formerly a member of the Institute of Economic Affairs (IEA) whose pro-market views are well known, and the Government Actuary Edward Johnston were also members. As well as being Government Actuary, Edward Johnston was at that time also President of the Pensions Management Institute.

It is perhaps significant that while the Treasury and the private sector pensions industry were both adequately, if indirectly, represented there was no represen-tative of the social security lobby such as a member of the SSAC. Nor does there appear to be a representative of the CBI, TUC or IoD, but then these groups all gave evidence in their own right.

The full Inquiry Team consisted of a mixture of ministers, outside advisers two of whom were actuaries, and the Government Actuary. The Treasury was usually represented ministerially by Sir Barney Hayhoe as well as by civil servants. Departments of Employment and Trade and Industry were members though they were not always represented ministerially as pensions issues were peripheral to their interests. These interests would sometimes be reflected in the Inquiry but apparently this did not lead in any sense to government departments pulling against each other.

In addition to the official members there was, as mentioned, a number of civil servants who contributed to the Inquiry's meetings. These included: Strachan Heppell (Permanent Secretary) who came to all the Inquiry meetings; Joe Ward (Undersecretary in charge of pensions policy), and Geoffrey Arton (Permanent Secretary, social security). These civil servants made significant contributions to the Inquiry's proceedings.

Although John Redwood and David Willetts were not co-opted onto the Inquiry they were effectively members. They came to virtually every meeting including informal meetings, and Nick Montagu kept them informed. John Redwood attended representing the Downing Street Central Policy Unit (CPU) to which he had been seconded from the merchant bankers, Rothschilds. By common consent he was very active. Either John Redwood or David Willetts would come along to meetings of the Inquiry, which was useful to Norman Fowler in two ways. First, it gave a flavour of the CPU's thinking. The CPU is so influential that it would be naive to ignore the direction of their thought. Secondly, as an actuary and investment adviser John Redwood had had considerable experience in the field of pensions from his time at Rothschilds. It might be thought that the presence of John Redwood and David Willetts, with their very close proximity to the Prime Minister, would inhibit free discussion among the Parliamentary members of the Inquiry, but Norman Fowler was sure this was not so. He described David Willetts as a very creative person with lots of ideas, adding that although he was not crucial to the Inquiry:

> Any government minister that has the slightest bit of sense and the slightest bit of aspiration to try to get his policies through will want to take the (Central) Policy Unit with him, and that's a fact of life. I mean, today if you're Secretary of State and you want to get your policies through, you will take quite a lot of trouble with the (Central) Policy Unit member who is looking after your area. (Sir Norman Fowler, 1993).

The three DHSS ministers in the Inquiry were free to feed in points that they wanted to, though in general they took the same line as that of the Secretary of State. The Treasury, on the other hand, did not always follow the same line as Norman Fowler; opposition took the form of Sir Barney Hayhoe from time to time intervening during the Main Team's deliberations with: 'I'm sorry. I can't allow this discussion to proceed.' if the discussion strayed into such areas as taxation. However, most Treasury opposition came after the Inquiry had completed its work.

The role of the Government Actuary, Edward Johnston, and his department was described as being of great importance to the Inquiry, not least when the policy-making process got beyond the Green and White Papers to the stage where it was necessary to know the cost implications of the final proposals. Indeed the Inquiry's secretary, Nick Montagu, was in daily contact with his opposite number in the Government Actuary's Department. In the course of the Inquiry the Government Actuary's Department produced such information as projections of what sums particular amounts of contribution might yield which were published in a background paper *Population, Pensions Costs and Pensioners' Incomes: A Background Paper the Inquiry into Provision for Retirement* (DHSS, 1984). The Government Actuary also produced an update of his previous quinquennial report showing what the cost would be and the effect of prices and earnings upratings. This was one of the first published documents. The second part of *Population, Pension Costs and Pensioners' Incomes* (DHSS, 1984), on the subject of pensioners' incomes, was by Guy Feigehen, who was a senior civil servant in the DHSS. However, from the evidence of Inquiry participants it is clear that the information produced by the Government Actuary had no impact on the direction of pensions policy decisions, implying that technical information and arguments played a supporting rather than decisive role in the policy-making process.

Procedure

(i) *Agenda:*The agenda resulted from discussions between Nick Montagu and Norman Fowler. Control obviously lay with the latter. The agenda was updated on a regular basis according to recent developments in the Inquiry. It covered a wide range of topics without ranging further than the Secretary of State wanted it to.

(ii) *Invitations for Evidence:* Shortly after the Inquiry into Provision For Retirement was announced in November 1983, invitations to submit evidence were sent out. Unfortunately the consultation procedure afforded only and two months for outside contributors to make submissions. Remarkably, by the closing date of January 31st 1984 for written evidence on the first of the parts into which the Inquiry was subdivided, written evidence from over 1,500 sources had been received (Kaye, 1981, p.44). Nevertheless, the consultation period was wholly inadequate, not least because the estimates of the budgetary impact of the proposals were not published until November 1985, which was after the consultation period had closed and indeed after the publication of the Green Paper in June 1985. Had either a Royal Commission or public inquiry been used the effective consultation period would have been considerably longer.

(iii) *Selection of evidence:* The broad criteria were the result of discussions between Norman Fowler and Nick Montagu. A lot of the evidence which came in was what in the civil service is known as 'casework' i.e. individual complaints and anecdotes; it was not evidence of the sort the Inquiry was interested in. There were hard luck stories on early leavers; a lot of people were in favour of a lower pension age; people who felt their state pension was too low. In any case, the Inquiry was concerned not with those already retired but rather with the current workforce. All of the said evidence was read by either Nick Montagu or Ian Alexander and was logged. If it came from a representative body it would probably be summarised. If it was evidence from a representative body that was going to give evidence it would be summarised in some detail. What was ultimately produced was a summary of points made under the headings plus approximate numbers of how many pieces of evidence referred to each heading. In addition, evidence from obviously important external bodies was passed to the Inquiry without being edited or summarised. Other evidence might be forwarded to the Inquiry in summarised form if the civil servants thought it worthy of the Inquiry's attention. Members of the Inquiry could call for evidence if they thought it appropriate.

(iv) *Minutes:* Nick Montagu produced cabinet-style minutes after every meeting which were then circulated. At the end of each discussion the Secretary of State would give a summing up which would go into the minutes. Where there were different points of view on an issue Nick Montagu produced minutes that reflected these points of view and the Secretary of State's summing up as chairman of the discussion.

Personal Pensions Sub Group.

A complete review of state and occupational pensions was called for with a particular slant towards the 'personal portable pensions' issue. Hence the Inquiry into Provision for Retirement had a Sub Group on personal pensions. Indeed the personal pensions solution was being considered as a policy option when the Inquiry was set up and it was to be looked at from a technical rather than political viewpoint. A separate Sub Group on personal pensions with slightly different, though overlapping, membership was set up at virtually the same time as the Main Team. As well sending out its own invitations for evidence: 'The Sub Group commissioned market research ... to assess the likely demand for personal pensions.' (DHSS, 1984a, para.2.1). Like the Main Team of the Inquiry, the Sub Group was chaired by Norman Fowler and supported by the same secretariat.

The Sub Group was purely advisory and devoted to personal and portable pensions. Its membership consisted of (now Sir) Mark Weinberg, Stewart Lyon and Marshall Field. However, the informal organisation of the Sub Group meant that it was frequently attended by non members who took an active part in its proceedings.

The Sub Group differed from the Main Team in that although it consisted of the same outside advisers plus Mark Weinberg, with the exception of Norman Fowler it had no politicians among its regular members. Politicians usually only attended when invited although they could attend at their discretion and, in any event, they were kept informed of developments within the Sub Group. Among those who also attended were John Redwood on behalf of the CPU, David Willetts of the CPS, and senior civil servants.

With regard to the the Sub Group's role, the evidence indicates that the personal pension solution had been decided upon before the Inquiry's proceedings commenced; the Sub Group was mainly concerned with practicalities. The relationship between the Sub Group and the Main Team was such that formally the Sub Group reported to the Main Team, although the membership was overlapping. In terms of producing pensions policy it is possible that the Sub Group was more innovative than the Main Team, the latter apparently acting mainly as a sounding board with which Norman Fowler could assess Cabinet reaction to the proposals that were emerging. It was the Sub Group which was mainly responsible for producing the Consultative Document on Personal Pensions, although its actual author was Nick Montagu.

That the Government Actuary, Edward Johnston, was not a member of the Sub Group implies that issues relating to the future of SERPS and its projected costs were not discussed in this forum and this adds weight to the assertion that the idea of personal pensions was not inextricably linked to the projected cost of SERPS, and the 2% Incentive and the National Insurance Rebate were not discussed here. This points to the choice of personal pensions flowing from a political rather than economic or actuarial preference.

Analysis of the Inquiry's Deliberation

In this section the evidence from interview data, correspondence and publications is analysed in an attempt to reveal something of the course taken by the Inquiry, its priorities and its contribution to the Green Paper (DHSS, 1985), the White Paper (DHSS, 1985a), and the final legislation: Social Security Act 1986. The analysis looks at the evidence in terms of the inputs and influences that could reasonably be expected to have had some effect on the Inquiry's course, and then in terms of the Inquiry's outputs. The available and unavoidably incomplete evidence is analysed according to what have appeared so far to be the main issues in the pensions debate and whose importance is confirmed by the correspondence between the DHSS and interested parties requesting evidence:

1. demography and the cost of SERPS;

2. personal pensions;

3. the early leavers problem, the age of retirement was also examined since, as will be seen, it was specifically mentioned by respondents as a factor.

An ideological shift occurred in the early 1980s that was epitomised by the New Right's concept of 'people's capitalism' in which the bulk of the population would be shareholders whose material well-being depended to far greater extent than before on their ability to secure sufficient income to purchase resources through the market. The role of the state would accordingly diminish. As a result the relative importance of ideology is a recurrent theme and will be highlighted in the course of examining the Inquiry's considerations.

i) Demography and the Future Cost of SERPS.

It was felt within the Inquiry into Provision for Retirement that the open-ended commitment of providing a GMP, stipulated by the Social Security Act 1975 as a condition of contracting out of SERPS, discouraged small employers from making arrangements for providing their employees with additional pensions and in turn this had encouraged membership of the state additional pension scheme. Consequently this aspect of the relationship between occupational pensions and SERPS was a major consideration. It had been accepted by members of the Inquiry that the way to get people out of SERPS was through 'personal portable pensions', because the people who belonged to SERPS, by and large, were people who worked for very small firms who could not create final salary occupational schemes. However, in interview, Sir Norman Fowler said that personal pensions would have been introduced regardless of any changes that may or may not have been made to the arrangements for SERPS:

> I would have proposed personal pensions irrespective of what had happened to SERPS because personal pensions seemed to me to be simply an extra option as far as the public was concerned. It of course was deeply unpopular with the occupational pensions industry. It was an option we would have wished to give to people come what may. (Sir Norman Fowler, 1993).

The way in which the Inquiry proceeded confirms the inevitability of contracted out personal pensions. But if this was so, why should a Secretary of State go to all the bother of holding a time consuming and expensive inquiry with a personal pensions Sub Group? As is shown in this Chapter, there were political and tactical motives for this.

A very considerable amount of the Main Team's time was spent on the reduction of the cost of SERPS not in the near future but into the next century. There was a radical view from the right that some finite term should be put on SERPS at the end of which it would be abolished regardless of the consequences. The alternative view, which had emerged from earlier internal inquiries, was that the conditions of SERPS should be modified. The consensus among members of the Inquiry was that modification might be justified but not outright abolition. At least one participant argued for more compassion on the grounds that it would take quite a long time to adjust to the new concept, saying in interview that 'It's rather like weaning someone off drugs'. The question of the trade off between SERPS and the Basic Retirement Pension costs was considered. There was no concern about the cost of the Basic Retirement Pension, although they did look at cost projections for raising the value of this pensions in line with earnings instead of prices.

It is interesting to speculate on the influence of demographic projections on the policy-making process. The Main Team sought evidence from the Government Actuary's Department and the NAPF on this matter, but Norman Fowler's public disagreement with the Prime Minister and the Chancellor of the Exchequer in November 1983 expressed in two speeches on November 22nd and 23rd 1983 (see Chapter 6) would seem to indicate that with regard to the future cost of SERPS he attached little importance to demographic arguments. However, in interview Sir Norman said:

With the kind of 'pay as you go' system that we have in this country, I think it would be irresponsible for a politician who has any pretensions to say he's looking at pensions provision not to actually look at the future debt, because future debt and how it's financed is what it's all about. (Sir Norman Fowler, 1993).

The implication is that although at some stage during the Inquiry the Secretary of State came to accept the logic of assessing the demographic data, it was only sought as part of the search for technical arguments to be used in support of political proposals concerning personal pensions.

(ii) Personal Pensions.

The occupational pensions interests were deeply suspicious of moves towards personal pensions and money purchase because of the unfortunate experiences of the 1970s when inflation eroded money purchase schemes. Sir Norman found that:

> ... there was a lot of inherent conservatism as far as the pensions industry was concerned, and a lot of people saying 'For goodness sake don't make changes because otherwise we'll get back into the situation where the Labour Party get in and they'll make changes and then we won't know what to do!' (Sir Norman Fowler, 1993).

Occupational pension providers were also frightened of anything that might be an alternative to the compulsory membership of occupational pension schemes. Those opposed to personal pensions had argued that it would be impossible or too expensive to run, but in some cases their real fears stemmed from the possible destabilisation of occupational pension schemes.

Such destabilisation would arise because group pension funds have cross-subsidies in-built so that the current younger contributors subsidise the current older contributors. If sufficient number of young contributors opted out of an occupational pension scheme to take out personal pension plans, group schemes would become unviable or collapse. Hence those opposed to personal pensions wanted opting out to be at the discretion of the employer rather than the employee. The Sub Group did a lot of work on this problem.

For those sympathetic to the views of the New Right, personal pensions were inextricably linked to 'people's capitalism'. Herein, it seemed, lay the solution to the predicted future escalation in the cost of SERPS: those people currently contributing to SERPS must be persuaded to use the market to provide for retirement by taking out personal pensions. Further indications that Norman Fowler's support for personal pensions was essentially ideological are contained in the two letters discussed below from the DHSS to organisations with a special interest in pensions policy, requesting that they submit evidence to the Inquiry into provision for Retirement. These organisations included the CBI, IoD, and NAPF.

The first letter was dated December 12th 1983 and was from Nick Montagu, Secretary to the Inquiry. A number of features serve to confirm that Norman Fowler was thinking of personal pensions as being the Inquiry's focal point. For example, the letter's heading:

INQUIRY INTO PROVISION FOR RETIREMENT
PERSONAL PORTABLE PENSIONS

and the sentence:

> The Secretary of State is anxious that the Inquiry should give priority in their considerations to the question of personal portable pensions, on which he hopes to reach a conclusion by the spring.

Then there is a list of what are described as 'Some of the main advantages of personal pensions ... '.

- they give people more control over their own pensions.

- employees would have a greater sense of involvement in their pension scheme.

- they would produce a fairer balance between people who leave a scheme and those who stay in it than the present arrangements.

- they help encourage job mobility.

At the end of the letter it states:

> The Government are sympathetic towards these aims *(i.e. advantages to personal pensions)* and want to examine what are the consequences of achieving them through portable pensions.

With the possible exception of encouraging job mobility, all the 'advantages' listed above are ideological, and at no point does the letter refer to the future of SERPS. Since none of the issues addressed has either economic or demographic dimensions, it is clear that the outcome of this first phase of the Inquiry was ideologically determined and was a *fait accompli*. This raises questions concerning the immediate origin of this new ideology. A clue might lie in the repeated use of the term 'personal portable pension' employed previously by Vinson and Chappell (Vinson and Chappell, 1983) and the 1983 CPRS report on pensions discussed in Chapter 5. On the whole the letter gives the impression that the Inquiry would prefer to receive evidence which was favourable to personal pensions.

After the first written submissions of evidence, representatives of some of those organisations were invited to give further evidence in a public session held in January 1984. There then followed a second letter from the Secretary to the Inquiry, dated January 19th 1984, inviting interested parties to submit evidence on other aspects of pensions provision. Six subject areas were listed as being of interest to the Inquiry:

- the impact of future demographic changes on pension provision;

- the interaction of state and private sector pension schemes, with particular regard for contracting out provisions;

- the impact of pension provision and personal savings on each other and on the economy;

- the income and services needs of older people;

- the age of retirement;

- the level and mix of retirees' incomes derived from social security, state pensions and occupational pensions.

The deadline for submissions was March 16th 1984.

Curiously, the IoD did not receive a second request for evidence. Its first submission on the subject of personal pensions came in the form of a response to the consultative document that resulted from the Sub Group's work.

The first letter (dated December 12th 1983) from Nick Montagu to interested parties, with its emphasis on ideological rather than economic or demographic reasons for introducing personal pensions, confirms Sir Norman Fowler's statement (above) that the introduction of personal pensions was not necessarily related to projected funding problems for SERPS. This is further reinforced by the content of the second letter dated January 19th 1984 which discusses the background problems, the first of which is the effect of demographic trends on future pension costs; the two phases of the Inquiry appear to be back to front. A logical Inquiry would have begun by requesting evidence on the background problems and then would have moved on to discuss possible solutions; with the Inquiry into Provision for Retirement, however, the Inquiry began by considering the solution personal pensions and then turned its attention to assessing the problems which personal pensions were supposed to solve. In other words, economic and demographic considerations were not important to the Inquiry; personal pensions were certain to have been introduced anyway, for purely ideological reasons. Ideology was of particular importance to 1980s pensions policy-making. The CPS had a considerable impact on policy with regard to personal pensions, but otherwise 'think tanks' seem to have had no significant effect.

To some extent the ideological forces present within the Inquiry were no more than a reflection of those in the wider policy community which occasionally found expression in the Inquiry. For example, although the Inquiry was not concerned with wider share ownership, some of those giving evidence may have thought it was and tried to turn the Inquiry round to their point of view.

(iii) Early Leavers

The problem of early leavers was considered, though not fully, since the drafting of the 1985 legislation on preservation was at an advanced stage when the Inquiry was set up. On November 29th 1983, just six days after the announcement of the Inquiry into Provision for Retirement, the DHSS had published a consultative document proposing legislation that would implement the OPB recommendation on revaluation of early leavers' contributions contained in its 1981 report (OPB, 1981) '(*The Times*, November 30th, 1983; *Pensions World*, 1983, p.788). 'Portability' should have ceased to be an issue even if personal pensions remained on the agenda for ideological reasons.

The repeated use of the term 'personal portable pension' in the first letter (December 12th 1983) asking for submissions of evidence to the Inquiry might suggest that Norman Fowler did not see the OPB recommendation as a complete solution and was willing to consider new ideas. This is reinforced by the third of the four 'advantages' of personal pensions set out in the above letter which notes the possibility that personal pensions would produce a fairer balance between leavers and stayers.

The early leavers issue became intertwined with that of personal pensions and the people's capitalism idea. The Sub Group initially referred to personal pensions as 'portable pensions', apparently reflecting both the concern with portability and the terminology used by Norman Fowler following from Vinson and Chappell (1983). Furthermore, advocates of personal pensions argued that their approach to pensions was superior to that of occupational pension schemes which could not provide adequately for early leavers. In time it was accepted that portability was not the problem, but this leaves the question of why Norman Fowler purposely raised the issue of early leavers in the Inquiry. It is hardly likely that Norman Fowler was dissatisfied with the measures on transferability and preservation of occupational pensions proposed in the Consultative Document (DHSS, 1984a) and which were enacted in the Social Security Act 1985; if he were so dissatisfied he would have cancelled the publication of this consultative document until the Inquiry had completed its tasks.

An alternative though speculative explanation is that the deliberate linking of the two issues of personal pensions and early leavers served to restructure the pensions policy community in a way that allowed Norman Fowler to take command of the pensions debate. The early leavers problem was one which was dominated by technical considerations, at which Vinson and Chappell had not shown themselves to be very adept, rather than ideological ones with which they were very persuasive. The effect would have been to make technical arguments more powerful than ideological ones. He would in this way have been able to introduce personal pensions on his own terms, using the early leavers problem as political justification. While the Inquiry provided a means by which Norman Fowler could review pensions policy in relative freedom from a meddlesome Prime Minister and Chancellor of the Exchequer, the early leavers problem provided a political device with which to justify his preferred measures. Otherwise, logically, the issue of early leavers should not have been considered by the Inquiry at all. At the very least, the repeated use of the term 'personal portable pensions' shows a deliberate and self-conscious acknowledgement of both the main British promoters of this term, Vinson and Chappell and, by implication, the Prime Minister who appears to have been a powerful force in the personal pensions cause. Its presence on the agenda is one of the more confusing aspects of this particular piece of policy-making.

(iv) Age of Retirement

Norman Fowler announced the Inquiry into Provision for Retirement by way of making a reply to the in the form of a response to the Social Services Committee's 1982 report (DHSS *Reply to the Third Report of the SSC on the Age of Retirement,* 1983). The government had only issued a holding reply to the SSC's report; something more substantial was called for, although it has to be said that there was no evidence of pressure for or expectation of a detailed government response. The SSC document (SSC, 1982) may have provided an additional political justification for the Inquiry into Provision for Retirement, a device for announcing it and a further means of changing the pensions debate and restructuring the policy community.

The SSC report was looked at in considerable detail and intensity but its influence on the policy outcomes was minimal. The reasons for not acting on any of its recommendations were political rather than economic. The SSC was also concerned over what would happen if someone chose to retire early and then got into financial difficulties.

Miscellaneous Considerations

(i) Treasury Influence

Ideology was undoubtedly very important to Treasury policy and evidence of both this and a long-term perspective can be found in economic policy as is demonstrated by the 1984 Treasury Green Paper *The Next Ten Years* which, with a telling show of confidence, concerns itself with next ten years' public expenditure (HM Treasury, 1984). It also confirms the considerable degree of control exercised by the Treasury over social policy. The main theme of this Green Paper was that hitherto governments had decided how much money to spend on programmes and then raised taxes accordingly. It argued that this should be the other way round:

> As public spending takes a larger and larger share of the GDP, so the public sector steadily encroaches on the rest of the economy. ... finance must determine expenditure, not expenditure finance....(HM Treasury, 1984, para.68).

This is basically a restatement of the ethos of the 1979 Public Expenditure White Paper (HM Treasury, 1979) in which it was asserted that state expenditure had increased faster than economic growth. The Treasury Green Paper continued:

> Wherever it is possible and sensible to do so, the Government is seeking to transfer the provision of services into the market sector. ... but over a wide range of services the only means of controlling the cost is for the government to limit the supply. (HM Treasury, 1979, para.26).

It is difficult to assess whether the Treasury Green Paper (1984) had any influence on the agenda for the Inquiry into Provision for Retirement. Certainly it was considered by the Main Team. This Green Paper restated the ethos that a social security system should be tailored to match the potential of the economy and not vice versa (HM Treasury, 1984, para.68) and could therefore be expected to contain at least implicit support for the idea of abolishing SERPS. But the assumptions on which the Treasury Green Paper's calculations for the next five years were based included the continued existence of SERPS and therefore it is difficult to interpret its content as a source of pressure for change originating from the Treasury. Nevertheless, the Treasury was as keen as DHSS ministers to reduce the future cost of SERPS given the falling contribution base and rising costs, but this enthusiasm for cutting costs extended only to modifying SERPS so as to reduce its emerging costs. The Treasury view was that some of the short-term changes being proposed would have considerable long term implications. This led, after the Inquiry process had been completed, to the Chancellor taking a higher profile in it all, and there were some extremely taut cabinet committee meetings.

(ii) Investor Protection.

In the Inquiry's earlier discussions they gave consideration to the possibility that stockbrokers and National Savings might be allowed to be pensions providers; the idea was to break the institutional stranglehold of the life offices. Additional reasons for involving National Savings in pension provision were that the Secretary of State had been impressed by the Independent Retirement Account which operates in the United States, and National Savings would partially alleviate the concern within the Inquiry about what might happen if people were indeed dependent on their own investment judgement for making adequate pension provision and they found themselves underprovided for; would they be allowed to depend on Income Support? It seemed to several members of the Inquiry that those promoting the idea of independence had an unrealistic faith in the possibility of educating the population at large to make investment decisions. However, as will be seen in Chapter 10, it was decided that permitting stockbrokers to become personal pension providers was not feasible. With regard to National Savings:

They weren't the least bit interested. I think we got a one line letter back which I wish I'd kept, actually it was a marvellous Civil Service letter! (Sir Norman Fowler, 1993).

The impending Financial Services legislation and its wider control of investments were not considered in the course of the Inquiry's deliberations, although the members of the Inquiry's Main Team and the Sub Group were amply qualified to tackle this area. Indeed Alex Fletcher, who was a member of the Inquiry in his capacity of Minister for Consumer Affairs, was later responsible for setting up a number of committees which carried out background work for the Financial Services legislation; Marshall Field was a consultant to the SIB and Sir Mark Weinberg was chairman of the Marketing of Investments Board Organising Committee (MIBOC) and a member of the Securities and Investments Board (SIB). MIBOC was absorbed into SIB, whereupon Sir Mark Weinberg became its Deputy Chairman (DTI Bank of England Press Release December 14th, 1985). The delays in implementing the Financial Services Act 1986 held up the launch of contracted out personal pensions until June 1988. This is explained in Chapter 10.

(iii) Investment Patterns.

The second letter from the DHSS to interested organisations and individuals requesting evidence specifically asked for evidence of the possible impact of pensions changes on investment patterns. However, participants say that in the course of the Inquiry no consideration was given to this matter. It is difficult to think of a reason for this; the diversion of millions of present and future SERPS contributors to personal pensions could only have a dramatic impact on the securities market as the corresponding demand for investment opportunities increased. This supports Walker's argument (Walker, 1990) that in the field of pensions, economic considerations are often not as important as ideological ones.

(iv) Sexual Equality.

There were submissions to the Inquiry from EOC who, according to one participant, were more concerned with getting equal pensions for women than with larger pensions for everyone. As the same Inquiry member succinctly put it: 'The (Main) Team was not in the equality business'. In fact the Green Paper (DHSS, 1985) did take account of gender by proposing a bias in annuity rates towards women, but this was not implemented.

Analysis

In the course of its work the Inquiry into Provision for Retirement published a background paper and a consultative document on personal pensions. These are discussed below. The Inquiry did not produce any final report, published or otherwise, that summarised its deliberations. Instead they produced a series of papers to provide a basis for discussion and there were minutes of those discussions. This series of minutes formed the basis of later discussions between the Secretary of State, ministers, senior civil servants and a body of outside advisers that was set up much later in early 1986 and is discussed below (DHSS, Press Release, 86/159).

When the review process was complete the Inquiry itself was closed but the Inquiry Secretariat continued to exist, becoming Norman Fowler's advisers on pension reforms. Drawing on the Inquiry's findings, the Secretariat carried the work forward on the Green Paper and the White Paper. This work was carried on independently of the Policy Division.

Inquiry Outputs

(i)Background Paper.

In June 1984 the DHSS published a background paper to the Inquiry entitled: *Population, Pension Costs and Pensioners' Incomes.* This contains two main sections covering the Government Actuary's projections for population, dependency ratio, earnings and pension costs for as far forward as 2038, and an economic assessment of how income will be distributed among pensioners and how future pensioners' incomes will compare with that of the paid workforce. In his introduction to this paper, Norman Fowler gives the appearance of having accepted the 'demographic timebomb' argument over which he disagreed with both the Prime Minister and Chancellor of the Exchequer (see Chapter 6) in November 1983:

> One of the main messages about the future in the Government Actuary's projections is that expenditure on pensions is set to rise significantly as pensioners increase in number and live longer, and as more of them get higher pensions both from the state and from their employers .... At the same time there will be a marked rise in the ratio of pensioners to workers, which becomes most marked from about 2010.... (Norman Fowler in: DHSS, 1984, p.1).

The SSAC, in its Fourth and Fifth Reports (SSAC 1986/7), disagreed with this assessment. This is discussed later.

(ii) Personal Pensions: A Consultative Document.

Of greater significance, since it contained Norman Fowler's the first proposals on personal pensions, was the publication in July 1984 of: *Personal Pensions A Consultative Document* (DHSS, 1984a). This small booklet afforded the first public insight into the direction the Inquiry was leading. It came out much sooner than the Green Paper because this task was completed first. The Inquiry into Provision for Retirement had:

> a study of personal pensions as its first task. The Inquiry set up a Sub Group to concentrate on this task. It took written evidence and held four public hearings; it also has advice from the Occupational Pensions Board. (DHSS, 1984a, ch.1.1).

The Consultative Document's key proposals (chap.3.1) were that:

(1) personal pensions, usually money purchase, should be available as a matter of right to all employees;

(2) the qualification for contracting out of SERPS, which for occupational pensions is the provision of a Guaranteed Minimum Pension, should for personal pensions be contribution-defined;

(3) special arrangements should exist so that where employees belong to employers' contracted out occupational pension schemes destabilisation of the occupational schemes does not ensue, and

(4) employers should not be obliged to contribute to employees' personal pension plans except to the extent of the employers' NI rebate. Responsibility for the failure of a personal pension plan to produce an adequate income will fall entirely to the employee.

The Consultative Document asks for comments on its proposals for personal pensions. However, it quite blatantly asks for favourable comments or comments which at least favour the introduction of personal pensions. For example:

> The Government would welcome comments on these approaches (for collecting contributions) or alternative proposals for the handling of personal pensions. (DHSS, 1984a, chap.3.29).

The above proposals are in part justified by the findings of a 1984 market research survey commissioned by the Sub Group. The project was carried out by Social Surveys (Gallup Poll) Ltd in June 1984 and was entitled: *The Demand for Portable Pensions: Report of research carried out for the Inquiry into Provision for Retirement* and:

> It showed public support for the idea (of personal pensions).... Eighty per cent of people not in schemes were interested in personal pensions. And a third of people in schemes wanted to pay more to get a better pension. People wanted more choice .... (DHSS, 1984a, chap.2.1).

There are so many indications that for ideological reasons the introduction of personal pensions was inevitable that it seems strange that market research should be used to test public acceptability. Furthermore, with evidence of such an overwhelming demand it is equally strange that it was felt necessary to create a generous system of incentives and National Insurance rebates. A possible explanation is that the market research was carried out primarily to test alternative ways of marketing personal pensions, including the offer of an Incentive and National Insurance Rebates.

In principle the Sub Group's phase of the pensions review was over. There still remained the 'problem' of SERPS for the Main Team to tackle, but in the mean time it was a question of studying the comments which the Consultative Document produced and then deciding the details of how personal pensions were to be administered. The Consultative Document received a generally favourable reception; the IoD's only qualification was that:

> ... the Government should urgently examine the role of 'guaranteed minimum pension' in occupational schemes, and the earnings-related 'additional component' in the state scheme, in order to make the choice of occupational scheme or personal pension more equal. (IoD, 1985a p.2).

The absence of a hostile reaction to the Consultative Document implies that Norman Fowler's ideas on personal pensions were at least broadly acceptable to the Prime Minister, in which case the revision that occurred between the Inquiry and the publication of the Green Paper (DHSS, 1985) must have been confined to SERPS.

Policy Outcomes.

The Inquiry produce neither policy recommendations nor a consensus among its participants:

> I don't think all of them would necessarily agree with every part of what was being said so at the end of the day they were my proposals. ... It was the minister putting forward the proposals having listened to everybody and having had the benefit of the expert advice around the table. ... It wasn't the aim to produce an agreed report in every detail. (Sir Norman Fowler, 1993).

Nevertheless, it is notable that of those participants interviewed only two did not acknowledge the feeling that the Inquiry had moved in distinct directions. Other participants, while agreeing that the production of a set of recommendations had not been their purpose, usually had a clear idea of what proposals the Inquiry was leading towards. They were accordingly surprised at the proposals which appeared in the Green Paper (DHSS, 1985). These proposals will be examined later, but it is possible here, in the context of studying the policy-making process, to discuss what happened between the ending of the Inquiry

86

and Green Paper's publication and why ideas which participants felt had gained acceptance during the Inquiry were discarded.

Representatives of the pensions industry were pleased that acceptance was secured for contracted out personal pensions operating on a money purchase basis. Previously this had been unthinkable; it had been dogma that to contract out a firm's scheme must be better than that provided by the state. They were also pleased that employees opting for personal pensions instead of their employer's scheme were not automatically entitled to a contribution from their employer since this would avoid the risk of destabilisation. On the other hand, some Inquiry members were looking to personal pensions as the answer to a larger number of problems. They were hoping that it would be possible to roll into it provision for the self-employed, the topping up pension for the employee with an occupational scheme, the contracting out vehicle for the man who was not in a pension scheme. It would be the same vehicle for everyone, creating a much simpler regime. However, the Inland Revenue saw tax avoidance problems and insisted that different types of pension provision should be maintained in separate compartments, each covered by different rules.

The most significant reversal concerned SERPS. On the whole, members of the Inquiry had been quite pleased with the Inquiry's acceptance of the need to modify rather than scrap SERPS and had believed this was to be the basis of the new pensions policy. However, according to Sir Norman Fowler, he commenced the Inquiry with the abolition of SERPS very much in mind. He had formulated proposals for the abolition of SERPS and its replacement with a mandatory personal pension provision whose contributions would be subject to the same tax relief as final salary occupational pensions. Early in 1985 Norman Fowler took his recommendations to a special cabinet committee known as MISC 111 and chaired by Margaret Thatcher. He met with fierce opposition from the Chancellor of the Exchequer. Nigel Lawson had initially been in favour of abolishing SERPS but realised at the very last minute that if SERPS were abolished and personal pensions made mandatory, rather than being phased out and replaced by voluntary use of personal pensions plans, the cost in terms of lost revenue from SERPS contributions and extra tax relief would have an enormous and adverse impact on the Public Sector Borrowing Requirement (Fowler, 1991, pp.216-217). In a year when it was hoped to cut the cost of social security this would not be acceptable. It was the Treasury's suggestion that SERPS should be modified rather than be abolished, but both Margaret Thatcher and Norman Fowler were firmly committed to the idea of abolishing SERPS. Hence the Green Paper *Reform of Social Security* was published on June 3rd 1985 with the proposal for the abolition of SERPS intact.

8 Formulation of a new pensions policy

The Green Paper *Reform of Social Security*

The Green Paper *Reform of Social Security* (DHSS, 1985) was published in three volumes in June 1985. With regard to pensions the emphasis of the Green Paper was on increased choice and personal responsibility.

Among the observations contained in the second volume of the Green Paper was one that SERPS should be replaced by:

> ... a new partnership between state provision and occupational and personal provision. ... This can only be achieved as part of a long process of reform. (DHSS, 1985, vol.2, chap.1.39 40).

After giving an assurance that the Basic Retirement Pension would remain in place (DHSS, 1985, vol.2, chap.1.41) the Green Paper explained that SERPS was to be phased out; men under 50 years and women under 45 years would, over a period of three years, be phased out of SERPS and into private provision, though for those just below the stated cut off ages a taper system was to be applied to increase the value of their pensions. All entitlements earned to date would be preserved (DHSS, 1985, vol.2, chap.1.41). Maximum freedom was to be allowed on the way in which provision was made (DHSS, vol.2, chap.1.43). The goal of portability by way of requiring the transferability of accrued pensions contributions (DHSS, vol.2, chap.1.51) is strikingly similar to ideas canvassed by the CPS and the IoD.

Responses to the Green Paper

When the Green Paper was published in June 1985 it was almost as a consultative document and comments were welcomed, albeit within a very short time scale. The main organisations responded predictably.

In September 1985 the CBI published its response to the Green Paper in which they tacitly agreed with the principle of introducing personal pensions

88

and the objective of restricting future growth in state pensions expenditure (CBI, 1985, para.1.8). However, they were very concerned that the abolition rather than modification of SERPS could greatly increase business costs because in the total absence of SERPS contributions to fund retirees, employers and employees would have to fund the future retirement of current workers *and* the SERPS pensions of current retirees. They suggested instead that the basis of SERPS pensions should be altered from the best 20 years to lifetime earnings and that a surviving spouse should only be allowed to inherit 50% of a deceased spouse's SERPS pension (CBI, 1985, para.1.9)

The first IoD response to the Green Paper came with a personal letter dated August 23rd 1985 to Norman Fowler from John Hoskyns (IoD, 1985c) who, following a break after leaving the Downing Street CPU, had replaced Walter Goldsmith as Director General:

> (The IoD) welcomes the decision to abolish the State Earnings-Related Pension Scheme. It shares the Government's concern over the financial burden … . (IoD, 1985c)

Not only were the same sentiments expressed the following month in the IoD's subsequent and more formal response to the Green Paper but, more ambitiously: 'The arguments for privatising SERPS … are equally valid for the basic national insurance retirement pension.' (IoD, 1985d, para.21).

The proposed abolition of SERPS met with such a hostile reaction both inside and outside the Cabinet that the proposal was withdrawn. Indeed the Green Paper's proposals were widely opposed by the main pensions institutions who favoured the existing system and by some who favoured change but felt the practical difficulties in the government's proposals were insurmountable (Kaye, 1987, p.18).

White Paper: *Programme for Action*

In December 1985, three months after the consultation period for Reform of Social Security, the White Paper *Programme for Action* (DHSS, 1985a) was published. This document was not as radical as the preceeding Green Paper. Despite support from the IoD, the Save and Prosper Group and Framlington, the proposal to phase out SERPS was replaced by one to modify it in view of representations from the NAPF, insurance companies, the CBI and other employer bodies (DHSS, 1985a, chap 2.13/14).

In order to reduce the cost of SERPS, the measures contained in *Programme for Action* (DHSS, 1985a) and implemented in April 1988 had the effect of limiting new membership and devaluing the worth of future contributions from 1.25% to 1% of revalued salary for 'lifetime average' rather than the 'best twenty years'. Those who retired before April 2000 will continue to accrue a SERPS pension at a rate of 1.25% per annum and receive a pension based on their best 20 years' earnings. The rate of accrual after April 1988 and for those workers who retire between April 2000 and April 2010 will be tapered and those retiring after that date will receive a pension based on 20% of relevant earnings under the new measures. It will be 2032 for women and 2037 for men that pre-April 1988 benefits will cease to be applicable. As a result of the reduced SERPS accrual rate contracted out pension schemes would only have to produce a GMP based on 20% of earnings after 1988/89, occupational pension schemes would be responsible for upgrading the post-retirement GMP in line with the RPI up to a maximum of 3%. Finally, and as the CBI had recommended, the surviving spouse rules were also changed so that until April 2000 it will be possible for either spouse to inherit their partner's state earnings-related pension up to a maximum. Thereafter a surviving spouse will only be permitted to inherit a maximum of half their partner's SERPS pension irrespective of which regime it accrued under. This means that as those born during the bulge of births of 1947 to the mid 1960s enter retirement, the cost will be reduced, easing the burden on the existing workforce (DHSS, 1985a chap.2.15).

The White Paper went on to propose that personal pensions should be allowable as means of contracted out pension provision (DHSS, 1985a, chap.2.48 50) and, although it was not fully implemented, said that until 1992 93 a 2% incentive should be paid to contributors to newly contracted out personal pension plans and newly created final salary and money-purchase occupational pensions schemes (DHSS, 1985a, chap.2.31). The implication is that the government was keen to motivate both employers and employees to avoid the use of SERPS as a means of additional pension provision, but in reality the targets were SERPS contributors and potential personal pensions providers. The actual implementation of this Incentive, which was limited to former SERPS contributors, is discussed below.

From the above changes to the Green Paper's proposals for SERPS the inference can be drawn that Margaret Thatcher and Norman Fowler must have backed down in the face of political and public pressure.

Two things happened between the publication of the Green Paper and that of the White Paper. First, there was the realisation that the Green Paper proposals for the abolition of SERPS and the implementation of compulsory occupational or personal pensions were less attractive to insurance companies than ministers and senior civil servants had supposed. Secondly, and perhaps more critically, there was a struggle between the DHSS and the Treasury. This arose from the Treasury's inflexibility on issues of taxation, the contracting out National Insurance rebate and the two percent Incentive and, in particular, the very real problem of switching from an unfunded to a funded pension scheme, causing the current source of contributions to dry up and current expenditure having to be funded from taxation. It was for this reason that the modification of SERPS was more attractive to the Treasury than its phasing out and replacement by mandatory personal pension plans. The resolution of this disagreement took the form of the White Paper *Programme for Action* (DHSS, 1985).

90

Creation of the Advisory Group

In March 17th 1986 Norman Fowler announced the setting up of an advisory group on personal pensions. In May he announced its membership in a press release which said that:

> The group's members will assist Ministers to strike the right balance between essential regulatory protection for personal pension holders and effective competition between providers. (DHSS, 1986)

The membership consisted of:

Mark Boleat	Director General of the Building Societies Association;
Roy Brimblecombe	Executive Director and Actuary of Eagle Star Insurance;
Jeremy Hebblethwaite	Director of Save & Prosper, Member of Marketing of Investments Board Organising Committee;
Mark Weinberg	Chairman, Allied Dunbar Assurance, Chairman, Marketing of Investments Board Organising Committee; Member, Securities and Investments Board.

Mark Weinberg had been a member of the Inquiry's Personal Pensions Sub Group and as such was the only member of the Inquiry Team whose services were retained by Norman Fowler.

Mark Weinberg's role was particularly important at this stage of the policy-making. The rules for marketing and management of investments were still in the process of being developed in readiness for the deregulation of financial institutions known colloquially as 'Big Bang' which was scheduled for October 1986. As will be seen in Chapter 10 the framework within which personal pensions would operate had to be developed now if they were to be launched in April 1987 as planned. As chairman of MIBOC (Marketing of Investments Board Organising Committee) Mark Weinberg had a considerable role in overseeing the preparation of the 'rulebooks' by which the as yet non-existent regulatory organisations, including Financial Intermediaries Managers and Brokers Regulatory Association (FIMBRA), Investment Management Regulatory Organisation (IMRO) and Life Assurance and Unit Trust Regulatory Organisation (LAUTRO), would have to operate.

Contracted Out Personal Pensions

The Social Security Act 1986 broke new ground in two particular ways:

1. henceforth it would be permissible for contributors to personal pension plans, if the plans were deemed 'appropriate', to contract out of SERPS or occupational pension schemes, and

2. an element of consumer choice in the field of pensions provision was introduced.

A third effect was that the previously oligopolistic market of pensions providers would in theory come to an end with a widening of the range of organisations that could provide means of pensions provision. As will be seen, in practice this measure has not been very effective.

It would seem reasonable to expect potential providers of personal pensions to eagerly accept the opportunity of exploiting a huge market under the following conditions:

1. the market consisted of approximately half the British workforce. These were people in full-time employment who did not have access to occupational pension schemes and currently contributed to SERPS. It would only need a fraction of these SERPS contributors to contract out by taking out personal pension plans for the result to be a commercial success;

2. personal pension providers' administrative costs would be minimal because it was agreed that the Inland Revenue would collect personal pension contributions and pass them to fund managers;

3. the main rival product to personal pensions, SERPS, was being adversely publicised by its sponsor, the DHSS. The return on SERPS contributions was already uncompetitive; it was to be made less favourable still by being reduced from 1.25% to 1.0% of annual relevant earnings while the maturity period was extended from 20 years to 40 years bringing SERPS into line with occupational pension schemes, and the pension calculation would be based not on the best twenty years but on whole working lifetime;

4. SERPS members who contracted out in favour of personal pension plans retain the right to contract back in to SERPS at a later date if they so desire. In fact this is an exceptionally generous provision which to some degree protects SERPS contributors from both the consequences of adverse pensions decisions and the low returns on the later contributions to a personal pension plan which only have a short time before retirement to increase in value, and

5. young workers not currently contributing were to be refused access to SERPS. They and any other full-time employees not contributing to occupational pension schemes would be obliged by law to contribute to a personal

pension plan. In practice SERPS has become a 'scheme of default' whereby people who do not contribute to an occupational pension scheme and fail to make alternative personal pension arrangements find themselves automatically contributing to SERPS. This feature, together with (4) above mean that SERPS will take rather longer to phase out than was originally envisaged.

Despite (4) and (5) above, it is difficult to imagine a more favourable set of circumstances for the launch of a new financial product. It is understandable that those engaged in the provision of occupational pensions had reservations about entering the personal pensions market. They feared that a recurrence of the high inflation seen in the 1970s, which severely eroded the value of annuities, would once again discredit the money purchase system of pension provision and the institutions that managed them. But this still left an array of financial institutions not currently engaged in pension provision some of which, in particular building societies, had only recently been empowered to offer a wide range of financial services to the public. Small financial institutions, including some friendly societies and building societies, might not have had the resources necessary to develop and market new financial products, but this still left a selection of clearing banks, merchant banks, life offices, unit trust managers and large building societies. They would surely embrace the opportunity to enter a market that was largely free from the oligopolistic domination of institutions whose reputations, expertise and sales networks would make it very difficult for a new entrant to succeed. Some of the potential personal pensions providers had been convinced that there should be a marketing incentive for personal pensions to ensure their initial success. It was no use just legislating for personal pensions and hoping the idea would become instantly popular. There had to be an incentive to encourage potential pensions providers to enter the personal pensions market and set up the necessary distribution networks.

It seems that the DHSS was similarly concerned about the success of personal pension plans. This should not have led to any further action; personal pensions were being promoted by a government that believed them to be inherently 'good' and which had faith in the unfettered market's ability to resolve issues of consumer choice. Hence Conservative politicians, in particular Norman Fowler, should have been content to do nothing but watch as contributors to SERPS contracted out in increasing numbers and new providers of personal pensions, embarrassed by their original misjudgement, belatedly entered this lucrative market. But the Government was not prepared to trust market forces; according to Ward (1991, pp.45-6). Ministers overruled advice of officials who opposed the flat-rate 2% Incentive in favour of a variable incentive which depended on age and gender. The result was that prior to the launch of contracted out personal pensions, a system of rebates and incentives was legislated into being in 1987.

The Personal and Occupational Pension Schemes (Incentive Payments) Regulations 1987 was enacted in order to make personal pensions an even more attractive proposition. On the assumption that half a million people would take out personal pension plans, it was predicted that in the tax year 1989/90 the cost of the 2% Incentive would be £800 million. The number of contributors benefiting from this ceased to grow after April 1990 and after April 1993 the expense would cease altogether. That the Incentive was only available to those who contracted out of SERPS by April 1990 suggests that it was intended as a marketing device to ensure sufficient initial demand to make the newly launched contracted out personal pensions products economically viable.

The Social Security Act 1986 should be seen mainly as the outcome of an ideological struggle and partly as a logical consequence of Treasury policy which had pressed continually for reductions in government expenditure and, therefore, the social security budget. However, it will be seen in Chapter 10 that the combined effect of the 2% Incentive and the unexpectedly large number (four million) of individuals who took out personal pensions plans was to undermine the zero cost principle which the Treasury imposed on the Inquiry into Provision for Retirement and Norman Fowler's Social Security Reviews generally and thereby undermine the Treasury's cost cutting mission. The implication is that the 2% Incentive's origins were political.

Contracted Out Personal Pensions: Regulations & How They Work.

The regulations allow personal pensions and money purchase occupational pension schemes to have contracted out status provided they satisfy minimum contribution requirements.

i) Eligibility

To be eligible to take out a contracted out personal pension plan the individual must cease contributing to either SERPS or a contracted out occupational pension scheme.

The minimum contribution was set at 4% and as this was less than the total of the available incentives and rebates payable until 1993, it was not necessary for a worker who had opted for a personal pension plan to make any contribution. Shortsighted contributors who took advantage of this offer are quite likely on retirement to find themselves underprovided for.

ii) Marketing Personal Pensions

As was explained earlier, in an attempt to ensure that personal pensions were successfully launched the DHSS introduced two financial inducements that were aimed directly at potential contributors and their employers and indirectly at potential pensions providers. These two inducements were the 2.0% Incentive mentioned above and a 5.8% National Insurance Rebate. The 2% Incentive is a contribution by the State to the contracted out personal pension plans of eligible workers during the period from April 6th 1988 until April 5th 1993. Where appropriate the state would pay an amount equal to 2% of a contributor's earnings between the lower and upper earnings limits directly into their personal pension plan. In addition to the 2% Incentive there was a 5.8% National, Insurance Rebate.

For the period from April 6th 1988 until April 5th 1993 the effect of an employee contracting out of SERPS into an appropriate personal pension plan was to produce a National Insurance rebate of 5.8% of earnings between the lower and upper earnings limits. This is made up of: 2.0% derived from the employee's contributions and 3.8% derived from the employer's contributions. An added benefit lay in the fact that the employee's 2% National Insurance rebate was subject to standard rate tax relief, as was the employee's main contribution to a personal pension plan or an occupational pension fund. Hence, when the standard rate of income tax was 25% the employee's 2% National Insurance rebate was grossed up to 2.67% of relevant earnings.

It is possible that the 3.8% rebate on employers' National Insurance contributions was a measure that had three aims:

1. to negate the hostility of those employers and managers of occupational pension funds who feared an exodus of scheme members. Some such employers have refused to contribute to defecting employees' personal pension funds. Among those workers whose employers have refused to contribute to personal pension plans are Members of Parliament. The effect of the 3.8% rebate is to make a nominal contribution to the employee's personal pension on the employer's behalf thereby minimising the damage done by some employers' hostility;

2. the employers' National Insurance rebate would make group personal pensions an attractive proposition for an employer currently contributing to SERPS. With the aid of this rebate it becomes possible for a small employer to offer an attractive pensions package to workers at little additional expense, and

3. if personal pensions were intended to be taken up by employees in occupational pension schemes as well as those contributing to SERPS (and there is evidence, discussed below, to suggest that this was the case), it may have been felt necessary to cushion employees against the impact of employers who refused to contribute to 'defecting' employees' personal pension plans. Such an approach would also confirm that the system of incentives was part of a campaign to encourage individuals to take responsibility for providing for their retirement instead of relying on collective provision.

The National Insurance rebate is exceptionally generous when it is seen in terms of what would have to be contributed to an occupational pension scheme in order to produce a pension equal to SERPS:

Table 8.1 **National Insurance Rebates**

Age	Men % of earnings	Women % of earnings
16 – 19	2.2	2.9
20 – 24	2.2	3.0
25 – 29	2.4	3.5
30 – 34	2.8	4.2
35 – 39	3.4	5.2
40 – 44	4.3	6.6
45 – 49	5.4	8.7
50 – 54	7.1	10.9
55 – 59	9.0	12.5
60 – 64	10.5	–

Source: Government Actuary's Review of: Certain Contracting Out Terms, March 1987.

A direct comparison between personal pensions and SERPS is difficult, but from the above figures it is obvious that the cost to the state of the National Insurance rebate will exceed the savings made by not having to provide a SERPS pension for those who contract out and will not be entitled to a GMP.

Personal pensions have a greater appeal to younger members of the work-force so that the overwhelming majority of SERPS contributors who contract out with personal pensions are likely to be at the younger end of the age range. The figures above show that men and women under the ages of 50 and 40 years respectively will receive more in the way of National Insurance rebate than it would have cost to purchase a SERPS entitlement. It was therefore inevitable that the National Insurance rebate would have an adverse effect on the National Insurance Fund unless the difference was made up by remaining SERPS contributors and tax payers. In his budget speech on March 20th 1990 the Chancellor of the Exchequer John Major said that National Insurance contributions had fallen by £2.5 billion in 1989/90 because of the National Insurance rebate given to the new holders of personal pensions.

The high cost of introducing the 2% Incentive was exacerbated by the fact that the number of people taking out: '… personal pensions (was) eight times that which had been predicted by the National Audit Office.' (NAO, 1990 chap. 3.18) and resulted in the Government Actuary recommending that National Insurance rates should be increased for contributors to personal or occupational pensions (Henke, 1991). Nor did the DSS understand the reason for the success of personal pensions:

> … the Department (of Social Security) have no data on the reasons why four million individuals have taken out personal pensions, or their future intentions. (National Audit Office, 1990 chap.3.21)

which must have made it difficult to estimate future demand. In fact, as suggested earlier, it is more probable that both sets of measures were attempts by the government to ensure that a contracted out non-occupational pension system of some description was in place before the 1987 General Election. This aim would have been achieved had the General Election been held in the October as was widely predicted. Instead it was held in June 1987 and it was in any case highly unlikely that FSAVCs would have been a commercial success.

It was originally intended that in order to create a level playing field on which occupational and personal pensions providers would compete, the 2% incentive would be payable to people who took out personal pensions in favour of either existing membership of occupational pension schemes or SERPS. In the event, because of fears of destabilising occupational pension schemes, the bill was amended as it passed through Parliament. Consequently the Incentive would only be paid to those who had not had been members of occupational schemes for a reasonable period of time. The amended conditions affecting eligibility for the 2% Incentive were not been publicised nearly as vigorously as the Incentive's existence. In consequence much confusion has surrounded this issue, with some former occupational pensions contributors being persuaded by less than scrupulous financial advisers to leave their occupational pension scheme in favour of a personal pension plan, and then belatedly discovering that they were not being credited with the 2% Incentive. In December 1993 the SIB announced that it was investigating this with a view to ordering that compensation be paid to ill-advised consumers.

The *Personal and Occupational Pension Schemes (Incentive Payments) Regulations* 1987 gave the conditions which a contributor to a personal pension plan had to satisfy in order to qualify for the Incentive. These regulations stipulated that the 2% Incentive was available to personal pensions contributors unless, between January 1st 1986 and April 5th 1993:

1. the member has been contracted out under another scheme by virtue of doing the same job;

2. another person, in the same employment by virtue of which the individual is contracted out, has been contracted out under another scheme;

3. the member would have been contracted out under another scheme but for his election not to join the scheme.

In other words the 2% is only available if a personal pension is the only alternative to SERPS (Pensions Management, July 1988, p.7).

When looked at together, the consequence of the two types of financial inducement described above is that the maximum total subsidy from the state to personal pension contributors and available for a period of five years is, according to Reardon (1989, p.26):

	%	%
Incentive		2.00
NI Rebate: employee's	2.00	
tax relief (25%) on above	0.67	2.67
NI Rebate: employer's		3.80
% of relevant earnings		8.47

The combined cost to the National Insurance Fund of the Incentive and the National Insurance Rebate for the period to April 1993 was much higher than had been predicted by the DHSS, in part because they had assumed that half a million people would contract out of SERPS by taking out personal pension plans. The actual number was 4 million and the National Audit Office calculated the cost to the National Insurance Fund as being £9.3 billion. Approximately £3.4 billion would be saved in SERPS pensions that would not now have to be paid, leaving a net cost of £5.9 billion (NAO, 1990, para.14). A scheme designed to relieve future tax payers of the 'intolerable' future cost of SERPS has ended up costing twice as much as it is likely to save.

iii) Contributions

Contracted out personal pensions have no 'defined benefit'. That is to say they do not guarantee some minimum level of benefit in the future. The only regulation affecting the benefit received from a personal pension is the restriction on the proportion of maturity value that can be taken as a tax-free lump sum. Yet in order to limit personal pensions' popularity as a tax avoidance vehicle it is necessary for government to control the extent to which individuals utilise personal pensions plans. Without restrictions personal pensions, with their complete exemption from income and capital gains taxes and partial exemption from income tax on contributions, would become the dominant mode of long-term saving. (PEPs are less tax efficient because there is no tax relief on contributions.) Hence it is necessary for control to be exercised over them by limiting contribution levels to a percentage of gross earnings.

iv) Benefits

Because there is no guaranteed return on contributions invested in a personal pension plan, the state is free from the role of underwriter which it performs for occupational pension schemes, while employers with contracted out money purchase schemes are released from the responsibility of ensuring sufficient funds for current employees' pension liabilities. This risk is borne entirely by the contributor with the size of the lump sum being a product of the level of contributions and, much less predictably, the performance of the underlying securities in which the contributions have been invested. In this way the contributor's well-being is linked to developments in the economy. Even less predictable is the rate of inflation in future years. An annuity may produce a generous income at the outset but have its value severely depleted after just a few years of moderately high inflation.

The contributor is responsible for monitoring the adequacy of their pension provision. In the event of apparent underprovision they should make extra contributions and, in the event of underperformance by the life office or other pension plan provider, transfer their accrued contributions to a better investment vehicle. Unfortunately, the adequacy or otherwise of accrued personal pension provision will often only become apparent in the last year of contribution because it is then that the termination bonus is calculated, and this can amount to almost half of the personal pension plan's maturity value. Obviously this too late to make worthwhile additional contributions. The decision to change to a better provider would not be simple since the additional administration costs would be considerable.

On maturity the contributor to a contracted out personal pension plan may take up to a quarter of the value as a tax-free lump sum subject to a preset limit. This contrasts unfavourably with the Section 226 personal pension which on retirement allows a maximum of one third of the contract's maturity value to be taken as a tax-free lump sum.

The holder of a mature personal pension plan will shop around for the best annuity rate rather than take whatever the life office providing the pension plan offered. The annuity must provide an income after retirement which is incremental in the same way as the GMP, i.e. in line with the Retail Price Index (RPI) up to a maximum but no decreases. Note that it is possible to move from one personal pension plan to another and from a personal pension plan to an occupational pension scheme and vice versa, although only one change per year is permitted by the Inland Revenue.

This produces a lower monthly income for women on the grounds of their greater longevity. The Green Paper (DHSS, 1985, vol.2) proposed that life offices should be obliged to offer unisex annuity rates so that men and women would be given the same weekly/monthly incomes for the same lump sums, as though no differences in longevity existed. However, this was not implemented for reasons described below.

The problems equalised annuity rates might have entailed would have included the need for life offices to carefully 'balance' their annuity sales so as not to have 'too many' women compared to the numbers of men on their books. This would not have led to any particular problem for the life offices; it is relatively easy to actuarily determine an appropriate mix of annuity holders. In any case the cost difference between providing annuities for men and women is not as great as might first seem to be the case; although men tend not to live as long as women, the way in which annuities are calculated assumes that all men will have a surviving spouse who will inherit a reduced income. Hence annuity rates for men have already been partially adapted to taking account of women's greater lifespan and the transition cost will not be as great as might otherwise have been the case. However, there would always be the danger of some offices targeting their marketing at men and leaving other personal pensions providers to either take on the excess of women customers or explain to them that their books were 'full'.

In any case, owing to demographic changes it is possible that the equalising of annuity rates for men and women would have had an impact in the longer term. As an increasing number of women spend more time in the workforce and consequently retire with full private pension in their own right, the cost of pensions may rise quite steeply. Currently, most private sector pensions are drawn by men whose partners inherit a portion of the full pension on their death. As an increasing number of retirees on private pensions are women, so an increasing number of number of private sector pensions will be drawn at the full rate for the lifespan of women. This would lead to an adjustment of annuity rates that would place the increased cost of retirement on the workforce and (possibly) employers but not on the state.

As a consequence of measures in the Finance Act 1987 personal pensions can commence providing the contributor with benefits anywhere between the ages of 50 and 75 years. This makes personal pensions an extremely effective tax saving vehicle and appears to facilitate flexible retirement. It is interesting to speculate on the possibility that at some point in the future unemployed older workers with adequately funded personal pensions plans will be encouraged to take early retirement and thereby be removed from the unemployment figures.

v) Administrative Costs

It is inconceivable that the state will indefinitely bear the cost and inconvenience of acting as a clearing house for personal pension contributions. Just as the National Insurance rebate and Incentive will be withdrawn after a fixed term, so it is likely that once enough institutions are sufficiently committed to personal pensions provision and dependent on it for an appreciable part of their profits, the Treasury will insist they provide and fund their own clearing agency for dealing with contributions. There is a precedent for this transfer of responsibility and cost; the Inland Revenue transferred the responsibility of calculating and collecting income tax from people in full-time employment.

9   A new philosophy of welfare

Introduction

The purpose of this Chapter is to link alternative pensions policies and proposals with their ideological bases. Particular attention will be given to the Green Paper *Reform of Social Security* (DHSS, 1985), the White Paper *Programme for Action* (DHSS, 1985) and the subsequent Social Security Act 1986 which were all preceded by the publication of an important paper by Vinson and Chappell in 1983 and the Inquiry into Provision for Retirement. In order to help understand the ideological origins of the 1986 pensions legislation this analysis will therefore make reference to the ideas promoted by the CPS (Vinson and Chappell, 1983) together with some examples of the evidence submitted to the Inquiry into Provision for Retirement by the NAPF and IoD. These organisations' positions provide extreme examples of the spectrum of approaches which were vying for policy makers' attention.

Social Security (Pensions) Act 1975

The substantial replacement of SERPS with contracted out personal pensions represented an ideological shift in terms of the respective roles of the state and the individual in pensions provision. In order to appreciate both the extent of this shift and the values that policy makers were seeking to reject this Chapter will begin with a brief description of the Castle plan in order to identify the values that underpinned SERPS.

Secretary of State Barbara Castle's plan for the State Earnings-Related Pension Scheme were contained in the White Paper *Better Pensions* (DHSS, 1974) and the subsequent Social Security (Pensions) Act 1975. The scheme had four key aspects:

1. the state would assume ultimate responsibility for ensuring that every retired worker would have both a basic and a contributory earnings-related pension, thereby reducing the extent of poverty among retired people:

    The proposals set out in this White Paper will fulfil the Government's pledge to bring an end to the massive dependence on means-tested supplementary benefit after a normal working life. (DHSS, 1974, p.iii, para.1)

2. the state would compel contracted out private sector additional pension schemes to preserve pension rights so that they approximately matched the benefits produced by the proposed SERPS;
3. the state would underwrite the private sector pensions in payment, and
4. discrimination in terms of access to occupational schemes on the basis of gender or occupational status would be ended:

> For too long women have been treated as second class citizens in pensions and benefit provision. An important part of this policy (*for equality of women*) is equality of treatment in the field of pensions and other benefits. This White Paper will fulfil that policy. (DHSS, 1974, p.iii, para.1)

and, speaking of the position in 1971:

> The inferior position of manual workers is particularly striking. ... For salaried workers on the other hand, flat-rate schemes were almost unknown. (DHSS, 1974, chap.3, para.53).

The Castle plan was therefore concerned with more than just pension provision; it was concerned with the alleviation of poverty among retirees, discrimination within the workforce and conditions of employment. As such it was consistent with much of the recent legislation which had been enacted by both political parties while in office (Jackson, 1977, pp.7-8). Examples of other legislation include: the Equal Pay Act 1970, the Industrial Relations Act 1971, the Contracts of Employment Act 1972, the Trade Union and Labour Relations Act 1974, the Employment Protection Act 1975, and the Sex Discrimination Act 1975 (Jackson, 1977). Both the formulation and implementation of this policy were consistent with the idea of a strongly interventionist state.

The state was generous in granting women both SERPS pensions which were calculated as though they and men had equal longevity, and a surviving spouse entitlement to the full SERPS pension of their husband. Yet it was content to provide an additional pension of only 25% of relevant earnings while the better occupational pension schemes were paying at least forty eightieths of full final salary. This implies that getting people, especially retired women, out of the supplementary pension system was a priority. By definition this was to be at least a medium term project which, because SERPS is unfunded, would amend the existing intergenerational contract. Ideologically speaking, SERPS came under attack on three main counts which are dealt with below:

i) Intergenerational Contract

The 'intergenerational contract' is a feature of the welfare system which recognises that most of the population will be productive for much of their lives but that at the beginning and the end they may be dependent on others. In the light of this, the current workforce is required to fund the education of today's children and young people and the state pensions of today's retirees, in exchange for which current workers, having already benefited from an education funded by a previous generation of workers, will themselves benefit in retirement from pensions funded by today's children who will have entered the labour force.

The term 'contract' is a misnomer since employees were not free to withhold their participation; the 1975 Act gave only the employer, not employees, some choice over the type of pension scheme to which they would contribute. Indeed, those associated with the New Right have sought to deny the very existence of this 'contract' on the grounds that a current workforce cannot bind a future workforce to what may be an onerous responsibility of funding future SERPS pensions (Barry, 1985, p.488). Nor in any sense is the 'contract' binding since, as seen with the Social Security Act 1986, the state is free to unilaterally alter the terms of membership. Nevertheless, this intergenerational relationship has been at the heart of some of the more important features of the post-war welfare state, particularly education and the basic and earnings-related retirement pensions.

There are advantages to having an unfunded or 'pay as you go' pension system, but those allied to the anti-collectivist New Right were hostile to it because 'pay as you go' locks people into an arrangement of state dependency, irrespective of genuine need' (Barry, 1985, p.488). In other words, intergenerational contracts such as that engendered by SERPS, restrict personal freedom to choose a method of pensions provision, without necessarily serving a welfare function. It might also be argued that the very requirement that, in order to contract out, occupational pensions schemes should provide a GMP is a restriction on the freedom of pension providers to produce pensions that the market demands, but the alternative situation would only afford true freedom to those whose employers' decisions or occupational status afforded them a choice in how to provide for retirement. As Beveridge failed to realise, it is not in the interests of the market to cater adequately either for those in low status low paid jobs, often employed by small labour-intensive firms or for those whose employment patterns are subject to disruption; in particular these people would have little choice in the quality of their provision for retirement and would tend to rely on traditional forms of savings such as building society accounts and endowment policies, despite their low yields.

For reasons explained in Chapter 3 a funded additional pension scheme, with its restrictions on deliberate cross-subsidies of the sort which a policy of re-distributing income would represent, would not have allowed an impact to be made on poverty among such groups as workers with broken career patterns. This welfare objective can only be tackled either through an unfunded scheme or by the state.

ii) Intragenerational Redistribution

Intragenerational transfers of resources are the basis of much of the taxation and income maintenance (though not usually pensions) systems. Intragenera-

103

tional distributions most commonly concern transfers between the working and non-working and between the taxed and untaxed sections of the population. These transfers are deliberate and carefully planned by government but, as explained in Chapter 3, in the context of pensions the distributions are not always so simple; the nature of the interaction between tax and pensions regulations is such that sometimes there are perverse transfers from the worse off to the better off. This is anathema to the New Right who favour the idea of a level playing field for competing methods of pensions provision. The ideal form of equality in the field of pensions provision would be for each individual to have their own personal investment portfolio.

iii)Ideological Shift

On May 3rd 1979 a Conservative government, led by Margaret Thatcher, was elected to office. According to Hall (1986, p.100) the Conservative electoral platform had repudiated the Keynesian consensus. Margaret Thatcher argued that: the state had grown too large, and thus inefficient; to fund the welfare state that the public wanted involved levels of taxes which right wing politicians believed people could not afford and which would sap work incentives. They also believed that political overload was occurring because of the state's readiness to intervene. Herein lay the origins of a search for a pensions policy that would allow the state to at least partially withdraw from its responsibility of providing additional pensions.

In truth the Keynesian/Beveridge approach had probably been abandoned by the Labour government of the late1970s; what the new Conservative government did was to formally disown it. A new ideology was needed to replace the discredited Keynesian/Beveridgism that had been the basis of many of the post-war developments in social policy, and that chosen was monetarism. According to Hall (1986, p.99):

> ... monetarism triumphed in Britain, not as economic science, but as political ideology. Its validity could not be proven in scientific terms, but to , those who were seeking to restore the authority of the state it seemed to offer a solution. ... It was a doctrine designed to justify an attack on the power of the unions. ... At worst it rationalised the use of unemployment as a weapon of labour discipline.

At the heart of monetarism was the New Right and their belief that the primary responsibility of government should be the maintenance of defence policy, foreign policy, law and order and a strong currency. Offe (1984, p. 289) explains the New Right thus:

> In Western Europe, Britain and the United States, its common denominator is its deep aversion to state intervention, control, and regulation. ... The New Right offers the market as the alternative to bureaucratic domination ... The New Right is oriented to achievement, effectiveness, efficiency

and productivity. It therefore denounces all those parasitic, hedonistic and counter productive forces that do not conform to the allegedly superior rationality of the market.

It follows that with the state minimally responsible for the distribution of resources through welfare mechanisms, people would assume responsibility for providing for their own welfare via the market. This might bring such advantages as consumer choice and downward pressure on prices. However, Offe (1984, p.290) comments that '(the New Right has) grandiose and, to say the least, unsupported hopes for the market place'.

A pensions policy consistent with this ideology would, in George and Wilding's (1985) terms, be essentially anti-collectivist and favour ideas of increasing personal responsibility and reducing dependency on the state. This view is sympathetic with the notion that to be a full member of society it is necessary to be economically active in as broad a sense as possible, i.e. not just by selling one's labour but through the ownership of capital. As will be seen, the ideological shift probably contributed to the triggering of the Inquiry and to the choice of solution.

At the forefront of promoting an individualistic approach towards pension were the Centre for Policy Studies (CPS) and the Institute of Directors (IoD), countered to some degree by the National Association of Pension Funds (NAPF). Their ideas are examined below.

Centre for Policy Studies

The Centre for Policy Studies is a right wing think tank founded by Margaret Thatcher and Sir (now Lord) Keith Joseph. Two of its members Nigel Vinson (now Lord Vinson of Roddam Dene) and Philip Chappell were particularly important in promoting the ideas of personal capitalism and of personal portable pensions through the timely publication of a short paper: *Personal And Portable Pensions For All* (Vinson and Chappell, 1983). They rejected the traditional Conservative view that occupational pensions should be essential to retirement provision, believing that 'the concentration of wealth into few hands is very dangerous democratically and politically' (Vinson, 1989). More importantly in Chappell's mind was the view that people were being deprived of responsibility for their own investment destiny the idea of a share owning democracy.

Nigel Vinson is one of the CPS's founder directors and is chairman of its Personal Capital Formation Group (more recently known as the 'Wider Ownership Group'). The Wider Ownership Group consists of:

> People who are interested in spreading and diffusing the ownership of wealth because the philosophical background to this is that a free society ... depends on well diffused, well spread economic power and the multiple patronage that flows from that. (Vinson, 1989)

It was in his capacity as chairman of the Wider Ownership Group that Nigel Vinson co-authored with Philip Chappell, also a Group member, the above mentioned

105

short paper. This paper was published in April 1983, several months before the announcement by Norman Fowler of the Inquiry into Provision for Retirement. Asked how he came to be interested in the field of pensions policy, Lord Vinson replied: 'I am interested philosophically in the ownership of wealth.' (Vinson, 1989), adding that he was surprised at the impact the CPS paper had had on pensions policy.

The CPS paper, *Personal and Portable Pensions For All* (Vinson and Chappell, 1983) was produced following a series of discussions within the Wider Ownership Group. Other members of the Group included Philip Darwin and Brian Kingham. Although he was not formally a member of this group, Graham Mather (then head of the Policy Unit at the IoD) took part in several of these Wider Ownership Group discussions.

The CPS paper expresses concern that a consequence of the prevailing method of pensions provision through pension funds is that most people experience ownership of capital at second hand which 'as such, is not ownership in the *motivational* sense' (Vinson and Chappell, 1983, para.2a) whereas personal pensions 'would give a new opportunity for twelve million people to have a real sense of involvement in the industrial success of this country' (Vinson and Chappell, 1983, para.2c). The view is presented that:

> There is an argument that in equity citizens should be treated similarly and their pension not be dependent upon the companies in which they happened to have worked. Consequently state benefits should be increased, company benefits abolished and each individual given the option to top up his state pension by way of tax-deductible additional voluntary contributions. This view is perhaps ahead of its time. (Vinson and Chappell, 1983, para.4b iii)

Vinson and Chappell (1983) adopted an indirect approach to further their aims for a share owning democracy in which control of capital was dispersed and choices between alternative forms of savings were tax neutral. They proposed that there should be a fundamental review of pension legislation. Its objectives would be to 'aid mobility', 'remove the penalty of changing jobs', and 'link individuals more closely with the wealth represented by their pension fund' (Vinson and Chappell, 1983, para.1a). The injustice affecting early leavers 'leads to ossification of employment patterns and harms the whole nation by inhibiting enterprise' (Vinson and Chappell, 1983, para.3a). No evidence is given to support this claim. In offering a solution to the early leavers problem brief consideration is given to the preservation of rights by increasing contributions (Vinson and Chappell, 1983, paras.4d & 6a) but the conclusion, similar to that of the IoD, is reached that 'this is likely to happen anyway but it is not a sufficient solution' (Vinson and Chappell, 1983, para.4d).

The forecast that legislation on preservation of accrued pension rights would be insufficient may have been accepted by Norman Fowler since he both introduced preservation measures in the Social Security Act 1985 and included the 'early leavers' problem on his agenda for the Inquiry into Provision for Retirement (see Chapters 5-7).

The rectification of the injustice to early leavers was seen as an:

opportunity, *if the political will is there*, not only for pension benefits to be put on a more equitable basis but also for people if they wish, to be given the chance to run their own personalised pensions ... (Vinson and Chappell, 1983, para.4a, *CPS' emphasis*)

thereby creating an opportunity, however impractical, for some individuals to manage their own investment portfolio while others might rely on an extension of the provisions of the Section 226 pension, which at the time was mainly applicable to the self-employed, to all workers. Also, in the words of Vinson and Chappell (1983, para.2b), 'such a policy would encourage job mobility without pension penalty or revenue costs except insofar (as) people might save more'.

Despite the repeated assurance that very few workers would be likely to leave their occupational pension schemes in favour of personal pensions, Vinson and Chappell express the view that *for the time being at least,* this should only be permitted with the employer's consent (Vinson and Chappell, 1983, para.5e). So in spite of the support of individual freedom, for example 'we regard freedom of the individual as more important (than employers' interest in a 'static' workforce) (Vinson and Chappell, 1983, para.6e), they still take the employers' side by saying they are against giving employees the right to opt out of employers' occupational pension schemes because it 'might ... put too great a strain on some pension funds or encourage employers to abandon the optional element of their funds' (Vinson and Chappell, 1983, para.5e). This would appear to be a concession to occupational pensions providers and sponsors. However, this reservation was ignored in the Social Security Act 1986.

An essential precondition to the operation any sort of market is the availability of information on which decisions are made. To satisfy this the CPS paper recommended that all pension schemes (personal and occupational):

SHOULD BE REQUIRED TO PUBLISH THEIR ANNUAL (DISCON-TINUANCE) VALUATION, AND ATTRIBUTE TO EACH MEMBER HIS APPROPRIATE SHARE IN UNITS AT THAT POINT IN TIME. (Vinson and Chappell, 1983, para.5, *CPS' Block Capitals*).

The paper goes on to argue in favour of encouraging a gradual move towards money purchase schemes (Vinson and Chappell, 1983, para.4b(i)). This is justified on the grounds that it would, firstly, progressively eliminate the subsidisation of the non-leaver. Presumably they intended that leavers should take their contributions and use them to start a personal pension fund rather than have their entitlement preserved (Vinson and Chappell, 1983, para.4b i). Note that legislation was subsequently introduced (1985) to ensure that early leavers got better value for their contributions. Secondly, it would reduce the 'enormous' risks to employers that occupational pension funds can entail (Vinson and Chappell, 1983, para.4bii).

The treatment of SERPS is surprisingly benign. SERPS is only briefly mentioned in the CPS paper and is neither criticised nor recommended for either winding up or replacement by private pensions. Indeed, there is a suggestion, apparently for those concerned about the ability of employers to fund occupational schemes, that they might use the integrated approach that combines SERPS with a proportionately reduced occupational pension (Vinson and Chappell, 1983, para.6bii). Yet the continued existence of SERPS seems contrary to the strong support given by the CPS to the merits of 'personal capital formation' and giving individuals control of their pension investment. Vinson and Chappell seems to support state involvement rather than campaign for its demise. One interpretation would be that the views of the pensions industry and a desire not to embarrass the government in the way that the 1983 CPRS paper almost did prevailed over ideological predelictions.

Some critics would argue that the main problem with Vinson and Chappell's proposals for spreading the ownership of wealth and dispersing economic power is that these two aims are mutually exclusive. In societies where wealth is widely spread, institutional investment is the norm; most individuals have neither the time nor the expertise to manage their own investments, and in any case the cost in fees of managing small funds would take a considerable part of any investment gains. As a result, economic control, far from being 'well spread', becomes concentrated in the hands of a small number of investment managers. This is reflected in the fact that most personal pension providers are large institutional investors such as life offices which, as a consequence of the expansion facilitated by the Social Security Act 1986 of personal pensions, have more assets under their control than ever before.

Many of the recommended measures were adopted in the Social Security Act 1986, though often not in a pure form. However, in some respects, chiefly in connection with SERPS, the CPS document is less radical than either the Green Paper *Reform of Social Security* (1985) or the eventual legislation the Social Security Act 1986.

Institute of Directors

In preparing its evidence for the Inquiry into Provision for Retirement the IoD adopted an assertive approach. In response to the Inquiry for Provision for Retirement's request for evidence, whereas the NAPF simply answered the questions posed in the Inquiry's letter, the IoD submission of January 31st 1984 took on the broader task of building a case for personal pensions, stating in para.1 that:

> As a leading advocate of the need for reform of the occupational pension system we believe that, given the necessary political will, the chance now presents itself fundamentally to alter the way in which pension provision is made. (IoD, 1984a, para.1)

The reference to 'political will' is strikingly similar to that made in the CPS paper (Vinson & Chappell, 1983, para.4a,) described above. The IoD submission continues:

> Underlying the Institute's support for the concept of personal portable pensions is a long-term commitment to the dissemination of wealth in society. ... If we accept that there is a lack of understanding in modern Britain of the wealth-creating processes which underpin our free enterprise economy then only by increasing involvement in the creation of wealth can we continue to secure the freedoms which society holds to be important. (IoD, 1984a, para.2)

Again, the IoD submission shows distinct similarities with the CPS paper (Vinson and Chappell, 1983). The above paragraph leaves little doubt that its authors are interested in more than merely promoting what it believes to be the most efficacious system of pension provision. Rather, as with Vinson and Chappell (1983), there is an ideological agenda.

In part, the IoD's ideological aims would be achieved by getting people to identify more closely with their pension contribution (IoD, 1984a, para.3). This might be achieved through an extension of the same philosophy that motivated the encouragement given to home ownership; this further transfer of choice and responsibility to individuals would be attained by 'extending to occupational pension investors the right to determine how their money is directed' (IoD, 1984a, para.4) and would thereby further the goal of individual independence. In addition: 'The object of our proposals is to bring about a flexibility that will allow individuals who wish it a greater freedom of choice of action' (IoD, 1984a, para.5).

This philosophy of individual freedom and self-determination resulted in an inadvertently progressive attitude towards occupational pensions. The IoD held that the employee, not the employer, should have control over occupational pension assets (IoD, 1984a, para.7) though they were careful to reassure the pensions industry that there was no desire to destabilise occupational pension funds (IoD, 1984a, paras.6 and 40). Nevertheless, the IoD was not content with the government's proposed action on early leavers which it saw more as a palliative than a solution: 'Complete portability of pension rights can deal with the early leaver problem fairly and completely' (IoD, 1984a, para.8). The IoD was keen to point out that personal pensions would be advantageous to women who experienced career breaks (IoD, 1984a, para.9) and would generally encourage job mobility (IoD, 1984a, para.10).

Like the CPS, the IoD submission expressed concern about the concentration of control of pension fund assets in too few hands, citing the 1983 Stock Exchange Survey on Share Ownership which showed that whereas in 1963 6% of equity was controlled by pension funds, in 1981 the proportion was 27% (IoD, 1984a, paras.11-12).

These aims would be achieved by disclosure and leaving options. On an annual basis occupational pension funds would provide employees with a statement of the discontinuance value of accrued contributions. This would assist the employee's decision-making and create an 'informed interest' in the fund's performance (IoD, 1984a, paras.13/14). The employee would be able to choose between the following options: transfer contributions to a new employer's fund; establish a personal pension portfolio; and use the transfer value as capital to start a business (IoD, 1984a, para.15). It is significant that these options do not include the taking out of a personal pension plan, including a S.226 pension arrangement, with a life office. Indeed:

> ... the Institute would like to see an expansion of the pensions market by permitting banks, building societies and unit trusts to offer their own tax-approved retirement provision funds. (IoD, 1984a, para.17)

It would seem that the IoD was not in favour of personal pensions options that entailed the further concentration of control of invested pension assets in the hands of a few powerful institutional investors.

Having declared that they did not intend to destabilise occupational pension schemes, the IoD made a recommendation that was potentially quite onerous for many employers: this was the recommendation that all occupational pension funds should be obliged to provide facilities for AVCs (IoD, 1984a, para.21) and it is entirely consistent with the idea of affording employees maximum choice regarding the level of additional pension provision.

There appears to have been a very pragmatic motive for the IoD recommendations: in summarising the combined impact of all the proposed measures the IoD concludes that: 'This approach will ease cost pressures on company schemes' (IoD, 1984a, para.28).

As was seen in Chapters 5 and 6, an element in the IoD Director General, Walter Goldsmith's, earlier speeches on the subject of pensions was that the cost of implementing the OPB's recommended improvements to occupational pension schemes (OPB, 1981 and 1982) should not be borne by employers. However, from the structure and overall content of the IoD submission it is difficult to believe that this advantage is more than a makeweight in an otherwise ideologically motivated document. Clear statements of this are given elsewhere in the submission:

> The Institute has based its approach on the belief that capitalism can only function successfully when the process of wealth creation is properly understood and as many people as possible are encouraged to participate in that process. (IoD, 1984a, para.39)

and:

> We now have the opportunity, if we can summon the will, to bring about a fundamental shift in attitude towards wealth in this country while widening

choice and strengthening the free enterprise economy. It is an opportunity not to be lost. (IoD, 1984a, para.41)

In one important respect the IoD expressed disagreement with the CPS:

> We do not find attractive the idea that an employee who wishes to contract out of his employer's scheme should have the right to contract into the State Earnings-Related Scheme. This is not the place to discuss the problems of SERPS but it is sufficient to say that there is mounting concern that the scheme will not be able to cope with the demands which even the present level of subscription is going to entail in the future. (IoD, 1984a, para.32)

The IoD was not, in the event, asked to submit evidence on the future of SERPS.

National Association of Pension Funds

Evidence of the NAPF's values concerning pensions policy are to be found in its submissions to the Inquiry into Provision for Retirement. The NAPF's first submission was dated January 5th 1984. In contrast with the IoD submission described above which had assertively built a case for personal pensions, the NAPF submission consisted of only of a series of answers to each of the questions posed by the letter from the DHSS asking for evidence. The quality of the arguments in this document is less than impressive, frequently defensive and, at times, spurious. They expressed support for the idea that an early leaver should be able to transfer their accrued contributions to a Section 226 contract (NAPF, 1984, para.4) but argued weakly that occupational pensions are indeed personal:

> The benefits for and in respect of each individual are based on *his* service and *his* salary. The benefits are therefore wholly 'personal'. What the individual does not have is his own 'pot of gold' and it is only in this context that the pension might not be regarded as personal. (NAPF, 1984, para.4)

The NAPF believed that personal pensions would give members less rather than greater control over their retirement income (NAPF, 1984, para.8) and that personal pensions would simply introduce new imbalances between those who selected good policies and investment advice and those who did not (NAPF, 1984, paras.11-12). The submission's one strong argument concerned the possibility that occupational pensions hindered job mobility:

> There is little evidence that pension rights hinder job mobility. Indeed such evidence as exists suggests that most employees do not take pensions into account at all when changing jobs. ... Why should pensions come under attack as a hindrance to job mobility rather than the payment of high (sometimes inordinate) salaries? (NAPF, 1984, para.13)

111

Finally, in order to demonstrate the lack of co-operation that characterised the NAPF submission:

> It seems to us it would be extremely difficult to enable personal pension arrangements to be used for contracting out purposes. We do not see it as our role to suggest solutions to this problem even if we could think of any. (NAPF, 1984, para.21)

This was a strange way to seek to influence policy-makers.

As described in Chapter 7 the NAPF, in its response to the Inquiry's second request for evidence, submitted only a one-and-a-half page document attached to which were five NAPF papers that had been written over the previous six years and whose subjects approximated those on which the Inquiry had sought evidence (NAPF, 1984a). Nevertheless, certain values are clearly presented in this document:

> It is accepted that there must always be a role for the state to protect the unfortunate, the unwary or the needy and a partnership of some kind will therefore be desirable ...Having actively assisted in the creation of the present partnership, implemented in 1978, NAPF would not seek to alter it. ... The NAPF does not consider it desirable for the state to become involved to any extent beyond its present commitment. (NAPF, 1984a, para.3)

Obviously the NAPF was keen for SERPS to continue in the 1978 mould. Although as an organisation the NAPF undoubtedly represents the interests of capitalism, it is a brand of capitalism which George and Wilding (1985) have called 'reluctant collectivism' because such capitalists, while believing firmly in the role of the market in distributing scarce resources, nevertheless recognise the valuable role which the state can perform in distributing welfare resources.

Reform of Social Security

Although some of the key ideas contained in the Green Paper *Reform of Social Security* (DHSS, 1985) were not actually implemented, it is here that the clearest exposition is to be found of the values underpinning the pensions measures contained in the Social Security Act 1986. The Green Paper posed no threat to the intergenerational contract on which the Basic Retirement Pension was founded:

> ... the basic national insurance pension will remain unchanged. ... the Government believe it is right for each generation of working people to provide the basic level of income to their predecessors in retirement. (DHSS, 1985, vol.2, chap.1.41)

However, this indulgence did not extend to SERPS:

The Government accepts the need to tackle the open-ended commitments of SERPS. ... we propose to replace SERPS by a new partnership between state provision and occupational and personal pension provision. (DHSS, 1985, vol.2, chap 1.39)

and,

'... those ... whose pension expectations are closely tied to (SERPS) will continue as at present' (DHSS, 1985, vol.2, chap.1.41).

In other words, it was proposed that workers who currently contributed to SERPS and were within fifteen years of retirement age would be allowed to benefit from continued membership of SERPS for the remainder of their working lives, while for younger members of the workforce:

... who can begin now to build up their own additional pension provisions through occupational and personal pensions, the Government that this, rather than state provision, should be the system of the future. (DHSS, 1985, vol.2, chap.1.41)

The essence of this proposal was to be the amending of the intergenerational contract between future workers and retirees; as the SERPS contribution base declined future SERPS pensions would increasingly be funded by tax payers until eventually there were no surviving SERPS retirees, at which point the 'contract' would expire.

In time this proposal would curtail the state's responsibility for the earnings-related pensions of workers who do not have access to occupational schemes. The means by which this objective is to be achieved is the replacement of SERPS with personal pensions to which employer and employee would, after a three year period of phasing in, be required to contribute a minimum of 4% of earnings. These would be money purchase schemes producing, for each contributor, a lump sum on retirement to be used to purchase an annuity. For reasons explained in Chapter 10 the three year phasing out of SERPS was abandoned in the subsequent White Paper in favour of modifications to the conditions of SERPS that would reduce the value of SERPS contributions, change the basis from best twenty years to working lifetime, and restrict new membership.

Money purchase-based pensions have distinct disadvantages such as those rehearsed in Chapter 3. Nevertheless, the Green Paper argues that money purchase schemes are distinctly attractive to employers in that they: '... offer a known level of commitment without the open-ended promise of a defined benefit scheme' (DHSS, 1985, vol.2, chap.1.47) while, for the employees: '... it gives an identifiable sum of personal savings which belongs directly to him' (DHSS, 1985, vol.2, chap.1.47). The sum may be identifiable in the sense that any surplus will accrue to the worker rather than the fund, but it will not be predictable. The accrual of surpluses to the member could provide a means of financing early retirement of older workers. It could even be sufficient to disqualify such unemployed older workers from claiming means-tested benefits.

The Green Paper (DHSS, 1985) offered no discouragement to employers who might be tempted by this advantage of predictable costs to wind up their existing salary related retirement pension schemes and direct all new contributions into personal pensions. If this were to happen at all, it would tend to affect those workers whose industrial strength was weakest. Those employed in monopoly industries would be able to withstand any such move by an employer, and this in turn would complicate the discrepancies between those with occupational pensions and those who did not have access to such schemes.

Great emphasis was laid on freedom of choice, except to the extent that there would a minimum level of contribution. Hence: '... any employee will have the right to opt for a personal pension instead of being a member of his employer's scheme' (DHSS, 1985, vol.2, 4 chap.1.50).

With regard to sexual equality, the Green Paper proposed that insurance companies should produce the annuity rates for women as for men (DHSS, 1985, vol.2, chap.1.54) but in the event it was not implemented.

It is arguable that there have always been latent contradictions between the ideology underpinning the welfare system and that which underpins the economy. For example, the values which support the economy, such as the work ethic, thrift, a fair day's work for a fair day's pay, run contrary to those of welfare such as everyone having some minimum standard of living and being allocated resources according to need rather than merit (Mishra, 1981). If this is the case, then because of the extent to which welfare decisions are based on either secret criteria or no criteria at all (Jones et al, 1978) it has usually been possible for the state to conceal both its own values and any emerging fracture in what society at large is led to believe is a consensus. Hence such latent contradictions would rarely become patent.

The post-1983 Conservative government provides a partial exception to this rule. In its Green Paper *Reform of Social Security* it has sought to explain the recent social security reforms in terms of: '... meeting genuine need' (DHSS, 1985, vol.1, chap.1.12) and making the system: '... simpler to understand and easier to administer' (DHSS, 1985, vol.1, chap.1.12). In this way the Conservative government has sought to obscure some of its real policy objectives. It is in the context of pensions policy that the Green Paper probably comes closest to disclosing the market-oriented objective of its proposals when it states that '... the social security system must be consistent with the Government's objectives for the economy' (DHSS, 1985, vol 1, chap 1.12); it may be that this objective was always present, but it was never more explicit than in the post-1979 period. It will be shown that although the Social Security Act 1986 gives the impression of moving some way towards introducing economic values and away from welfare values as the underpinning to earnings-related pensions policy, it does not depart from the principles enunciated by Beveridge in 1942.

Social Security Act 1986

Contracted out personal pensions as provided under the Social Security Act 1986 enable the individual to provide for retirement via the market by contributing at least some minimal percentage of income to a pension fund managed for their benefit. Responsibility for selecting appropriate investments usually falls to the fund managers. The said contributions are invested with the object of producing a maximum return. A personal pension plan can be an individual or group entity. On retirement the fund (or the individual's portion of it) is liquidated to produce a lump sum for the purchase of an annuity which provides an income until death for the retiree and a reduced income for any surviving spouse. The main contrasts with occupational pensions are that:

1. personal pension schemes are contribution-defined whereas occupational pension schemes, as explained in Chapter 3, are benefit-defined. Hence with personal pension funds an employer is not at risk in periods of poor investment return of having to top up their occupational pension fund's assets in order to maintain its solvency. This also excludes the possibility of a cross-subsidy from young to older workers;

2. personal pensions are fully portable in the sense that when job changes occur it is possible to continue contributing to the same personal fund except where it is a group scheme. There is no need to leave contributions in one's former employer's occupational pension fund where they will be subject to a maximum revaluation of five per cent per annum irrespective of the performance of the underlying securities. Hence there is no question of early leavers subsidising long stayers;

3. the employee bears all the risk of the personal pension fund failing to produce a sufficient lump sum to buy an adequate annuity. After retirement the provider of the annuity is responsible for providing an income which is incremental in the same way as the GMP, i.e. in line with the RPI up to 3% per annum but no decreases (Kaye, 1987, pp.22-23). Beyond this the employee is still responsible if, through price inflation, the annuity ceases to be adequate. This contrasts with the situation for occupational pension funds where the employer is responsible for ensuring that the fund produces sufficient assets during the employee's working life to produce an adequate pension, and the state is responsible after retirement for ensuring that the pension keeps pace with price inflation.

As the Social Security Act 1986 takes effect and the state begins its gradual withdrawal from the provision of earnings-related pensions, the impact will be that while earnings levels will still determine an individual's ability to make contributions to either or both an occupational scheme and private pension provision, the return on the sums invested will be the product of the condition of the economy generally and of corporate profitability in particular.

Changes in corporate profitability manifest themselves in the dividends and capital growth attached to equity investments. This is influenced by, among other factors, industrial relations. Just as company profits suffer as a consequence of industrial disputes and 'excessive' wage demands, so dividends and capital gains accruing to investors, including the sponsors of pension funds, will also be adversely affected.

To the post-1979 Conservative governments an important factor in precipitating industrial unrest is that workers' interests and values are not linked sufficiently to those of their employers; for example, too few employees realise the 'advantages' of working for a highly profitable company, seeing instead opportunities for yet higher wage claims. Even with occupational pension schemes employees are shielded from the adverse effects of the economy by the employers' responsibility to make good any deficit between current assets and future liabilities. Personal pensions might be seen as strengthening the link between the workers' interests and company profits. In this scenario personal pensions are seen as placing pressure on workers to avoid industrial action that reduces corporate profitability and sometimes results in redundancies by making them identify with the values and objectives of their employers. This can be viewed in either of two ways:

i) *as a market form of distributive justice*

in which the state, in theory if not in practice, is reducing to a minimum its role in allocating resources throughout society, in this case from the workforce to the retired population. In this instance there is not necessarily an intention of altering the behaviour of the actors, but rather to allow individuals the freedom to exhibit whatever economic behaviour they will, and to be rewarded or sanctioned by the 'hidden hand' of the market.

ii) *as a mode of domination*

it is a form of incorporation whereby workers as trade union members are being constrained from causing the economic disruption described above which in the late 1970s and early 1980s allegedly fuelled inflation and job losses. In contrast with the above option this is most certainly an attempt by government on behalf of capitalism to modify the behaviour of the working class by forcing a convergence of capitalist and proletarian interests. In this way workforce discipline is in theory maintained by the threat of low profitability leading to poor returns on invested personal pension funds and thus to lower pensions. If the prospect of lower pensions is too distant for it to affect the behaviour of most workers, the requirement of the 1986 Act that contributors to both occupational and personal pensions be provided with annual statements of the value of their accrued contributions would provide the necessary feedback to make workers conscious of the extent to which their prosperity was linked not just to their ability to secure higher wages but to the prosperity of the economy as a whole.

It is notable that in preceding years concerted efforts were made by the government to educate the public on the merits of capitalism and personal share ownership by encouraging them to buy not only their own homes but also shares in the 'privatisation' issues and to take out personal equity plans. This would have paved the way for the acceptance of personal pensions and made a large proportion of working class people dependent for their material well-being on their *individual investment decisions* as private citizens and not just their *collective industrial actions* as members of trade unions. The same government was responsible for introducing draconian legislation aimed at altering the behaviour of trade unions and their members, suggesting that tying the prosperity of workers to the performance of the economy forms part of a new mode of domination which is as important as the introduction of a market-oriented form of distributive justice. At the heart of this mode of domination is the goal of committing members of the working class to New Right values. Unfortunately, there may be adverse aspects for those less well able to use market methods to make provision for retirement. For example, extending 'choice' and 'responsibility' to consumers may sounds attractive in marketing terms but in an adverse economic climate these terms will probably become synonyms for *blame*.

In a system founded on consumer choice, where underprovision results from either insufficient contributions or a failure of the market, it may be argued by policy makers and welfare professionals that the individual should have sold his or her home, bought a cheaper one and invested the surplus in a personal pension. Instead, the consumer made a choice to enjoy other things, such as better housing than could actually be afforded, and now expects the taxpayer to keep them in a lifestyle to which they are not entitled. Alternatively if the individual is in a type of work which frequently entails early retirement or was in a declining industry, it may be argued that they should have realised the probability of not being able to work until pensionable age and made extra provision accordingly.

It may be alleged that the individual should have known from the annual statements that they had underprovided and responded by making additional provision and/or changing investment vehicles. In practice the provision of annual statements on investment performance and the current worth of pensions provision may be of little use or meaning to most people. The unknown value of the termination bonus is further complicated by the fact that the value of accrued pension provision increases geometrically not arithmetically and is dependent on future unknown earnings, making it difficult for most people to assess at interim stages in their working lives whether their pension provision is adequate.

In other words, the individual who discovers too late that their retirement is underprovided for may find difficulty in claiming any allowance or benefit from the state, even where underprovision occurs as a consequence of unforeseen and sustained high rates of inflation during the post-retirement period when the retiree is incapable of making further provision. Hence reliance on the state will be cut. There will therefore be a fall in the incidence of intra and inter generational distributions of resources, and pensions will afford less opportunity for either planned or inadvertent transfers. Where personal pensions are used in preference to occupational pension schemes, there will be an end to some of the intragenerational transfers that are built into employers' schemes.

Conclusion

The main effect of the Social Security Act 1986 has been to alter the relationships between the state and the individual; and the economy/employment market and the individual. Individuals without continuous access to occupational pension schemes throughout their working lives could previously have depended on the state for provision of an additional pension; the restrictions on new entrants to SERPS mean that in time the only pension retirees will receive from the state will be the Basic Retirement Pension whose values continues to decline as a proportion of retirees' incomes. Instead they will be dependant on personal pensions which in turn depend on the performance of the economy and underlying securities for their level of return. However, this represents no more than a return to the principles of Beveridge who, in 1942 had advocated the provision of a basic pension that did not stifle individual initiative (Beveridge, 1942).

Beveridge had made it plain in his report that individuals should not be discouraged from making personal provision for old age and, from his proposals, it is clear that the state contributory pension was intended to cover only basic needs:

> The State in organising social security should not stifle incentive, opportunity responsibility; in establishing a national minimum, it should leave room and encouragement for voluntary action by each individual to provide more than that minimum for himself and his family. (Beveridge, 1942, para.9)

In this way the state avoided competing with existing private sector pension arrangements. Beveridge would have preferred to have seen a 'funded' state pension scheme which was, by definition, self-financing. In the event what emerged was a 'pay as you go' scheme in which the contributions of the current workforce provided the basic pension. However, personal pensions and additional voluntary contributions have the potential to achieve Beveridge's aim admirably.

The effect of the 1986 Act has not been as radical as might be thought, partly as a consequence of the reliance on large institutions to provide personal pension plans. There will nevertheless be a widening in the variations in retirement incomes as a result of differences in life offices' investment performances and inability, particularly on the part of the low paid, to discriminate between pension providers.

118

If those most closely identified with the New Right had had their way, what could have happened was that the welfare basis that underpins SERPS would be replaced completely by something much more compatible with a capitalist ideology in which individuals provided only for their own retirement, possibly with the aid of personal investment portfolios, and the state's underwriting of occupational pensions might well have ended. Instead, SERPS is to continue in modified form, the state will continue to underwrite occupational pensions, and contributions to personal pension plans are being handled by the large financial institutions to which Walter Goldsmith, Nigel Vinson and Philip Chappell took exception.

The traditional means by which resources are transferred from one part of the population to another – social security – is being partially replaced by an extension to the fiscal welfare system through the introduction of the NI rebate and the 2% Incentive. Hence the unfunded nature of SERPS, which results in present contributors providing pensions for previous contributors, is being replaced by personal pensions whose contributors' future pensions are in part funded by, on the one hand, contributors to SERPS who do not benefit from the NI rebate, the 2% Incentive or tax relief on their contributions, and on the other hand, contributors to occupational pension schemes who receive a NI rebate (reduced by an amount necessary to purchase a GMP) but do not benefit from the 2% Incentive. The intergenerational contract has not therefore been abolished, and intragenerational transfers continue in a more complex form that before.

10 Implementation of a new pensions policy

Introduction

When examining personal pensions the Social Security Act 1986 cannot be looked at in isolation. There were several pieces of legislation whose implementation was to affect the 1986 Act's success and these will be examined in the course of this chapter:

i) *the Financial Services Act 1986*

ii) *the Building Societies Act 1986*

iii) *the Social Security Act 1986*

In terms of policy formulation and implementation there are respects in which at least two of these Acts overlap; as mentioned in Chapter 7 the minister responsible for the Financial Services Act 1986 was (later Sir) Alex Fletcher, and he appointed Marshall Field and Sir Mark Weinberg to chair committees that did detailed work on self-regulation for the financial services legislation (DTI Cmnd 9432). These three men were all members of the Inquiry into Provision for Retirement which contributed to the Social Security Act 1986. This factor appears to show a merging of two hitherto distinct policy communities. Welfare and financial policies had previously been made by different sets of people and were governed by different sets of values. Except to the extent that both types of policy required ratification by the Cabinet and Parliament, the policy-making processes took place in entirely different spheres. In the constitution of the Main Team and the Sub Group of the Inquiry into Provision for Retirement it can be seen that capitalist methods and values were being employed to solve a welfare problem. Given that Sir Alex was a member of the Conservative Cabinet and Sir Mark Weinberg and Marshall Field are leading figures in the city, it is hard to imagine these three people being in favour of anything but the phasing out or abolition of SERPS and its replacement with personal pensions.

The provisions of these three Acts interacted to shape the introduction of contracted out personal pensions. Other pieces of legislation which were to prove significant and will be considered briefly here were the Social Security Act 1985, the Finance (No.2) Act 1988 and the Personal and Occupational Pension Schemes (Incentive Payments) Regulations 1987.

Some of the rules and regulations affecting contracted out personal pensions are contained in the Social Security Act 1986 and the Finance (No.2) Act 1988. However, a noteworthy aspect of the Social Security Act 1986 is that it contains very little detail about how the implementation of the new pensions policy would be effected. Much of this was decided later and implemented through a series of Statutory Instruments. The following Statutory Instruments were made on June 25th 1987, laid before Parliament on July 6th 1987 and came into force on April 6th 1988:

SI 1099   Contracting Out (Transfer) Amendment Regulations 1987
SI 1101   Money Purchase Contracted Out Regulations 1987
SI 1105   Occupational Pension Scheme (Disclosure of Information) (Amendment) Regulations 1987

The following were made on June 25th 1987, laid before Parliament on July 6th 1987 and came into force January 4th 1988:

SI 1109   Personal Pensions (Appropriate Scheme) Regulations 1987
SI 1113   Abatement of Benefit Regulations 1987
SI 1115   Incentive Payments Regulations 1987

Financial services regulations affecting the marketing of personal pensions and upon which the implementation of the Social Security Act 1986 was dependent were delayed by problems described below. As a consequence, problems were created for the Secretary of State and indeed the Cabinet whose collective response was to 'muddle through'. Despite the inconvenience that must have been caused to the few providers who were eager to launch their new products, there seemed to be little complaint or embarrassment each time a new introduction date for contracted out personal pensions was announced.

This is significant because although contracted out personal pensions were launched on July 1st 1988 amendments to the Finance Bill and to Part 10 of the guidelines which deals with monitoring of contributions were still being dealt with in June 1988. Compared with the 1975 legislation and regulations, those which created and now regulate contracted out personal pensions are very complex. Furthermore, the 1986 legislation is much more dependent on and interactive with other pieces of legislation.

Related Legislation and its Impact

i) Social Security Act 1985

The Social Security Act 1985, which received royal assent on June 22nd 1985 established three principles which were to be crucial to the introduction of the Social Security Act 1986:

1. it provided early leavers (whose problems were discussed in Chapter 3) with the right to a transfer value in respect of their accrued occupational pension contributions, although it did not create the right to have a transfer accepted by a new employer);

2. pension schemes would be required to disclose information to new members on joining as well as statements of benefits annually and on request to existing members (OPB 1981 para.10.6). This was to be essential both to the working of contracted out personal pensions and the general principle that the individual should accept responsibility for the adequacy of their own pension provision. The OPB justified these proposals in its 1981 Report on the grounds that such disclosure would lead to an improvement in the benefits provided by occupational pension schemes:

    The objective (of information disclosure) is to create a climate of opinion in which early leavers' rights gain prominence. We regard the requirements on information we have recommended as an essential minimum. (OPB, June 1981, Para. 10.11)

3. in response to two reports by the Occupational Pensions Board (OPB, 1981, 1982) the Social Security Act 1985 also provided that the value of early leavers' accrued pension contributions should be subject to some form of protection. Occupational pension schemes would in future be obliged to revalue such contributions in line with the Retail Price Index up to a maximum of 5% per annum. Given that earnings rise faster than prices this is probably less than what might be considered a reasonable annual rate of growth. Unfortunately the legislation was founded on a misconception on the part of the Conservative government. They believed the problem to be one of inflation affecting the value of pension rights accrued with early employers, ignoring other factors such as length of service and product- ivity and other wage increases. In fact very few salaries and wages increase by price inflation only (Kaye 1987, p.55). Hence it legislated that employers should inflate ex-employees' pensions to afford limited protection against price inflation. Nevertheless, this will play an important role in improving the return on contributions for the majority of workers whose working lives are spread between several employers and whose contributions, if not redeemed, could likewise be spread between several occupational pension funds. At the same time it

will increase the cost of occupational pensions by depriving funds of an important source of surpluses which were particularly valuable during the late 1970s and early 1980s when redundancies were at high levels.

The same 1985 legislation – the Social Security Act 1985 – required pension schemes to provide transfer values on a basis which was equitable with deferred pensions and other preserved benefits, though it stopped short of requiring occupational pension schemes to unconditionally accept the transfer values of new employees' pension rights accrued in previous employment. This was in line with what the OPB had recommended (OPB, 1981 paras. 9.32; 9.33). Mandatory transfer would have been at least inequitable. Where a new employee had previously belonged to a less well managed pension scheme the value of his or her contributions in relation to salary would be less than those of existing members. This would require either of two measures:

1. the trustees could dilute any surplus within the fund to make up the deficit, but this would reduce the funds available to improve pensions for existing and future retirees, or

2. on recruitment the employer could pay a lump sum into the pension fund to cover the initial deficit in the transfer value of the new employee's pension contributions.

The situation would be especially acute in industries with high labour turnovers or where job changes involved high salary increases. Mandatory transfers would therefore benefit 'high flyers' at the expense of low paid workers. Where the new employee begins work on a significantly higher wage than was received in their previous employment, on the basis of which their previous pension contributions were calculated, the transfer value of their accrued contributions may not be adequate to produce a pension based on final salary unless as before either the new employer contributes a lump sum to make up the deficit or the pension fund's assets are diluted. The latter option has the potential to deprive existing members of improvements in pension levels by creating a cross-subsidy between employees of the sort described in Chapter 3.

It can be seen that by introducing the right to a transfer value the authors of the Social Security Act 1985 seemed to recognise the early leavers problem but without insisting that occupational pension schemes provide a total solution. When seen from this point of view this measure does not make very much sense; it cannot possibly be effective. However, it would make sense if it was known at the time by policy makers that the right to opt out of occupational pensions and into personal pensions was soon to be introduced. It would be necessary to have this requirement to provide a transfer value in place so that contributors to occupational schemes would have a basis on which to make their choice between keeping their existing arrangement or opting for a personal pension with a provider of their own choosing. The same can be said regarding the provision for annual disclosure of information to contributors; it provides occupational pension contributors with information essential for making a choice between their existing scheme and personal pension. As it would take some time for many fund managers to put the necessary arrangements in place for producing and disclosing these types of information, such advance notice was at least helpful and probably essential in ensuring a smooth introduction of personal pensions. The Social Security Act 1985 received the royal assent six months before the publication of the Green Paper *Reform of Social Security* and was probably drafted sometime before the Inquiry into Provision for Retirement had been completed.

Hence, by introducing the right to a transfer value the Social Security Act 1985 recognised the early leaver problem without insisting that the sponsors of occupational pension schemes provide a total solution. Similarly, the preservation of the value of accrued occupational pensions contributions seems only a partial answer to the problem; why could not the value of such contributions be increased in line with the growth of the pension fund as a whole? It is as though the DHSS, with the certain knowledge of the shape of the forthcoming Social Security Act 1986, saw personal pensions as the permanent solution to these dual problems. It is difficult otherwise to explain why the early leavers problem took up so much of the Inquiry's time; if Norman Fowler had regarded the problem as being 'solved' he would not have allowed it so prominent a place on the agenda unless it was needed as a 'makeweight' to strengthen the case for personal pensions.

ii) Finance Act 1986

The Finance Act 1986, which received royal assent on November 7th 1986, introduced a new investment/tax avoidance device known as Personal Equity Plans (PEPs). According to Nigel Lawson's successor as Chancellor of the Exchequer, John Major, £750,000,000 was invested in 300,000 new PEPs in 1989/90 (Budget speech March 20th 1990). In practice the tax advantages offered by PEPs were of greatest value to the prosperous in society. However, political objective was for this investment innovation would be of value to all investors whether large or small. The populist way in which PEPs were promoted showed clearly Nigel Lawson's desire to educate a large part of the general population into accepting that stock market investment was not the exclusive preserve of the very wealthy. The introduction of PEPs coincided almost exactly with the dramatic fall in the use of National Savings as a fund-raising borrowing device. In the late 1980s, particularly during the rise in interest rates, the Government failed to offer personal savers attractive investments in this field. When taken in conjunction with the ascendancy of PEPs this suggests that the state has been moving out of savings and encouraging savers to rely on the private sector, not least by taking risks on the stock market. In so doing the Chancellor of the Exchequer Nigel Lawson and the Treasury were promoting the principle of 'popular capitalism' which, aided by the advertising by PEP providers and the Conservative government's ongoing privatisation programme,

124

probably helped establish the idea of personal investment portfolios in the public consciousness and thereby prepared the ground for personal pensions.

iii) *Building Societies Act 1986*

The Building Societies Act 1986 made it possible for building societies to administer and market personal pension plans. To some degree this was in order to equalise banks and building societies, banks having previously made inroads into the home loans market. The more important aim, however, was to increase the range of financial services (including personal pensions) providers and thereby maximise competition. As is shown below, the success of the Act in this respect was very limited.

Henceforth, banks, building societies and unit trust management companies would be permitted to enter the personal pensions market. It was hoped that the resulting competition would lead to minimal management charges and arrangement fees and maximum consumer choice and returns on investment. Indeed, such was the commitment to widening the range of providers that consideration was given by the Inquiry Sub Group to allowing stockbrokers to provide personal pensions. However, it was felt that stockbrokers were not a sufficiently homogeneous group for it to be safely assumed that they would all possess the necessary intellectual and material resources to cope with this type and scale of responsibility to investors. In particular, members of the Inquiry saw a danger that some of the smaller firms might tempted to enter this market but find themselves unable to cope with demands on their expertise and resources.

Where building societies have become pension providers they have tended to act as representatives of life offices. This is because for small organisations, which many building societies are when compared to other financial institutions, the cost of designing and setting up a range of personal pension products and recruiting and training staff to provide good quality advice to consumers was prohibitive. Life assurance companies on the other hand were more than willing to train building society staff to sell their products and thereby secure an increased market share. Hence it was only the major merchant and clearing banks and the largest of building societies that were able to enter the market with their own versions of personal pension plans. Despite this limitation there was a proliferation of personal pension products.

Among the first of the new pension providers to market unit trust linked personal pensions was Rothschilds, the investment arm of the merchant bank. In 1986, before the regulations affecting personal pensions had been devised let alone publicised: "... the company made a conscious decision to go for personal pensions whilst deciding against PEPs." (Ellis, 1988, p.31).

iv) *Financial Services Act 1986*

This is the legislation that preceded the City 'revolution' known as 'Big Bang'. Of particular relevance here are two issues:

1. in a move which was consistent with the Conservative government's view that the state's role in the market should be minimal, provision was made in this Act for practitioner-based regulation of the provision of financial services. However, like the Social Security Act 1986, the Financial Services Act provided only a framework within which this regulation was to take place. These regulations would focus on the advertising of and advising on investments, the disclosure of information concerning the costs of policies, restrictions on who could sell such investments as personal pensions and laws against people claiming to be 'independent' advisers when in reality they were contracted to particular providers of financial products. This is dealt with at length below and it will be seen that the problems arising during the implementation of this legislation were to have major consequences for the introduction of contracted out personal pensions;

2. the Financial Services Act 1986 and its subsequent regulations laid down that a personal pension was to be treated as an investment and created the framework that was to govern the marketing of personal pensions and the giving of investment advice. A distinction was made between occupational and personal pensions.

As a consequence of the Financial Services Act 1986 contracted out personal pensions, in contrast with contracted out occupational pensions, would not to be regarded as an 'investment' under the terms of the Act. This was mainly for the practical reason that if occupational pensions were regarded as an investment, the act of an employer encouraging employees to join or remain in an occupational scheme would constitute investment advice and would be an offence unless the employer was registered with the appropriate regulatory body. This would create the unmanageable situation of every employer with an occupational pension scheme having to be registered as an investment adviser and supervised by the Financial Intermediaries Managers and Brokers Regulatory Association (FIMBRA). Indeed there are legal purists who argue that although an occupational pension scheme does not constitute an investment for the contributing employee, the employer, by exhorting the employee to join the occupational pension scheme, is in effect advising them not to take out a personal pension plan and therefore is giving investment advice after all.

A second justification for not treating occupational pensions as an investment related to the GMP and the final salary basis of most schemes. Since it is the employer's responsibility to ensure that a pension fund's assets are sufficient to fund future liabilities it could be argued that the pension fund is the employer's investment rather than the employees'. This is supported by the fact that the level of benefit received by a retiring employee is normally based on final salary rather than investment performance. It must be noted that such an argument strengthens the case against occupational pension funds having worker trustees. Perhaps more importantly, it is an argument which undermines both workers' and retirees' claims on pension fund surpluses. If, as may now be

126

happening, this view becomes widely held by employers, it would make it very difficult for trade unions to secure better occupational pensions for future and present retirees.

Problems of Implementation

It is difficult now to imagine personal pensions without the regulatory framework set up by the Financial Services Act 1986, and yet the fact is that they had existed since the 1950s without any apparent difficulties and with few, if any, scandals. Similarly, unit trust managers and life offices had marketed their services in the past with minimal regulation, dealing either directly with the public or through insurance brokers who were neither regulated nor required to be qualified. Why was it suddenly necessary for financial products, including personal pensions, to be controlled by a stiff regulatory system? One reason is that contracted out personal pensions involve a move away from the security of protected final salary schemes into a field where pensions provision is relatively speculative and amenable to undesirable methods of selling, especially if the range of providers was widened. Hitherto the marketing of personal pensions had been almost exclusively directed at the self-employed. When making such complex financial decisions as are necessary in choosing a personal pension plan, members of this group can reasonably be expected to possess either the necessary skill and judgement or, failing this, easy access to independent professional advice. By contrast a large proportion of future personal pension holders will possess neither the requisite judgement nor access to reliable independent advice. Hence the need for regulation even though it undoubtedly impeded the launch of contracted out personal pensions and probably clashed with the government's first instinct for open competition and regulation by market forces. What actually emerged was a compromise that would achieve the desired regulation while minimising the role of the state: self-regulation was developed and extended to pension providers and to the new breed of financial advisers, descended quite often from the previously unregulated , insurance brokers.

The agency primarily responsible for devising and implementing the regulations is the Securities and Investments Board (SIB) whose Deputy Chairman, Sir Mark Weinberg, had been a member of the Sub Group to the Inquiry into Provision for Retirement. The SIB is a private company empowered by the Financial Services Act 1986. While retaining overall responsibility the SIB delegated the job of producing the rule books and the task of day to day regulating to several practitioner-based regulatory organisations which the Act had created. These regulations had to be approved by the SIB and then by Office of Fair Trading (OFT). If the OFT objected to any rule the Department of Trade could become involved and had the power to overrule the former.

Producing acceptable rulebooks proved to be a complex task and was not completed in time. The difficulties that arose were later to be a major obstacle to the introduction of personal pensions in the form laid down by the Social

Security Act 1986. As a result, Norman Fowler's successor as Secretary of State, John Moore, delayed the launch until July 1st 1988. The repeated delays and the fact that July 1st rather than April 6th was chosen as the launch date confirms the level of confusion.

Delays seem to have arisen from conflicting errors made by the Department of Trade and Industry (DTI) and the SIB. When in 1987 the DTI published its rules it was discovered that they had overlooked the need to provide for the regulation of a particular type of fund ('umbrella funds'). The confusion was made worse by the fact that some of the SIB rules directly contradicted each other. The result of this disorder was that the date on which contracted out personal pensions finally became operational was the fourth date that had been announced (April 1987, April 1988, then January 1988 and finally July 1st 1988). It was this DTI confusion that delayed the launch of 1986 style personal pensions.

According to the trade magazine *Pensions Management* the result was that: "You can count on the fingers of one hand the number of pensions providers launching personal pensions on July 1st" (Ellis, July 1988, p.31). Understandably, prospective members of FIMBRA put off registration until the regulations with which they would have to comply became clear. This contributed to FIMBRA producing a deficit of £3.4 million during the first nine months of operation. By March 1988 it had only 5,496 members instead of the projected 7,500, and in November 1988 there were more than 1,000 member who were still trading on interim authorisations (*Pensions Management*, November 1988). Apart from the largest life offices and banks, most new entrants to the personal pensions market would have found this state of affairs discouraging because as a result they were unable to establish a network of intermediaries through which their products could be retailed.

Legislation and implementation of the new arrangements for private sector pensions provision in the 1980s were characterised by disarray and indecision. The Social Security Act 1986 seemed to finalise the overall pattern for future pension provision with only the details to be worked out, but what followed during the next two years seems to indicate that politicians and civil servants were "making it up as they went along".

Responses to Implementation Problems

In the first half of 1987 two sets of measures affecting private pensions provision were announced. They both were characterised by haste and confusion that must have beset the Conservative government in the months preceding the 1987 General Election. In what appeared to be a compromise aimed at ensuring that something in the way of a contracted out personal pension system was in place sooner rather than later, the Chancellor of the Exchequer announced in his 1987 Budget speech that with effect from October 26th 1987 Free Standing Additional Voluntary Contributions (FSAVCs) would come into being. Soon afterwards Norman Fowler announced that when contracted out personal pensions were eventually introduced it would be possible for individuals to backdate their personal pension contributions to the beginning of the tax year.

i) *Free Standing Additional Voluntary Contributions (FSAVCs)*

Since April 1987 all employers' occupational pension schemes had been obliged to facilitate Additional Voluntary Contributions (AVCs) so that members of any occupational pension scheme could make extra retirement provision, in the form of either added years or money purchase, through additional voluntary contributions to their employer's scheme. For the benefit of members of occupational pension schemes who wished to make additional voluntary contributions but not via their employer's AVC facilities FSAVCs were created. In fact FSAVCs were only available to members of occupational schemes. The 'free standing' nature of what was created by the Finance Act 1987 meant that from October 1987 an occupational scheme member could make extra provision for retirement by contributing to a private fund, though an employer was prohibited from contributing to such a fund.

A peculiar aspect of FSAVCs is the way they are benefit-limited. As with personal and occupational pensions, in order to minimise the exploitation of FSAVCs as a means of tax-free savings rather than genuine pensions provision some form of restrictions had to be placed on their use. In view of the money purchase basis of FSAVCs the obvious form of restriction would have been to limit contributions, as with personal pensions, and indeed this was done. However, it was decided that in addition a benefit limit should be imposed. The result is that the managers of an FSAVC fund are responsible by law for ensuring that a contributor's combined potential benefit from their main scheme and their FSAVC does not exceed two thirds of their final salary. If benefits do exceed this level the employee loses part of their occupational pension. Nor can the benefit be commuted to cash except in a few prescribed circumstances where the main scheme is also commuted for the same reason. Such circumstances include ill-health. It is also possible to liquidate an FSAVC in order to transfer the value to an employer's occupational scheme, for example where an employee changes jobs or where it is decided to use an AVC instead.

These regulations are obviously unwieldy and seem contrary to the principle, implicit in the notion of people's capitalism, of reward being dictated by the market. The FSAVC is singularly unsuitable for SERPS contributors, and yet they had been Norman Fowler's main target. It might therefore have been the intention to give pensions providers the opportunity to begin their entry the personal pensions market without further delay and with a product that could be modified to form an 'appropriate personal pension'. If this was the intention then it failed, largely because of the remarkable restrictions devised by the Inland Revenue.

As stated, FSAVCs became operational in October 1987. Given that the personal pensions regulations contained in and flowing from the Social Security Act 1986 were introduced just nine months later in July 1988, it is difficult to

129

imagine why FSAVCs were even considered let alone legislated into being. Indeed, as mentioned in Chapter 7, several external members of the Inquiry into Provision for Retirement had been hoping that the outcome would be a single multi-role personal pension product that would combine provision for the self-employed, a topping up pension for the employee with an occupational scheme, and the contracting out vehicle for the employee who was not in a contracted out occupational pension scheme. If this idea had been adopted the FSAVC debacle would probably not have emerged.

It was provided that personal pensions could be used by occupational pensions contributors in precisely the same way as FSAVCs but with contribution and not benefit restrictions. Therefore FSAVCs do not completely substitute for personal pensions in the sense of providing a contracted out pension for current SERPS contributors; nor does an FSAVC qualify for the tax relief on the National Insurance rebate, and they are benefit-limited where personal pensions are only contribution-limited.

ii) Backdating of Contributions and Tax Allowances

Then, before FSAVCs had even had a chance to fail, Norman Fowler hit upon a peculiar way of ensuring personal pensions were introduced as soon as possible: he announced just before the 1987 General Election that workers who were not members of employers' occupational pensions schemes in January 1988 would be able to backdate their contributions to a personal pension plan to April 1987 (i.e. for the full tax year 87/88) and collect the 2% Incentive. In so doing he seemed to overlook the fact that the regulatory agencies would not be ready to authorise the financial intermediaries who would retail personal pensions; until such times as they were, individuals would be obliged by existing law to continue contributing either to SERPS or to employers' schemes. It was SERPS contributors whom it was hoped would be attracted by the possibility of personal pension provision. However, as SERPS does not refund or transfer accrued contributions and the overwhelming majority of SERPS contributors are not so highly paid as to be able to make double provision for retirement in a given year in order to benefit from the 2% Incentive and the tax relief, it difficult to see how this measure could have been effective. Those who would have taken out a personal pension could have done so the following year anyway and under existing regulations would be able to back date their contributions for taxation purposes.

To recapitulate, it seems that pensions policies were developing simultaneously in the Treasury and the DHSS, but this does not imply either inter-departmental rivalry or a conspiracy. The 1987 Budget will have been approved by the Cabinet and this makes it certain that Norman Fowler consented to the FSAVC proposals. Similarly, it is inconceivable that Norman Fowler could have acted unilaterally in facilitating the backdating of the 2% Incentive. This has cost implications and therefore must have had the consent of the Chancellor of the Exchequer, the Prime Minister, and probably that of the Cabinet. As suggested earlier, it is more probable that both sets of measures were attempts by the Government to ensure that a contracted out non-occupational pension system of some description was in place before the 1987 General Election. This aim would have been achieved had the General Election been held in the October as was widely predicted. Instead it was held in June 1987, and it was in any case highly unlikely that FSAVCs would have been a commercial success.

What is demonstrated is that the dynamics which were driving policy developments at this time were ideological and political. That such organisations as the CPS and IoD appeared to have no role is a reflection not of their loss of influence but of the fact that with the appropriate pensions legislation in place their work was done. Economic interests were irrelevant. As has happened so often since 1983, with the rights of schools and hospitals to 'opt out' and the introduction of the community charge, post-1983 Conservative governments first of all announced their radical new proposals affecting pensions policy and only then did it set about the task of trying to produce measures that would make the policy work. The account of FSAVCs and backdating bears this out, with the possibility that the proposals might not be practical never seriously being considered, not even when implementation problems began to occur. The regulations affecting FSAVCs, by restricting both contribution and benefit limits and prescribing a cumbersome mechanism by which they should be monitored, appear to have been hastily cobbled together and further demonstrate the extent to which politicians were 'making it up as they went along'.

Some of the Effects of Implementation

With effect from July 1st 1988 contracted out personal pensions became fully operational. The marketing exercise to promote them had been going on for some time, and there was a rapid increase in the numbers of financial advisers whose offices are now a common sight.

The effect of allowing alternative methods of pensions provision was to confront SERPS and occupational pensions contributors with a baffling array of products whose characteristics sometimes defied direct comparison. For example in the realm of personal pensions there are such options as 'with profits' insurance schemes or there are unit-linked pension plans where units in a fund are purchased at prices dependent on the value of the underlying investments. Hence even when share prices are falling and the most sensible thing to do is hold cash, units will be bought by contributors contracted to pay regular monthly sums (which is why it is useful to also have a deposit-based FSAVC pension).

There are three main types of personal pension provision:

First, there is the insurance-style personal pension plan which is not radically different from the endowment policy that has for decades provided an inefficient but reliable means of saving for thrifty working class people. This method of provision is associated with high setting up costs that are borne by the contributor (whereas in an employer's money purchase scheme it is the employer who bares the costs) and penalties for withdrawing accrued contributions. Contributors to personal pension plans are supposed to monitor the value of their accrued contributions and decide whether it is appropriate to transfer to a higher-yielding pension provider. However, because the first 18 month's contributions to a personal pension plan are taken up mainly by fees and set-up costs it could seem to many contributors to be cheaper to persist with their current low-yielding scheme than to either withdraw accrued contributions and transfer them to a new fund or leave those contributions with the original provider and take out a second personal pension plan with a new provider. The contributor's decision-making is made yet more difficult because of the way in which accrued contributions are valued. The gains from 'with-profits' insurance-type pensions plans give a return which is relatively modest but assured. Each year's bonus, once awarded, cannot be forfeited through adverse market performance in subsequent years. However, in addition to the annual bonus, insured personal pension plans pay a terminal bonus on maturity. The size of this bonus has a very significant impact on the retirement income of the contributor but it is not known until the plan nears maturity. In the late 1980s termination bonuses were in the order of 50%; in ten years from now they could be a mere 10%, but then again they might be in the region of 60%, depending on such factors as investment performance. The point is that the speculative nature of personal pensions might make AVCs a good form of retirement provision in addition to the basic retirement pension and an occupational pension. However, personal pensions as a main method of retirement provision must be regarded with caution.

To some degree the dominance of life offices in the personal pensions market will frustrate the Government's intention of increasing competition. More significantly for protagonists of 'people's capitalism' such as the IoD and the CPS, this style of personal pension does not diffuse the investment power held by institutional investors.

Secondly, there are unit trusts. As an approach to personal pension provision these afford a little more flexibility to contributors in that the penalties of changing from one fund to another are less than those associated with the insurance approach. Nevertheless, as before, control over investment remains vested in the hands on a few managers of the largest funds. Personal pensions plans based on unit trusts have a propensity to produce a greater return if properly managed and are closer to the New Right idea of 'every man his own capitalist'. However, gains through unit-linked personal pensions are very limited if consumers make regular contributions instead of carefully timing their investments. But few personal pensions contributors are going to realise this or feel able to make the necessary investment decisions. Furthermore, unit trust-based personal pensions plans still leave vast funds in the control of a limited number of investment managers. The only way in which the diffusion of investment control desired by the supporters of a pro-market ideology including members of the CPS could be attained is through self-administered pension funds, which in principle would not be radically different from PEPs.

Thirdly, there are Contracted Out Money-Purchase Schemes (COMPS). These allow employers to offer a defined contribution occupational pension scheme as an inducement to employees. Such schemes pre-date the Social Security Act 1986 but it is only since April 1988 that they have had been able to contract out of SERPS. From the employee's point of view a COMP scheme operates in much the same way as a personal pension plan except that there are no set-up or management costs to be deducted from contributions. From the employer's point of view the absence of a defined benefit basis means that a COMP scheme carries no liability to top up the fund in the event of the fund's underperformance. Such a pension scheme could be provided on an insured or managed basis, although a managed fund would probably still rely on a life office to provide insurance cover for death in service.

Consumer Choice

The introduction of consumer choice in pensions provision is probably a dubious gain for most contributors. While it is possible to describe 'ideal types' of contributor who are undoubtedly better suited to one form of provision than another, most potential personal pension contributors do not fit neatly into any particular category, which makes their choice of pension provision very difficult. There tend also to be lots of 'unknowns' in the calculation. For example, the rules of an occupational pension scheme will specify a percentage by which the pensions received by retirees will be increased in each year of retirement. It is quite common for an occupational pension scheme to also give discretionary increases in the pensions. The potential or current occupational pension scheme contributor who is considering the option of a personal pension plan can have no knowledge of what discretionary increases will be made in the distant future, and yet such increases can be very valuable. Most obviously, the potential personal pension contributor can have no knowledge of the stock market's future performance. Problems of choice are compounded where new providers are involved because there would be no track record of investment performance to enable the potential customer to make an informed decision. Furthermore, as a consequence of the Financial Services Act 1986 (and the Social Security Act 1985), providers of both personal and occupation pensions are required to make annual disclosures to contributors. The Life Assurance and Unit Trust Regulatory Organisation (LAUTRO) and SIB worked together during the latter part of 1987 to produce rules for product disclosure. However, although such information is obviously intended to facilitate decision-making, the likelihood is that these disclosure regulations will make choosing an appropriate vehicle for pension provision even more complicated for most employees.

133

11   Current issues

Introduction

In recent years considrable attention has focussed on the legal basis of occupational pension schemes. The central concern has been the ability of occupational pension schemes and the legal framework which governs them to afford adequate protection to their intended beneficiaries. This concern originated in the 1980s when, after a period of high inflation and heavy redundancies, many occupational pension funds found themselves to be in surplus. The question of who 'owned' the surplus became an important legal issue. However, the issue which has recently soared to the top of the policy agenda has been that of pension regulation. This occurred when it was discovered that pension funds to which Robert Maxwell had access had been plundered despite the body of trust law and, to a lesser degree, the network of regulatory agencies that were supposed to prevent such abuses. At about the same time, evidence was starting to emerge that the self-regulatory organisations were not performing as effectively as they might in order to defend the interests of potential and actual contributors to personal pension plans. Currently, private pensions provision is controlled by trust law and the self-regulatory organisations created by the Financial Services Act 1986.

Trust Law

Those who would reject trust law in favour of an all-embracing pensions act usually point to the haphazard way in which the former evolved. Trust law has its origins in the days of the Crusades. This was an age when women were not able to own property since they themselves were chattels, and so when a wealthy man went off to the Holy Land to fight for the Christian cause he would leave his property in the hands of a friend. The said friend would manage these resources as though they were his own although the beneficiaries would be the absent crusader's family. This 'trustee' had the power to acquire and dispose of property provided he was acting in the interests of the beneficiaries and not his own. It sometimes happened that a crusader would return from war several years later only to find that his estate had been plundered by the trusted friend. Under Common Law, as imposed by William the Conqueror, there was no adequate remedy for this wrong. However, there existed a branch of law known as 'Equity' which enabled a plaintiff to apply for a discretionary remedy where the Common Law produced a patently unfair outcome. It was in this way that trust law developed, so that the relationships between the person who sets up a trust (settlor), the people who will manage the trust (trustees) and those who are intended to benefit from the trust (beneficiaries) would be regulated.

From these beginnings trust law evolved into a device to enable wealthy fathers to make handsome settlements on their daughters while at the same time discouraging money-grabbing suitors. For reasons described above, a woman could not hold property in her own name and so any marriage settlement made by her father automatically became the property of her husband since technically she was owned by him. To avoid this situation some fathers, instead of transferring the ownership of property to the daughter's husband, set up a trust fund to hold assets for the benefit of the daughter and her husband but, in the event of the daughter's death, the terms of the trust required that the property did not pass to her surviving husband. Instead, the property either benefited any children the woman may have had or, failing this, would revert to her blood relatives. The trust might hold such property as investments providing a regular income, a house or farm etc. In this way daughter's well-being was enhanced and the family fortune could be kept relatively intact and safe from fortune hunters.

It was only a short step from being the basis of marriage settlements to being a tax-saving device. Death duty was payable each time property was transferred from the estate from the deceased to a beneficiary. Trusts provided a means of reducing this liability using a process sometimes called 'leap frogging'. If grandfather left his estate to his son and he in turn left the estate to the grandson, tax would be paid once when the grandfather died and again when his son died. If instead the grandfather put most of the estate in trust for the benefit of his son with the conditions that his son would have full benefit from the property during his lifetime and on his death the trust would cease to exist and the property would then be transferred to the grandson, tax would only become payable when the trust was dissolved and ownership passed to the grandson. Hence death duties would only be paid by alternate generations within a family. It was from these beginnings that the case law which forms the basis of pensions law was born.

Financial Services Act 1986

Since July 1988 and the implementation of the pensions measures contained in the Social Security Act 1986, the field of pensions policy has become the focal point of yet more pressure for change. Most notable among these has been the apparent failure of the Financial Services Act 1986 to afford protection to pension schemes' contributors. Under the Financial Services Act 1986 a three tier system of regulation has been established. The first tier consists of the Secretary of State for Trade and Industry. The next tier consists of the Securities and Investment Board (SIB) which is not of a government agency but rather a company set up by institutions in the financial sector. The third tier consists of the self-regulatory organisations (SROs) which are licenced by the SIB to carry out the process of regulating member organisations. These SROs include the Financial Intermediaries, Managers and Brokers Regulatory Association (FIMBRA), the Investment Management Regulatory Organisation (IMRO), the Life Assurance and Unit Trust Regulatory Organisation (LAUTRO) and the Securities and Futures Authority (SFA). The SROs have responsibility for formulating the criteria which an intending organisation must satisfy in order to become a member authorised to practice this type of business. SROs also produce the rules which, having been approved by the SIB, govern their members' business conduct. The point is that the SIB stands between the SROs and the government of the day. Should any SRO be negligent in its supervisory functions, it will be the SIB and not the DTI that will have the responsibility of bring order to the situation.

Robert Maxwell

The most notable example of both trust law and self-regulatory organisations apparently failing to do their respective jobs came with the death of communications tycoon Robert Maxwell. He died on November 5th 1991 while on a cruise in the Canary Islands, having apparently fallen from his yacht, the Lady Ghislaine, in the early hours of the morning. His body was found by a helicopter later that day. At first Robert Maxwell was mourned, with leading figures expressing their regret at his demise. But within a few weeks the scale of the damage he had done to his companies' past and present employees' pension funds had emerged. An estimated £400 million had been removed from the pension funds designed to benefit past and present employees, of which the receiver of Robert Maxwell's private estate told the Social Security Select Committee that he expected to recover only £8.75 million.

It has to be said that all the legislation and regulation in the world will not prevent someone of Robert Maxwell's strength and determination from doing as he wishes with pension fund assets. Perhaps one of the few measures that can be taken is by institutional investors and boards of directors to prevent situations arising where one man can achieve such absolute and unquestioned dominance over a company and all the assets under its control.

With this in mind, the two main problems appear to have been:

1. the failure of the Maxwell pension schemes' trustees to properly monitor and, where appropriate, prevent illegal transactions involving pension fund resources, and

2. the failure of IMRO – the self-regulatory body responsible for fund management – to identify some of the pension fund transactions which Robert Maxwell carried out as suspicious and worthy of further investigation. The SIB and IMRO have inspection and enforcement powers but they

appear to have been very reluctant to use them except where there was either indisputable evidence of fraud or at least very convincing complaints from consumers. Indeed, the SIB can go to court in order to obtain information deemed necessary to further their investigations. Even if all the relevant information concerning the Maxwell pension fund transactions had been available, it is likely that the different regulatory organisations involved would each have possessed different pieces of information concerning the institutions they were regulating, without any single agency in a position to collate this data so as to create a complete picture. In June 1993 the SFA fined Goldman Sachs, the investment bank that had acted as Robert Maxwell's stockbroker, £160,000 in respect of breaches of regulations (Atkinson & Whitebloom, 1993). In the same month the fund management company Invesco was fined £750,000 for mismanagement and failing to comply with City regulations when handling Mirror Group pension funds (Whitebloom, 1993b).

In June 1992 a £2.5 million relief fund was set up by the Secretary of State for Social Security, Peter Lilley, to relieve hardship among retired members of the occupational pension funds plundered by Robert Maxwell. This fund did nothing for most members of the Maxwell pension schemes, including Mirror Group Newspapers whose membership totalled 33,000. Rather, it was aimed particularly at the 4,000 members of the Maxwell Communications Works pension scheme and the 240 members of the Headington Pension Plan since these schemes were unable to make any payments to their members (Thomson, 1992). However, in October 1992 the pension funds were given the loan of £100 million by the Department of Social Security in the form of a concession that deferred the collection of National Insurance contributions (Atkinson, 1992a). Mirror Group Newspapers put forward a scheme under which the shortfall in its pension fund would be rectified over a period, of several years.

By March 1993 the £2.5 million relief fund was nearly exhausted. Furthermore, the Maxwell Pensioners' Trust, set up in July 1992 under the chairmanship of Sir John Cuckney, had only raised £6 million in donations from institutions (Whitebloom, 1993). The chief problem, according to Sir John, was the institutions' fears that a donation to the trust fund would be interpreted as an admission of liability (Atkinson, 1992). Another factor was that the Maxwell Pensioners' Trust did not have charitable status and therefore did not afford tax relief to donating companies. Indeed some companies have articles of association which prohibit the making of donations to non-charities. By April 1993 the administrators, Arthur Andersen, had recovered £100 million of the £400 million that had been removed from the various Maxwell pension funds (Whitebloom, 1993a).

Clearly this was not a satisfactory method of defending the interests of workers and retirees, not least because of the cost of putting right the damage; in the first year after Robert Maxwell's death the accountancy and legal costs of tracing the missing funds accrued at a rate of £300,000 per working day, and this was deducted from the recovered pension fund assets thereby reducing the resources available for pension fund contributors (Lawrence & Willcock, 1992). Nor is it tolerable that the financial security of current and future retirees should in any way depend on the charity of city institutions. In truth it is highly unlikely that a Conservative government would allow these present and future Maxwell retirees to suffer to any great extent, but the reality is that they have been made to suffer by the uncertainty of whether the state will in time bear the cost of the missing Maxwell pension fund assets.

Two inquiries were set up as a consequence of the Maxwell affair. In July 1992 the Chancellor of the Exchequer, Norman Lamont, asked the recently appointed chairman of the Securities and Investment Board Andrew Large to carry out an internal inquiry. The Secretary of State for Social Security, Peter Lilley appointed Professor Roy Goode of Oxford University to chair the Pension Law Review Committee that was to examine the shortcomings of pension and trust law. The SIB quickly produced a 127 page report which was published in May 1993, while Professor Roy Goode was granted an extension until September 1993.

Professor Roy Goode's terms of reference were:

> To review the framework of law and regulation within which occupational pension schemes operate, taking into account the rights and interests of the scheme members, pensioners and employers; to consider in particular the status and ownership of occupational pension funds and the accountability and roles of trustees, fund managers, auditors and pension scheme advisers; and to make recommendations. (Goode, 1993, vol.1, p.711)

The Committee took evidence from individuals and organisations with a relevant interest or expertise in the field of pensions. Visits were made to Australia, Canada and the USA to examine the ways in which these countries had regulated their private sector pensions.

In its report the Pension Law Review Committee concluded that trust law should continue as the basic framework for occupational pension schemes. Nevertheless, they favoured the additional safeguard of a Pensions Act which empowered a Pensions Regulator to impose further regulations and structure. They also supported providing pension scheme contributors with clearer information concerning the activities of their pension scheme and the worth of their accrued pension contributions. With regard to the administration of occupational pension schemes the Committee recommended that minimum solvency requirements should be laid down in law together with restrictions on the withdrawal of surpluses. Apparently recognising the nature of the trust which holds pension fund assets, the Committee recommended that employee trustees should be able to appoint further trustees. At the moment only the employer possesses this right of appointment.

The appointment of a pensions regulator represents a move away from self-regulation in the sense that it would put very considerable powers of intervention in the hands of one person who is situated outside the pensions industry. This regulator would have to approve the refund to an employer of any pension fund surplus. If worker trustees are given the right to appoint further trustees, this would reduce the incidence of employers appointing disproportionate numbers of senior managers whose real purpose is to defend the interests of the employer rather than those of the trust. In his report the head of the SIB, Andrew Large, supports the Goode Committee's idea of a pensions regulator. The SIB report recommends the creation of a new 'super policeman' to regulate the City. This would involve the SIB taking a much more active role as regulator. In addition, under the SIB scheme the subsidiary regulatory organisations would lose their relative independence and become branches of the SIB.

All this casts doubt on the feasibility of self-regulation, certainly in its present three tier form. There has been mounting criticism of self-regulation for the City, and this has been accompanied by a measure of support for the idea of a single omnipotent agency along the lines of America's Securities and Exchange Commission. Such criticism was fuelled by the news in 1991 that not only was FIMBRA facing insolvency but neither the SIB nor the Government had any statutory duty to rescue it. What this brings home is the extent to which the Government is able to distance itself from any liability to consumers where breaches of SIB and SRO rules has taken place. In the light of the Treasury's and Department of Social Security's refusal to give a firm commitment to underwrite the interests of contributors to the Maxwell pension schemes, the implications for contributors to occupational and personal pensions is clear. Only electoral pressure and a moral duty will compel the state to protect the interests of pensions contributors.

The chief executive of the Prudential Corporation said of self-regulation in 1992:

> It is time to face up to the fact that this approach does not work, and to revert to the conventional, proven statutory basis for regulation.
> Mick Newmarch cited by: Kane & Atkinson (1992)

Mick Newmarch was speaking in the wake of a series of financial scandals such as Maxwell, Guinness, Blue Arrow, Barlow Clowes and BCCI. In each case the appropriate regulatory body had done nothing about the situation until it was too late to protect the interests of innocent consumers. In the case of the Maxwell pension funds, even where the liquidators succeed in tracing the securities that belonged to the pension funds but which were sold or used as security by Robert Maxwell in order to raise cash, it may not be possible to recover them if the purchasers can prove that they acted in good faith. Hence the interests of the Maxwell pensioners will not have been protected.

12 Conclusion

The purpose of this book has been to produce an account of the pensions policy-making process. Consideration has been given to social and economic factors behind the policy shift that lead from the Social Security (Pensions) Act 1975 to the pensions measures contained in the Social Security Act 1986. The interview data collected from participants in the Inquiry into Provision for Retirement has been essential to this research, revealing the limitations of written sources and, albeit with some reservations, the value of off-the-record comments by well-informed interviewees.

Concern over the cost to the state of retirement pensions, most recently that of SERPS, is not a new phenomenon (Walker, 1990). Indeed, almost as soon as Beveridge' pensions proposals were in place doubts began to be expressed, resulting in the setting up of the Phillips Committee which reported in 1954. A number of factors have combined to cause grave concern among the post-1979 governments with regard to what has been referred to as the 'burden of dependency'. In addition to the failings of occupational pensions mentioned above, the most widely publicised focus of attention is the set of demographic changes predicted to occur over the next fifty years. The two main aspects of this are the increase in longevity and the change in the dependency ratio.

The increase in longevity is something Beveridge had not foreseen when making his recommendations for what became the National Insurance Act 1948. At that time a significant proportion of workforce could be relied on to die within a few years of retiring, if not while still in employment. Hence without any increase in benefits, the population's improved life expectancy has meant that financing the state flat-rate pension has become a more expensive proposition than was originally envisaged. However, the trend for more women to spend a greater part of their lives as active members of the paid workforce and the increase in productivity that has been produced by new technology have more than negated this and there is no reason to suppose that it will not continue to do so. In any case, merely transferring part of the cost of pensions provision from the public sector to the private sector in the belief that the former is inherently 'bad' while the latter is inevitably 'good' (Reddin, 1986 p.11) is not a solution.

Post-War Pensions Policy

Pensions policy in the post-war period has in many respects been very consistent. At every stage the state seems to be trying to minimise its responsibility for pensions expenditure. On the one hand, it has tried to persuade the market to absorb as much of the responsibility for pensions as possible, if need be by tax inducements. Tax inducements probably affect the willingness of potential sponsors and providers of pensions to enter the pensions market by reducing the real cost. But why use tax inducements to persuade the private sector to take only the 'better' customers while the state keeps the 'worst'? It would probably be cheaper and more equitable for the state to be the major provider of all pensions. On the other hand the state has tried to persuade people to accept responsibility for making additional provision for their retirement, even though a significant proportion of the population will have insufficient or no opportunity to make such provision.

Retirement pensions have throughout much the post-war period been dominated by economic and ideological rather than social considerations. An example of this is the recurring theme of government concern at the potential 'burden' the cost of retirement might one day comprise. This might owe something to the need of governments to justify decisions based on ideological criteria by reference to apparently value-free lines of reasoning. Hence the shift away from a flat-rate basis for contributions towards a progressive scale was explained in terms of its merits to the workforce and future retired population instead of in terms of successive governments' preference for progressive bases of taxation as a means of inflation-proofing state income. In this way ideological choices are presented as 'sensible' or unavoidable courses of action. Arguably, this may be exacerbated by the interests of a capitalist economy, on whose prosperity all governments depend for resources. These interests are often in direct contrast with those of the majority of the population. However, the economic and consensual rationales of policy-making were to be abandoned in favour of one which was more plainly ideological.

Pensions Policy-Making

It was apparent in Chapter 2 that no real 'pensions policy community' existed at the time when the proposals for the Social Security (Pensions) Act 1975 were taking shape. Consequently, the Labour governments of 1974/75 enjoyed relative freedom from the pressure of interest groups and had a clear tactical advantage over representatives of a straitened pensions industry.

By contrast, Chapters 5 and 6 showed how the ideas behind the 1986 pensions legislation became compelling precisely because of the efforts of well-placed individuals and the pressure groups to which they belonged. There were three significant differences between policy-making in the mid 1970s and that in the 1980s:

First, in 1974/75 pensions policy appears to have emerged from within government and the DHSS, with interest groups being consulted at a late stage in order to secure their support. In the 1980s, however, a readily identifiable pensions 'policy community' had come into existence, and it was from within here that influential ideas on pensions policy emerged. Indeed, it was shown that Norman Fowler handed over control of the 'pensions debate' to the policy community and that the Inquiry into Provision for Retirement was probably a means of wresting it back.

Secondly, the nature of the contact between politicians, and interest group became very informal. In the 1960s and 1970s there had been the occasional pretence of informal relations with, for example, the Prime Minister Harold Wilson inviting trade union leaders to Downing Street for beer and sandwiches, but the reality was very different. By the early 1980s this had changed dramatically. As shown in Chapters 5 to 7 the pensions policy community that had formed was very much a face to face community in which standing depended on individual rather than organisational status. The trade unionists invited to Downing Street for beer and sandwiches in the 1960s and 1970s were important because of the organisations they represented; it appears that most members of the pensions policy community in the 1980s were representatives of organisations because they were personally important. As a result, some organisations did not have access to the pensions policy community because they did not have well-connected people among their supporters.

If holding an ideologically 'correct' stance were the main qualification for membership of the pensions policy community, the ASI might reasonably have been expected to play an important role; they had been among the first to promote the concept of personal pensions and their position has certainly been in line with the New Right perspective. However, ideological 'correctness' was not sufficient as a qualification. Crucially, the ASI never found its way into the mainstream of Thatcherite ideology from which it would have been able to influence government policy – it never became 'one of us'. An important reason for this failure may be ASI members' lack of personal contact with members of what was very much a face-to-face policy community. By contrast the CPS, having been founded by Margaret Thatcher and Sir Keith Joseph, was totally adapted to the Thatcherite ideology, and its supporters had ample face-to-face contact with Conservative politicians, holding seminars attended by Cabinet ministers. Similarly, the IoD had shown its willingness to adapt to the Thatcherite ideology when in 1983, one month after the publication of the CPS paper on personal pensions (Vinson and Chappell, 1983) its Director General, Walter Goldsmith, began defending the personal pensions cause, having previously defended occupational pensions. In addition, the IoD had considerable contact with Conservative politicians as evidenced by the informal relations between its Director General and Norman Fowler. For example, the IoD submission of evidence to the Inquiry into Provision for Retirement which begins: 'Dear Norman...' and ends: 'Yours sincerely, Walter' (IoD, 1984). Hence the ASI seems to have worked hard at producing and publishing appropriately market-oriented policy ideas but failed to 'sell' those ideas either to members of the policy community or to Conservative politicians.

Thirdly, and finally, the climate in which the ideas behind the 1986 Act developed was very different to that which prevailed in 1974/75. The early 1970s, under both Labour and Conservative governments, had been a period of social reform, particularly with regard to employment law where the position of workers was improved. Changes included the Equal Pay Act 1970, the Industrial Relations Act 1971, the Contracts of Employment Act 1972, the Trade Union and Labour Relations Act 1974, the Sex Discrimination Act 1975 and the Employment Protection Act 1975 (Jackson, 1977, pp.7 8). By the late 1970s the emphasis was changing; a Labour government was attempting to lower workers' expectations through wage restraint and making an abortive attempt to restrict industrial action with Barbara Castle's White Paper *In Place Of Strife*.

Structural Change

This emphasis on controlling the workforce was continued in 1979 by the first Thatcher government but, by the early 1980s the means of effecting this control had changed from the simple use of repressive legislation that regulated the labour market to a broader ranging and more ideological campaign that combined legislation to constrain workers from industrial action with measures aimed at tying their fortunes more closely to corporate profitability. Parallel changes in social security legislation limited the amounts of supplementary benefit available to the families of striking workers. As if to reinforce workers' disincentive to take industrial action, a process of economic restructuring, loosely based on the rationale of monetarism, was allowed to take place which in the period up to 1982 cost at least three million people their jobs and placed a strong downward pressure on wage levels.

However, it was seen that outside the spheres of labour relations and law and order, the state was beginning to withdraw from it traditional roles in society. This withdrawal was in part motivated by a belief promulgated by the New Right that the state's spending activities were reducing the ability of 'the market' to meet real demand for goods and services at competitive prices, and the government's response was manifested by such measures as those compelling the NHS to sub-contract cleaning and catering functions to the private sector, the denationalisation of selected state industries, the introduction through the Financial Services Act 1986 of self-regulation for financial institutions and practitioners and, of course, the introduction of personal pensions as a contracting-out vehicle. This would bring about the phased privatisation of additional pensions for those workers without access to occupational pension schemes and introducing an element of choice for those who were members of occupational pension schemes. More importantly, these policies effected permanent structural changes to the welfare system; whereas the reforms to employment law enacted by both Conservative and Labour governments of the 1970s were incrementalist in nature and did little more than adapt the existing legislative framework to contemporary needs, the changes that characterised Conservative government policies of the 1980s were aimed at radically altering existing frameworks by underpinning them with a completely new set of values, derived from the New Right. Although the institutions, including state pensions, might continue to function, they would henceforth be fundamentally altered by the ideological shift that had taken place.

It is possible that the privatising of a number of state enterprises in a way that attracted novice investors was part of an educational programme designed to persuade workers to accept the linking of their future financial well-being to the vagaries of the economy which, since 1982, had experienced continuous growth in most sectors. What is certain is that social reform in terms of extending the welfare activities of the state had been abandoned. Social policy issues were increasingly determined by ostensibly economic criteria whose origins were undoubtedly ideological. As was shown in Chapters 5, 6 and 8, when the economic crises had abated, political decisions affecting welfare issues continued to be justified using an economic rationale, even though the state of the economy by 1983 was so strong that, in contrast with 1970s, no economic imperative existed. Hence the Green Paper *Reform of Social Security* (DHSS, 1985) justifies its proposals with such arguments as: 'The Social Security system must be consistent with with the Government's objectives for the economy.' (vol.1, chap.1.12). This position reflects the fact that social security accounts for a major portion of the: '... current heavy tax burden on individuals and companies.' (vol.1, chap.1.12). The motivation therefore was ideological, and from 1983 the ideological basis of welfare policy was only thinly disguised.

Policy Community

With regard to the changes that lead to the 1986 pensions legislation, Heclo and Wildavsky's (1974) concept of a 'policy community' has been essential to this research in drawing attention away from the obvious formal contacts between pressure groups and government and highlighting instead the informal links between significant individuals. An organisational approach raised the possibility that such organisations as the IoD behaved like political parties, producing ideas on pensions purely because some internal struggles had allowed the holders of that view to defeat opponents. It is probable that the IoD was a forum in which individuals could express and exchange ideas on pensions without any acrimony.

One organisation that certainly was not part of the pensions policy community was the TUC, but in February 1983 Len Murray, General Secretary of the TUC, optimistically claimed that:

> It was the TUC which really opened up discussion of a subject which had previously been shrouded in mystery. The TUC was in the lead in putting it (pensions) on the agenda. (Murray, 1983)

In fact the measures in the 1986 legislation began to develop when the OPB published two reports in 1981 and 1982. These had been commissioned before the implementation of the Social Security (Pensions) Act 1975, in March 1978 and February 1977 respectively, suggesting that since the late 1960s the subject of pensions had never really been off the agenda. The OPB reports were requested by David Ennals during the previous Labour government and concerned the adequacy of occupational pension schemes. But instead of acting to legislate the OPB proposals or some derivative thereof into existence, the post-1979 Conservative government, in keeping with its non-interventionist approach and general sympathy with industry's attempts to cut costs, chose to wait for the pensions industry to formulate its own approach to the early leavers problem. Nothing happened in either the pensions industry or government; the pensions industry was not about to legislate against itself and the government was probably afraid that no matter what measures it introduced to improve the quality of occupational pensions, the cost of the improved pensions would have to be borne by employers, employees or both, and therefore be guaranteed to be unpopular. It was at this stage that interest in the subject of pensions policy began to widen, with the Prime Minister commissioning a study by CPRS and such bodies as the SSC taking an interest. What followed was to demonstrate Margaret Thatcher's political strength through her ability to bring about an ideological shift, and the ability of a 'policy community', having adapted to this ideological shift not merely contribute to the policy-making through consultation, but to control that process, determining whose ideas should be allowed to come to the surface, whose ideas should be quietly submerged and which individuals should be excluded from the process altogether.

It was seen that after 1982, organisations such as the IoD and the CPS appeared to move to the forefront of the pensions debate. Other bodies such as the SSC produced lengthy and detailed reports which were all but completely ignored. But closer inspection showed that with the possible exception of the CPS, whose political status is unique, what was crucial about the pensions policy community was not the organisations but significant individuals who were amongst their members. As was shown in Chapter 5, the pensions policy community seemed to rely on these organisation as conduits for their ideas and to bring them into contact with other members of the pensions policy community. In particular, the IoD probably brought together people whose claim to recognition rested outside their IoD membership. They will often have held competing views on pensions but nevertheless had a respect for each other.

These significant individuals often had membership of several organisations which gave them connections with several overlapping networks through which to promote their ideas and respond to the ideas of others. More than this, they sometimes belonged to more than one policy community. For example, certain members also belonged to what may have been a 'financial' policy community; after their involvement in the Inquiry into Provision for Retirement, Alex Fletcher, Marshall Field, and Mark Weinberg became involved with the preparations for implementing the Financial Services Act 1986 which would bring about the deregulation of the City, known as 'Big Bang', as described in the previous Chapter.

When looking at the membership of the Inquiry into Provision for Retirement it was notable that such groups as the IoD and the CPS achieved remarkably little influence over pensions policy-making. The Inquiry's outside members were selected because they were experts in the field of pension provision; their qualifications for membership of the Inquiry are beyond reproach and yet, almost inevitably, those connected with finance were members of the same policy community as the IoD Director General, Walter Goldsmith, who after April 1983 had been a conspicuous campaigner for both personal pensions and personal capitalism. The IoD was therefore probably more than just an interest group but also a point of intersection at which individuals with material, political and ideological interests in pensions policy could come into contact with each other. In the course of interviewing members of the pensions policy community the researcher was struck by the frequency with which different interviewees not only showed an awareness of and respect for each others' ideas but often acknowledged knowing each other. One possibility is that owing to similar social backgrounds they shared a common culture and set of 'values' which led to a form of cohesion (Whitley, 1974, p. 65).

An interesting dimension of the Inquiry's membership was the continuous presence of David Willetts of the CPS and John Redwood of the Downing Street CPU on secondment from Rothschilds. The CPS and the CPU were probably the only two organisations to possess influence in their own right rather than by virtue of the personal status of their members. The presence of these two people despite their lack of official membership demonstrates both the influence their organisations possessed, such that they had to be taken seriously by Norman Fowler, and the fluidity that seemed to characterise the pensions policy community.

Elitism vs Pluralism

It appears that whereas pensions policy-making in the 1970s was essentially elitist, with decision-making confined to a handful of ministers and civil servants, by the early 1980s it had become a pluralist process with a number of different and competing organisations and individuals all contributing policy ideas. A characteristic of pluralism is that it can be very difficult for any one individual or group to achieve dominance and this created problems for Norman Fowler who needed to assert control over the flow of policy ideas before introducing his own proposals. His was approach was to set up the Inquiry into Provision for Retirement whose high profile and openness allowed members of the pensions policy community to feel fully involved through their submissions as though they were continuing to contribute to the policy-making process; in this respect the Inquiry gave the appearance of being pluralist. In fact Norman Fowler was restoring the elitist approach to pensions policy-making. When calling for evidence the Inquiry always specified issues it wanted to be informed about, thereby rendering illegitimate evidence not given formally to the Inquiry and contributions that did not conform to the terms of reference. Furthermore, in carefully selecting to serve on the Inquiry members of the policy community who were technically rather than ideologically oriented and generally in line with his ideas, Norman Fowler gave the appearance of reshaping rather than excluding this policy community; he granted membership to a sufficient number of leading actors for other members not to feel that their interests were going to be completely neglected. However, as was explained in Chapters 7 and 8, Norman Fowler and his ministers and civil servants did not implement the ideas produced within the Inquiry because Norman Fowler already knew what policies he was going to adopt. In other words, despite appearances, the actual policy-making process was as elitist as that employed by Barbara Castle in 1974.

Ideological, Material and Political Interests

It was seen in above and in Chapter 9 that the main dynamics within the policy community were: ideological, material and political interests. Material interest did not appear to be very influential, at least in a direct sense, but ideological and political interests were certainly important. Those with a political interest included Norman Fowler, Margaret Thatcher, Nigel Lawson and, to a lesser degree, Nigel Vinson and Philip Chappell whose association with the CPS gave them access certainly to the Prime Minister and probably to other ministers. Political interest, while important, was not sufficient to carry the proposal for the abolition of SERPS. But ideological interest appears to have been an even more important force. It was this which brought together those with a strong political interest such as the Prime Minister, ideologues such as Nigel Vinson, Philip Chappell and Walter Goldsmith. The measures that emerged in the subsequent legislation partially satisfied all these interests. The ideologists were pleased to see the beginning of the phasing out of SERPS, even though it was not combined with the disestablishment of pension funds. Those with a material interest, such as Mark Weinberg, Marshall Field and Stewart Lyon must have been delighted with the shape in which personal pensions as they emerged; far from threatening the future profitability of life offices the form which most personal pension plans would take could increase their role in pensions provision, and even Mark Weinberg's Hambros (subsequently Allied Dunbar) and John Redwood's Rothschilds stood to gain significantly as they had both developed alternative pensions products so as to be capable of exploiting either the institutionally managed personal pension or the CPS/IoD 'personal pot of gold' in the form of either a share portfolio or a unit trust holding. The policy outcome represents a victory for finance capitalism over New Right ideology but, of equal importance, it appears to represent a victory for the established pensions providers against whom Vinson (1989) and Vinson and Chappell (1983) railed.

Bibliography

Adam Smith Institute (1983), *Privatizing Pensions: A Report to the Secretary of State for Health and Social Security* Restricted Publication.

Adam Smith Institute (1988), *Enlightenment: Changing Pensions*. More flexible structure for a changing market, London, ASI (Research) Ltd 1988.

Age Concern (1974), *Memorandum on the White Paper 'Better Pensions' and a policy for a future state pension* Mitcham, Age Concern.

Aitken, I. (November 7th, 1988), 'Lawson's leak to plug a bolt hole' in *The Guardian*.

Alcock, P. (July 1985), 'Welfare State: Safety Net or Poverty Trap?' in *Marxism Today*, pp. 9-14.

Alcock, P. (July 11 1989), *The End of the Line for Social Security* paper given at: the Social Policy Association Conference, University of Bath.

Anon. (November 20 1986) 'A mirror down the hall' *The Guardian*

Anon. (July 1988) 'Two Per Cent Or Not Two Per Cent' in: *Pensions Management* p.7.

Anon. (October 23 1992) 'Maxwell receiver has low hopes' in: *The Guardian*.

Association of Consulting Actuaries, (September 14 1983), Contribution to DHSS Conference on Early Leavers, reported in: 'DHSS Conference on Early Leavers' *Pensions World* Vol. 12 October 1983 pp. 705-6.

Atkinson, A.B. (April 15th 1988), *Turning The Screw: Benefits For The Unemployed 1979-1988* paper given at the IFS Conference: The Economics of Social Security.

Atkinson, D. (October 29th 1992), 'City urged to make up Maxwell funds shortfall' in: *The Guardian*.

Atkinson, D. (October 31st 1992), 'Maxwell pension fund victims left to face uncertain future' in: *The Guardian*.

Atkinson, D. (May 26th 1983), 'Old system bequeathes a legacy of squabbling' in: *The Guardian*.

Atkinson, D. and Whitebloom, S. (June 17th 1983), 'Goldmans fined for Maxwell dealings' in: *The Guardian*.

Atkinson, D. and Whitebloom, S. (May 26th 1993), 'Large reputation at stake' in: *The Guardian*.

Atkinson, D. and Whitebloom, S. (May 26th 1993), 'City regulator gets tough' in: *The Guardian*.

Bachrach, P. and Baratz, M. (1970), *Power and Poverty: Theory and Practice*, OUP, New York.

Bacon and Woodrow (1993), *Pay and Benefits Pocket Book*, NTC Publications, Henley

Barber, W.J. (1967), *A History of Economic Thought*, Pelican, London.

Barry, N. (1979), *Hayek's Social and Economic Philosophy*, Macmillan, London.

Barry, N. (1985), 'The State, Pensions and Philosophy of Welfare' in: *Journal of Social Policy* Vol. 14(4) pp. 465-490.

Barry, N. (1990), *Welfare*, Open University Press, Buckingham.

Bean, P. *et al* (1985), *In Defence of Welfare*, Tavistock Publications.

Beavis, S. (April 10th 1993), 'Major asked to halt plan to use £481m pension fund cash for pit closures' in: *The Guardian*.

Benjamin, B. *et al* (), Pensions: The Problems of Today and Tomorrow London, Allen and Unwin 1987

Beveridge, Sir W. (1943), *Pillars of Security*, George Allen and Unwin, London.

Bevins, A. (November 23rd 1983), 'Fowler challenges arguments for cuts' in: *The Times.*

Bevins, A. (November 23rd 1983a), 'Ministers criticize absent Thatcher over spending cuts' in: *The Times.*

Bishop, G.F. *et al* (1983), 'Effects of Filters on Public Opinion Surveys' in: *Public Opinion Quarterly* Vol. 47(4) 1983 pp. 528-546.

Blackstone, T. and Plowden, W. (1988), *Inside The Think Tank* William Heinemann, London,

Blair, D. (September 11th 1982), 'The proposed central fund - the present position' in: *Pensions World* Vol. 11 pp. 507-8.

Blom-Cooper, L. (February 18th 1991), 'Not enough for government to pass the buck' in: the *Financial Times*.

Bose, M. (June 1985), 'How Portable Can Pensions Be?' in: *Director Magazine* (IoD) June 1985 pp. 58-66.

Bose, M. (June 4th 1988), 'Last act before the revolution' in: *The Guardian*.

Bose, M. (February 13th 1988), 'A word in your ear: jargon' in: *The Guardian*.

Bosenquet, N. (1983), *After the New Right*, Heinemann, London.

Bourke, L. (June 8th 1983), 'Pensions' in: *The Times.*

Bourke, L. (September 15th 1983a), 'Fowler poised to improve deal for pension leavers' in: *The Times.*

Bracewell-Milnes, B. (1985), *A Working Paper On Reducing Public Spending*, IoD Policy Unit, London.

Bracewell-Milnes, J.B. (1987), *Are Equity Markets Short-Sighted? Short-Termism' and its Critics*, Director Publications, London.

Bradshaw, J. (April 15th 1988), *Trends in Dependence on Supplementary Benefits Benefits For The Unemployed 1979-1988* paper given at the IFS Conference: The Economics of Social Security April.

Brimblecombe, R. (11 October 1982), 'Insured pension schemes in the United Kingdom' *Pensions World* Vol. pp. 597-601.

Brown, M, (March 22nd 1974), 'CBI ponders Mr Adamson's offer of resignation' in: *The Times.*

Brummer, A. (November 4th 1992), 'Growing case for Square Mile policing' in: *The Guardian*.

Brummer, A. (May 26th 1993), 'Making time for root and branch reform in the City' in: *The Guardian*.

Brunet, E. (April 6th 1974a), 'Changes in the offing' in: *The Times*.

Brunet, E. (June 1st 1974b), 'The options open to Mrs Castle' in: *The Times*.

Brunet, E. (September 14th 1974c), 'Pensions are back in the political limelight' in: *The Times*.

Brunet, E. (November 9th 1974d), 'Needed: a non-partisan package' in: *The Times*.

Brunet, E. (January 11th 1975a), 'Finding common ground between the parties' in: *The Times*.

Brunet, E. (February 8th 1975), 'Changes needed in rules for past employees' in: *The Times*.

Brunet, E. (February 15th 1975), 'Minimum benefits could pose some problems' in: *The Times*.

Brunet, E. (March 1st 1975), 'Mrs Castle heeds the industry's views' in: *The Times*.

Bulmer, M. (ed.) (1984), *Sociological Research Methods (2nd edition)*, Macmillan, London.

Burden, T. and Campbell, M. (1985), *Capitalism and Public Policy in the UK*, Croom and Helm, London.

Brown, J. and Small, S. (1985), *Occupational Benefits as Social Security*, PSI, London.

Centre for Policy Studies, (October 12th 1983), Contribution to DHSS Conference on Early Leavers September 1983, reported in: 'DHSS Conference on Early Leavers' *Pensions World* Vol. pp. 656 and 704.

Chappell, P. (1988), *Pensions and Priviledge*, CPS, London.

Charlton, P. (June 3rd 1982), 'Census data shows ageing population' in: the *Guardian*.

Child Poverty Action Group (1985), *Burying Beveridge. A Detailed Reponse to the Green Paper 'Reform of Social Security'*, CPAG, London.

Clare, J. (October 19th 1983), 'Pensioners unaware of cash deal' in: *The Times*.

Clarke, N. (May 7th 1993), 'Plunder and the pension fund' in: the *Guardian*.

Confederation of British Industry, Contribution to DHSS Conference on Early Leavers (September 13th 1983), reported in: 'DHSS Conference on Early Leavers' *Pension World* Vol. 12 October 1983 pp. 708-9.

Cutler, T. *et al* (1986), *Keynes, Beveridge and Beyond*, RKP, London.

Dahl, R. (1970), 'A Critique of the Ruling Elite Model' American Political Science Review Vol. 52 June 1958 pp. 463-9 cited in: Bachrach and Baratz *Power and Poverty: Theory and Practice*, OUP, New York, p. 9n.

Digby, A. (1989), *British Welfare Policy - Workhouse to Welfare*, Faber and Faber, London.

Andrew Dilnot *et al*, (1984) *The Reform of Social Security*, Clarendon Press, Oxford.

Drummond, M. (June 3rd 1974), 'Pension funds concerned over business rents' in: *The Times*.

Ellis, B. (1989), *Pensions in Britain 1955-1975*, HMSO, London.

151

Ellis, C. (July 1988), 'Will the new providers please stand up?' in: *Pensions Management*, p.31.

Ellison, R. (April 1982), An open letter to Professor Gower *Pensions World* Vol.11, pp. 222-4.

Ermisch, J. (1982), 'Resources of the Elderly' in: *Retirement Policy - the Next Fifty Years* (Joint Studies in Public Policy No. 5) Ed. Michael Fogarty, Heineman, London.

Estes, C. *et al* (July 1982), 'Dominant and Competing Paradigms in Gerontology: 'Towards a Political Economy of Ageing' in: *Ageing and Society* Vol. 2(2) pp. 151-64.

Eversley, D. (1982) 'The Demography of Retirement - Prospects to the Year 2000' Chapter 2 in: *Retirement Policy - the Next Fifty Years* (Joint Studies in Public Policy No. 5) Ed. Michael Fogarty, Heinneman, London.

Family Policy Studies Centre, (1988), An ageing population (Factsheet No. 2) FPSC, London.

Michael Fogarty (ed), (1982) *Retirement Policy - the Next Fifty Years* (ed.) Joint Studies in Public Policy, No. 5, Heinneman, London.

Fowler, N. (July 12th 1983), 'Pensions - The Voice of Government' Address to the NAPF Summer Conference, May 8th 1983 reported in: *Pensions World* Vol. 12 July 1983 pp. 380-2.

Fowler, N. (September 3rd 1983a), Speech to the Society of Pension Consultants Savoy Hotel London, November 5th 1983. Reported in: 'An individual touch "could pay" ' in: *The Times* (see also DHSS Press Release 85/308 below).

Fowler, N. (December 11th 1983b), Letter in: *The Sunday Times*.

Fowler, N. (1991), Ministers Decide London, Chapmans.

Franey, R. (undated, circa 1984), *Past Caring*, GLC Welfare Rights London.

Freethy, N. (November 1988), 'Pensions and Priviledge Revisited' in: *Pensions Management*, pp. 19-22.

Gamble, A. (1981), *An Introduction to Modern Social and Political Thought*, Macmillan, London.

Gamble, A. (1988), *The Free Economy and the Strong State*, Macmillan, London.

Gaselee, J. (June 1985) 'Suit Yourself' *Director* (IoD Magazine) p. 47.

George, V. and Wilding, P. (1985) *Ideology and Social Welfare*, Radical Social Policy, London.

Ginsberg, N. (1979) *Class, Capital and Social Policy*, Critical Texts in Social Work and the Welfare State, Macmillan, London.

Golding, and Middleton, S. (1982) *Images of Welfare*, Martin Robertson, London.

Goldsmith, W, (January 1982), 'The Impact of Pensions on Boardroom Decisions' A speech to the Autumn Conference of the NAPF November 1981, in: *Pensions World*, pp. 20-22.

Goodin, R. (1985), 'Self-Reliance Versus the Welfare State' in: *Journal of Social Policy* Vol. 14(1) 1985 pp. 25-47.

Gough, I. (1979), *The Political Economy of the Welfare State*, Macmillan, London.

Government Actuary's Department, (October 1983), Contribution to DHSS Conference on Early Leavers (September 13th 1983), reported in: 'DHSS Conference on Early Leavers' *Pensions World* Vol. 12, pp. 706-7

Gower, L.C.B. (April 1982), 'Investor Protection' in: *Pensions World* Vol. 11, pp.200-1.

Gray, J. (1986), Liberalism, OUP, London.

Groves, D. (July 11th 1989), *Sex and the Personal Pension* paper given at: the Social Policy Association Conference, University of Bath.

Guillemard, A-M. (ed.) (1983), *Old Age and the Welfare State* Sage Publications.

Gwilt, G.D. (October 14th 1974), 'Two Aspects of the White Paper on Pensions' in: *The Times*.

Haberman, S. (1987), 'Future Pensions Expenditure' in: Bernard Benjamin *et al Pensions: The Problems of Today and Tomorrow*, Allen and Unwin, London, pp. 165-188.

Haberman, S. (1987), Future Dependency' in: Bernard Benjamin *et al Pensions: The Problems of Today and Tomorrow*, Allen and Unwin, London, pp. 189-195.

Hall, P. (1986), *Governing the Economy - the Politics of State Intervention*, Polity Press, London.

Hall, S. and Jacques, M. (1983) *The Politics of Thatcherism*, Laurence and Wishart, London.

Halsey, A.H. (ed.) (1988), *British Social Trends since 1900*, Macmillan, London.

Hannah, L. (1986) *Inventing Retirement*, Cambridge University Press, Cambridge.

Harrison, D. (November 1988) 'Fair Dues for All' in: *Pensions Management*, pp.29-36.

Haviland, J. (November 24th 1983) 'Treasury seeks £90m. saving' in: *The Times*.

Hawkins, D.I. and Coney, K.A. (1981), 'Uninformed Response Error in Survey Research' in: *Journal of Marketing Research* Vol. 3, pp. 370-374.

Healy, P. (March 9th 1974), 'Cost of bigger pensions rules out family allowance rises this year, Mrs Castle says.' in: *The Times*.

Hedderwick, C. (May 1981), 'Review of the Scott Report on Public Sector Pensions and Job Security: U.K.' in: *Benefits International*, pp. 27-8.

Helowicz, G. (1987), 'A Look at the Past' Chapter 1 in: Bernard Benjamin *et al Pensions: The Problems of Today and Tomorrow*, Allen and Unwin, London, pp. 1-14.

Helowicz, G. (1987), 'Pension Fund Investment' in: Bernard Benjamin *et al Pensions: The Problems of Today and Tomorrow*, Allen and Unwin, London, pp. 83-115.

Hencke, D. (February 1st 1989), 'Thatcher goaded into setting pace for "premature" overhaul of the NHS' in: the *Guardian*.

Hencke, D. (January 3rd 1991), 'Pensions opt-out cost soars' in: the *Guardian*.

Heyes, T. (October 1982), 'U.K. pension funds - the next ten years' in: *Pensions World* Vol. 11 pp. 581-3.

Heyes, T. (October 1983), 'Early leavers: A contribution to the debate' in: *Pensions World* Vol. 12, pp.640-1.

Hill, M. and Bramley, G. (1986), *Analysing Social Policy*, Basil Blackwell, London.

Hockey, J. (February 4th 1988), Research Methods Seminar: *Interviewing* Doctoral Programme in British Policy Studies, University of Sheffield.

Hodge, P. (July 1988), 'The 1988 Pensions Explosion' on: *Pensions Management*, p.43.

Hogwood, B.W. and Gunn, L, A. (1984), *Policy Analysis for the Real World* Oxford University Press, Oxford.

Hoinville, G. 'Carrying Out Surveys Among the Elderly' in: *Researching the Elderly (Special Issue) Journal of the Market Research Society,* Vol. 25(3) pp. 215-293.

Hudson, K. (1982), *Help the Aged: Twenty-one years of experiment and achievement,* The Bodley Head, London.

Hunter, H. (August 10th 1988) 'Occupational pension schemes could be in jeopardy through burden of new legislation - NAPF' in: *The Guardian.*

Institute of Directors (March 1984) 'IoD campaigns for take-away pensions', *Direct Line* No. 12 p. 4

Institute of Directors (January 1985a), 'Make personal pensions more attractive, says IoD', *Direct Line* No. 22 p. 2.

Institute of Directors (July 1985b), 'The Welfare Burden' *Direct Line* No. 28 pp. 1-2.

Jackson, J. (1977), *Occupational Pensions - The New Law,* The New Commercial Publishing Company, London.

Jackson, P.M. (1985), 'Economics of an aging population' in: *Journal of Epidemiology and Community Health,* Vol. 39 pp. 97-101

Jackson, T. (December 9th 1983), 'Employers see need for change in pension law' in: *The Financial Times.*

James, C. (June 1984), *Occupational Pensions: The Failure of Private Welfare,* Fabian Society Tract No. 497, Fabian Society, London.

James, H. (June 1983), 'Pensions - The contemporary and future scene', A report of Henry James' address to the NAPF Annual Conference May 1983, in: *Pensions World* Vol. 12 pp. 378-9.

Johnson, M. (1982), 'The Implications of Greater Activity in Later Life' Chapter 6 in: *Retirement Policy - the Next Fifty Years,* Joint Studies in Public Studies No.5, Ed. Michael Fogarty, Heinneman, London.

Johnson, M. *et al* (1981), *Ageing Needs and Nutrition: A Study in Community Care,* PSI, London.

Johnston, E. (January 1982), 'The terms for contracting-out NAPF Autumn Conference 1981' in: *Pensions World* Vol. 11, pp. 18-20.

Johnston, E. (October 1982), 'Pensions costs in the long term' in: *Pensions World,* pp. 569-571.

Johnston, E. (March 1983), Summary of: 'The future cost of pensions' a talk given at Pensions in 1983 - FT Conference, London, February 9-10th 1983, reported in: *Pensions World* Vol. 11, p. 145.

Jordan, B. (1987), *Rethinking Welfare,* Basil Blackwell, London.

Kane, F. (April 27th 1983), 'Ex-tycoon admits pensions fraud' in: *The Guardian.*

Kane, D. and Atkinson, D. (November 4th 1992), 'City' incapable of stamping out fraud' in: *The Guardian*

Kaye, G. (1987) 'Current Regulations', Chapter 2 in: Bernard Benjamin *et al Pensions: The Problems of Today and Tomorrow,* Allen and Unwin, London, pp. 15-30.

Kaye, G. (1987) 'Retirement Benefit', Chapter 3 in: Bernard Benjamin *et al Pensions: The Problems of Today and Tomorrow,* Allen and Unwin, London, pp. 31-43.

Kaye, G. (1987), 'Current Problems in Pensions Provision' Chapter 4 in: Bernard Benjamin *et al Pensions: The Problems of Today and Tomorrow*, Allen and Unwin, London, pp. 44-65.

Keegan, W. (1989), *Mr Lawson's Gamble*, Hodder & Stoughton, London.

Labour Party (1981), *Social Security*, The Labour Party.

Lascelles, D. (October 20th 1983), 'The smoke of battle thickens', the *Financial Times*
.

Laurance, B. and Willcock, J. (November 5th 1992), 'The fortune hunters' in: *The Guardian*.

Lawson, N. (1992), *The View from No. 11*, Bantam Press, London.

Life Offices Association & Associated Scottish Life Offices (October 1983), Contribution to DHSS Conference on Early Association Leavers, September 13th 1983, reported in: 'DHSS Conference on Early Leavers', *Pensions World*, Vol. 12 p. 706.

Lindblom, C.E. (1959), 'The science of muddling through' in: *Public Administration Review*, Vol. 19, pp. 79-88.

Laurance, B. and Willcock, J. (November 5th 1992), 'The fortune hunters' in: *The Guardian*.

Lindsay, D. (Campaign for Equal Retirement Ages) (November 5th 1992) Letter to Editor in: *The Guardian*.

Lister, R. (April 15th 1988), *The Politics of Social Security: An Assessment of the Fowler Review* paper given at the IFS Conference: The Economics of Social Security.

Lister, R.(July 1989), *A Revolution Of Reducing Expectations: Social Security Policy In The 1980's* paper given at the Social Policy Association Conference, Bath.

Baroness Lockwood (June 1982), 'Sex equality in pension schemes' in: *Pensions World* Vol. 11 pp. 321-7.

Lynes, T. (1985), *Maintaining the Value of Benefits*, Family Income Support Part 7, PSI, London.

Lyon, S. 'The Outlook for Pensioning' speech made on October 25th 1982 reported in: *Pensions World* Vol. 12 January 1983 pp. 41-43 and February 1983 pp. 93-97.

Lyon, S. (July 1983), 'Pensions - can we afford the existing commitment?' Talk given to the Annual Conference of the NAPF Brighton, May 1983 reported in: *Pensions World* Vol. 12 pp.454-8.

McRae, H. (June 30th 1988), 'A practice pension funds should put on the retired list' in: *The Guardian*.

McKelvey, K.M. *et al* (1985), *Hosking's Pension Schemes and Retirement Benefits*, Sweet & Maxwell, London.

McPherson, M. and Raab, C. (1988), *Governing Education: and A Sociology of Policy Since 1945*, Edinburgh University Press, Edinburgh.

Marsh, D. (ed.) (1983), *Pressure Politics: interest groups in Great Britain*, Junction Books, London.

Meacher, M. (1986), Introduction to: *Social Security - the Real Agenda. Fabian Society's Response to the Government Review of Social Security*, Fabian Tract No. 498, Fabian Society, London.

Means, R. 'Public Policy and Older People - Where Are We Going?' in: *Journal of Social Policy* Vol. 16(4) 1987 pp. 543 - 550.

Midwinter, E. (2985), *The wage of retirement: the case for a new pensions policy*, Centre for Policy on Ageing, London.

Miliband, R. (1983), *Class Power and State Power*, Verso, London. London, Verso 1983

Wright Mills, C. (1956), *The Power Elite*, Oxford University Press, New York.

Minns, R. (1980), *Pension Funds and British Capitalism*, Heinnemann, London.

Victor Morgan, E. (1984), *Choices in Pensions*, Institute of Economic Affairs, London.

Murray, L. (March 1983), 'Trades Unions in the pensions fields' extracts from talk given at: Pensions in 1983 - FT Conference London, February 9-10th 1983 reported in: *Pensions World* Vol. 12 pp. 147-151

National Association of Pension Funds (October 1983), Contribution to DHSS Conference on Early Leavers September 1983, reported in: 'DHSS Conference on Early Leavers' *Pensions World* Vol. 12 pp. 642-3.

O'Connor, J. (1973), *The Fiscal Crisis of the State*, St Martins Press, New York.

Occupational Pensions Board (October 1983), Contribution to DHSS Conference on Early Leavers September 1983, reported in: 'DHSS Conference on Early Leavers' *Pensions World* Vol. 12 pp. 645-6.

Offe, C. (1984), *Contradictions of the Welfare State* ed. John Keane, Hutchinson Educational, London.

O'Higgins, M. (1987), 'Egalitarians, Equalities and Welfare Evaluation' in: *Journal of Social Policy* Vol. 16(1) pp. 1-18.

Oldfield, M. (March 1983), 'Transferability' extracts from a paper given at: Pensions in 1983 - FT Conference London February 9-10th 1983, reported in: *Pensions World* Vol. 12 pp. 151-2.

Oldfield, M. (April 1983), 'Choice in pension arrangements' extracts from a speech given to: The Joint BPF/NAPF Conference - Property in a Democracy, reported in: *Pensions World* Vol. 12 p. 222.

Oldfield, M. (June 1983), 'Address to the Annual Conference of the NAPF' May 5th 1983, reported in: *Pensions World* Vol. 12 pp. 377-8.

Oppenheim, A.N. (1966), *Questionnaire Design and Attitude Measurement*, Heinnemann, London.

Pauley, R. (February 11th 1985), 'Pensions proposals studied in Cabinet' in: the *Financial Times*.

Peet, R. (1984), 'Government Proposals for New Pension Schemes', *Post Magazine and Insurance Monitor*, Vol. 135 part 35, September 26th 1974, p. 2561 cited by Eric Shragge, pp. 148-9.

Pensions World (March 1982), 'Investor protection docment' in: *Pensions World* Vol. 11 p. 112.

Pensions World (April 1982), 'Review of contracting-out terms' in: *Pensions World* Vol. 11 pp. 175-179.

Pensions World (June 1982), '1982 NAPF Annual Conference' in: *Pensions World* Vol. 11 pp. 316-9.

Pensions World (July 1982), 'Pensions and employment mobility' in: *Pensions World* Vol. p. 431.

Pensions World (September 1982), 'National Insurance financing into the next century' in: *Pensions World* Vol. 12 p. 541.

Pensions World (November 1982), 'Legislation on OPB Reports' in: *Pensions World* Vol. 11 p. 635.

Pensions World (February 1983), 'Transferable Plan' in: *Pensions World* Vol. 13 p.135.

Pensions World (March 1983) 'Pensions in 1983 - FT Conference' in: *Pensions World* Vol. 12 pp. 145-152.

Pensions World (April 1983) 'Choice in pension arrangements' in: *Pensions World* Vol. 12 p. 222.

Pensions World (May 1983) 'IoD Propose Three Point Pension Charter' in: *Pensions World* Vol. 12 p. 306.

Pensions World (June 1983) 'TUC guidance on investment in South Africa' report of TUC contribution to the 1983 NAPF Annual Conference in: *Pensions World* Vol. 12 p. 382.

Pensions World (October 1983) 'DHSS Conference on Early Leavers' in: *Pensions World* Vol. 12 pp. 642-709.

Pensions World (November 1983), 'Other views on early leavers' in: *Pensions World* Vol. 12 pp. 714-717.

Pensions World (November 1983) 'A new pension plan from Lord Banks' in: *Pensions World* Vol. 12 pp. 741-742.

Pensions World (December 1983), 'Government pensions policy' in: *Pensions World* Vol. 12 p. 788.

Phillipson, C. (1982) *Capitalism and the Construction of Old Age*, Critical Texts in Social Work and the Welfare State, Macmillan, London.

Phillipson, C. and Walker, A. (eds) (1986), *Ageing and Social Policy: A Critical Assessment* Gower, London.

Pilch, M. (March 1982), 'Retirement policy - the next fifty years' in: *Pensions World* Vol. 11 pp. 145-150.

Pilch, M. and Wood, V. (1979), *Pension Schemes*, Gower Press, London.

Pilch, M. (March 1982), 'Retirement policy - the next fifty years' in: *Pensions World* Vol. 11 pp. 145-150.

Sir Alastair Pilkington (April 2nd 1974), 'Inequity between pensions' in: *The Times*.

Pirie, M., 'State pensions and the alternatives - economic and political reality' extracts of a speech given at the: Pensions in 1983 - Financial Times Conference, London, February 9-10th 1983 reported in: *Pensions World* Vol. 12 pp. 146-7.

Plant, R. (1984), *Equality, Markets and the State*, Fabian Society, London.

Plant, R. (1985), 'The very idea of a welfare state' chapter one of: Philip Bean *et al In Defence of Welfare*, Tavistock Publications, London.

Reardon, R. (1989), *Planning Your Pension*, Allied Dunbar Library Money Guides, Longman, London.

Reddin, M. and Pilch, M. (1985), *Can we afford our future?* and Age Concern Publications, Mitcham.

Reddin, M. (1986), 'Cost and Portability' in: *Social Security - the Real Agenda. The Fabian Society's Response to the Government Review of Social Security*, Fabian Tract No. 498, Fabian Society, London.

Rigby, B. (July 1983), 'Pension - will business get the right deal?' Summary of speech by the Director-General of the CBI to the Annual Conference of the NAPF, Brighton, May 1983, reported in: *Pensions World* Vol. 12 pp. 453-4.

Riley, B. (September 1st 1983), 'Call to improve pensions paid to early leavers' in: the *Financial Times*.

Riley, B. (December 1st 1983a), 'Alarm over rising cost of pensions' in: *Financial Times*.

Riley, B. (April 18th 1991), 'Pension funds press for action on sex equality' in: the *Financial Times*.

Robinson, R. (1986), 'Restructuring the Welfare State An Analysis of Public Expenditure 1979/80-1984/85' in: *Journal of Social Policy* 15(1) pp. 1-21.

Rogers, E. (January 1982), 'Protection for Early Leavers' NAPF Autumn Conference, November 1981 in: *Pensions World* Vol. 11 pp. 9-16.

Rose, D. (January 11th 1989), 'Big money turns the key' in: *The Guardian*.

Shore, P. (January 1982), 'A view from Westminster' in: *Pensions World* Vol. 11 pp. 16-17.

Short, E. (September 12th 1983), 'EEC pension directive criticised in: *The Financial Times*.

Short, E. (September 12th 1983), 'Call for freer pensions market' in: *The Financial Times*.

Short, E. (September 15th 1983), 'Pensions law likely to change' in: *The Financial Times*.

Short, E. (September 15th 1983), 'Law on job-changer' pensions near' in: *The Financial Times*.

Short, E. (September 16th 1983), 'Sides line up in pensions debate' in: the *Financial Times*.

Short, E. (October 7th 1983), 'Portable pension scheme launched by Save and Prosper' in: *The Financial Times*.

Short, E. (November 10th 1983), 'Occupational pensions industry faces major changes in coming year' in: *The Financial Times*.

Shragge, E. (1984), *Pensions Policy in Great Britain - A Socialist Analysis*, RKP, London.

Silverman, D. (1985), Qualitative Methodology and Sociology, Gower Publishing, Aldershot.

Slaughter, J. (July 3rd 1988), 'New Plans Shake Up Old Guard' in: *The Observer*.

Slaughter, J. (July 3rd 1988), 'New plans shake up the old guard' in: *The Observer*.

Slaughter, J. (July 3rd 1988), 'Call-up time for volunteerers' in: *The Observer*.

Smith, B.A. and Townsend, P. (1955) *New Pensions For The Old*, Fabian Research Series No. 171, Fabian Society, London.

Smith, B.A. and Townsend, P. (1986), 'Introduction: Challenging Government Assumptions' in *Social Security - the Real Agenda*, Chapter One, Fabian Society, London. The Fabian Society's Response to the Government Review of Social Security Fabian Tract No. 498.

Smith, G. (November 20th 1974), 'Conservatives give terms for pension approval' in: *The Times*.

Smith, T. 'Recalling Attitudes: An Analysis of Retrospective Questions in the 1982 GHS' in: *Public Opinion Quarterly* Vol. 48(3) pp. 639-649.

Society of Pension Consultants (October 1983), Contribution to DHSS Conference on Early Leavers September 1983, reported in: 'DHSS Conference on Early Leavers', *Pensions World* Vol. 12 pp. 704-5.

Spicer, S. (April 1990), 'The Power to Influence' in: *Pensions Management* Vol. 19 pp. 36-37.

Stanworth, P. and Giddens, A. (eds) (1974), *Elites and Power in British Society* Anthony Giddens (eds.) Cambridge University Press, London.

Stein, N.P. (1988-99), 'Reversions from Pension Plans: History, Policies and Prospects' in: *Tax Law Review* Vol. 44 pp.259-334.

Stephenson, H. (October 14th 1974), 'Crisis Budget time for Mr Healey' in: *The Times*.

Stone, M. (January 30th 1974a), 'Pensions: the Government's impossible deadline' in: *The Times*.

Stone, M. (August 2nd 1974b), 'Safeguards for pensions legislation' in: *The Times*.

Stone, M. (October 22nd 1974c), 'Legal and General plea for pensions safeguard' in: *The Times*.

Stone, M. (February 21st 1975), 'Guidelines on pensions for minister' in: *The Times*.

Stone, M. (March 14th 1975), 'Pension fund feeling the pinch' in: *The Times*.

Thomson, R. (June 28th 1992), 'Lilley bails out 4,000 Maxwell pensioners' in: the *Independent*.

The Times (May 9th 1974a), 'Reserve pension plan scrapped' in: *The Times*.

The Times (May 9th 1974b), 'Decision to drop reserve pension plan "flat-footed and doctinaire" Tory says' in: *The Times*.

The Times (May 9th 1974c), 'Pensions decision causes angry turmoil' in: *The Times*.

The Times (June 27th 1974), 'Pension funds attack freeze on office rents' in: *The Times*.

The Times (August 21st 1974), 'Tories propose flexibility in retirement age' in: *The Times*.

The Times (August 23rd 1974), 'Tory pensions proposals criticized' in: *The Times*.

The Times (October 1st 1974), 'Mrs Castle puts pensions back in the fray' in: *The Times*.

The Times (October 12th 1974), 'Green light for a package of pensions measures' in: *The Times*.

The Times (October 25th 1974), 'Pension payments "hidden taxation", Mr Powell says' in: *The Times*.

The Times (December 18th 1974), 'State pension scheme is criticized as inadequate' in: *The Times*.

The Times (February 28th 1975a), 'Business Diary: Rotherham sound' in: *The Times*.

The Times (February 28th 1975b), 'A Good But Expensive Bill' in: *The Times*.

The Times (February 28th 1975c), 'Labour makes two concessions on occupational pension schemes' in: *The Times*.

The Times (March 19th 1975), 'Second Reading of the Social Security (Pensions) Bill March 18th 1975' in: *The Times*.

The Times (March 19th 1975a), 'Bill a blank cheque drawn on future' in: *The Times*.

The Times (March 19th 1975b), 'Mrs Castle seeking to abolish discrimination against women in occupational pension schemes' in: *The Times*.

The Times (March 19th 1975c), 'Business Diary: Tax gathering' in: *The Times*.

The Times (March 20th 1975), 'Rapid action hoped for on pensions' in: *The Times*.

The Times (April 29th 1983), 'Heavy fund investment abroad' in: *The Times*.

The Times (May 25th 1983), 'Mortimer denies Labour would take over savings for investment' in: *The Times*.

The Times (September 3rd 1983), 'An individual touch could pay' in: *The Times*.

The Times (November 30th 1983), 'DHSS consultative document proposes legislation to protect job changers' in: *The Times*.

The Times (May 2nd 1985), 'Employers split on cost of earnings-related pension' in: *The Times*.

Timmins, N. (February 28th 1986), 'Private sector next in line' in: *The Times*.

Townsend, P. 'The Structural Dependency of the Elderly' in: *Ageing and Society* Vol. 1(1) 1981 pp. 5-20.

Trade Union Congress (October 1983), Contribution to DHSS Conference on Early Leavers September 13th 1983, reported in: 'DHSS Conference on Early Leavers' *Pensions World* Vol. 12 pp. 707-8.

Muriel Turner Asst. Gen. Sec. (1987), Address to CBI Conference on the Social Security Act 1986 cited in: *TUSIU Pension Extra*.

Van Den Brink-Budgen, R. (1984), 'Freedom and the Welfare State: A Multi-Dimensional Problem' in: *Journal of Social Policy* Vol. 13(1) pp. 21-39.

Vinson, N. and Chappell, P. (April 1983), *Personal and Portable Pensions - For All*, Centre for Policy Studies, London.

Vinson, N. and Chappell, P. (September 28th 1983), 'Financing pensions in a weak economy' in: *The Times*.

Walker, A. (1980), 'The Social Creation of Poverty and Dependency in Old Age' in: *Journal of Social Policy* Vol. 9(1) pp. 49-75.

Walker, A. (1981), 'Towards a Political Economy of Old Age' in: *Ageing and Society* Vol. 1(1) pp. 73-94.

Walker, A. (1983), 'The Social Production of Old Age' in: *Ageing and Society* Vol. 3(3) pp. 387-395.

Walker, A. (1984), *Socialist Planning: A Strategy for Socialist Welfare*, Basil Blackwell, London.

Walker, A. (April 18th 1985), 'Getting the Elderly to Pay' in: *New Society*, pp. 76-78.

Walker, A. (December 2nd 1987), *The Future of Social Policy* Inaugural Lecture, University of Sheffield.

Walker, A. (November 23rd 1988), 'Means to an end of state pensions' in: *The Guardian*.

Walker, A. (1990), 'The Economic "Burden" of Ageing and the Prospect of Inter-generational Conflict' in: *Ageing and Society*, Vol. 10 pp.377-396.

Walker, C. (1983), *Changing Social Policy the case of the Supplementary Benefits Review*, Bedford Square Press, London.

Ward, S. (September 12th 1987), 'Come to the Pensions Revolution' in: *The Guardian*.

Ward, S. (February 6th 1988), 'Shop around now for a pension plan' in: *The Guardian*.

Ward, S. (February 1991), 'Cost of personal pensions' *Pensions World* Vol. 20 No. 2 pp. 45-6.

Webber, M.M. (1970), 'Explorations into Urban Structure' *et al* University of Pennsylvania Press, 1964 cited in: Peter Worsley, *Introducing Sociology* 1st Edition, Penguin Books, Harmondsworth, p.40.

Whitebloom, S. (March 2nd 1993), 'Aid for MGN pensioners running out' in: *The Guardian*.

Whitebloom, S. (April 20th 1993), 'First Maxwell payouts are on the way' in: *The Guardian*.

Whitebloom, S. (June 7th 1993), 'Mirror pension redress nearer' in: *The Guardian*.

Whitebloom, S. and Atkinson, D. ((May 26th 1993), 'City regulator's takeover bid' in: *The Guardian*.

Whitley, R. (1974), 'The City and Industry: the directors of large companies, their characteristics and connections', Chapter 4 in: *Elites and Power in British Society* edited by Philip Stanworth and Anthony Giddens, Cambridge University Press, London.

Wilkie, D. (1987), 'Funded Pension Schemes - Macroeconomic Aspects' Chapter 5 in: Bernard Benjamin *et al Pensions: The Problems of Today and Tomorrow*, Allen and Unwin, London, pp. 66-82.

Willetts, D. (January 21st 1988), Seminar: *The Work of the Downing Street Policy Unit*, University of Sheffield.

Williamson, N. (1987), 'The New Right', Spokesman Press, London.

Wood, D. (August 22nd 1974), 'Tory plan to benefit women and elderly' *The Times*.

Wooton, B. (1985), 'The Moral Basis of the Welfare State' chapter two of: Philip Bean *et al In Defence of Welfare*, Tavistock Publications, London.

Worsley, P. (1970), *Introducing Sociology* (1st Edition) Penguin Books, Harmondsworth.

Young, H. (1989) *One of Us*, Pan Books, London.

Young, H. and Sloman, A. (1984), *But, Chancellor: An inquiry into the Treasury*, BBC Publications, London.

Other Publications:

Chronicle - Encyclopaedia of the 20th Century, (1989), Collins, London.

Directory of Directors (1988, 1989 and 1990), Reed Information Services Ltd., East Grinstead, 1988, 1989 and 1990.

Ellison, R. *Pensions Law and Practice*

Who's Who? 1988, 1989 and 1990.

Government Publications:

Central Statistical Office, *Social Trends* No. 21, HMSO, London. 1991

DHSS

Social Insurance and Allied Services Cmnd 6404, London, HMSO 1942.

Provision for Old Age Cmnd 538 London, HMSO 1958

Strategy for Pensions -

The Future Development of State and Occupational Pensions White Paper Cmnd 4755, London, HMSO September 1971.

Better Pensions: Fully Protected Against Inflation, White Paper, Cmnd 5713, London, HMSO 1973.

Growing Older, White Paper, Cmnd 8173, London, HMSO 1981.

Social Security Statistics, London, HMSO 1981

Reply to the Third Report from the Social Services Committee Session 1981-82 on The Age of Retirement Cmnd 9095, London, HMSO November 1983.

Population, Pension Costs and Pensioners' Incomes A Background Paper for the Inquiry into Provision for Retirement, London, June 1984.

Personal Pensions - A Consultative Document, London, HMSO July 16th 1984a.

Reform of Social Security, Green Paper, Cmnd 9517-9, London, HMSO June 3rd 1985.

Occupational Pensions: The Contracting-Out (Transfer) Regulations 1985 Press Release 85/24, London, HMSO September 9th 1985.

Pensions Policy: Speech by Norman Fowler Press Release 85/308, London, HMSO November 5th 1985.

Programme for Action, White Paper, Cmnd 9691, London, HMSO December 1985.

Social Security Act, 1985

New Protection for Early Leavers' Pensions Press Release 85/350, London, HMSO December 11th 1985.

Social Security Act, 1986.

New Information for Occupational Pensioners Press Release 86/42, London, HMSO February 12th 1986.

Norman Fowler Announces Membership of Advisory Group on personal Pensions Press Release 86/159, London, HMSO May 15th 1986.

New Rights for Members of Occupational Pension Schemes Press Release 86/206, London, HMSO June 25th 1986.

Pensions Simplified Press Release 86/296, London, HMSO September 24th 1986.

Occupational Pensions - New Regulations Press Release 86/306, London, HMSO October 7th 1986.

Reforming Social Security: Draft Regulations about Personal Pensions Press Release 86/370, London, HMSO November 24th 1986.

Occupational Pensions - New Regulations Press Release 86/408, December 15th 1986.

Reforming Social Security: Consultations on Personal Pensions Press Release 86/414, London, HMSO, December 17th 1986.

New Pension Choices Coming Soon Press Release 87/118, London, HMSO March 17th 1987.

Reforming Social Security: An Early Start For Personal Pensions Plus New Freedom To Boost Retirement Savings Press Release 87/121, London, HMSO March 18th 1987.

Reforming Social Security: New Pensions Regulations in Place Press Release 87/241, London, HMSO July 7th 1987.

Reforming Social Security: New Timetable for Personal Pensions Press Release 87/241, London, HMSO August 26th 1987.

Department of Trade and Industry

Review of Investor Protection Report (Gower): Part One. Cmnd 9125, London, HMSO January 1984.

Building Societies: A New Framework Green Paper Cmnd 9316, London, HMSO 1984.

Financial Services In The United Kingdom A new framework for investor protection Cmnd 9432, London, HMSO January 1985.

Merger of Securities and Investments Board (SIB) and Marketing of Investments Board Organising Committee (MIBOC) DTI/Bank of England Press Pelease: London, HMSO December 19th 1985.

Government Actuary's Department

Occupational Pension Schemes 1967: The Third Survey by the Government Actuary London, HMSO 1967.

Occupational Pension Schemes 1971: The Fourth Survey by the Government Actuary London, HMSO 1972.

Review of Contracting-Out Terms London, HMSO, March 1987.

Government Actuary's Quinquennial Review National Insurance Fund Long-Term Financial Estimates HC451, London, HMSO July 1982.

Government Actuary's Quinquennial Review National Insurance Fund Long-Term Financial Estimates 1986 Report, London, HMSO 1987.

National Audit Office

The Elderly: Information Requirements for Supporting the Elderly and Implications Personal Pensions for the National Insurance Fund London, HMSO 1990.

Occupational Pensions Board

Solvency, Disclosure of Information and Member Participation in Occupational Pension Schemes Cmnd 5904 and 5904-I, London, HMSO February 1975.

Equal Status for Men and Women in Occupational Pension Schemes Cmnd 6599, London, HMSO August 1976.

Improved Protection for the Occupational Pension Rights and Expectations of Early Leavers Cmnd 8271, London, HMSO June 1981.

Greater Security for the Rights and Expectations of Members of Occupational Pension Schemes Cmnd 8649, London, HMSO October 1982.

Social Security Advisory Committee

Second Report 1982/83, London, HMSO January 1983.

Fifth Report 1986/87, London, HMSO 1987.

Social Services Committee

Second Report 1981/2: Public Expenditure on Social Services HC306-1, London, HMSO July 1982.

Third Report 1981/2: The Age of Retirement HC26-1, London, HMSO October 1982a.

HM Treasury

The Government's Expenditure Plans 1980-81 White Paper, Cmnd 7746, London, HMSO November 1979.

The Next Ten Years: public expenditure and taxation in the 1990s Green Paper, Cmnd 9189, London, HMSO March 1984.

Miscellaneous Government Publications

Report of the Committee to Review the Functioning of Financial Institutions (Wilson Committee) Cmnd 7937, London, HMSO June 1980.

Inquiry into the Value of Pensions (Scott Report) Cmnd 8147, London, HMSO February 1981.

Hansard (various years 1973-1986).

Pension Law Reform vols. 1 and 2 Report of the Committee chaired by Professor Roy Goode Cmnd 2342-1nd2, London, HMSO, September 1993.

Evidence submitted to Inquiry into Provision for Retirement

Institute of Directors Submission of Evidence to the Inquiry into Provision for Retirement January 31st 1984

National Association of Pension Funds Submission of Evidence to the Inquiry into Provision for Retirement January 31st 1984

National Association of Pension Funds Submission of Evidence to the Inquiry into Provision for Retirement March 30th 1984

Responses to the Green Paper *Reform of Social Security*

Confederation of British Industry Response to Green Paper September 1985

Institute of Directors Informal response August 23rd 1985

Institute of Directors Formal response September 1985